Enduring Bonds

Enduring Bonds

INEQUALITY, MARRIAGE, PARENTING,
AND EVERYTHING ELSE THAT MAKES
FAMILIES GREAT AND TERRIBLE

Philip N. Cohen

UNIVERSITY OF CALIFORNIA PRESS

University of California Press, one of the most distinguished university presses in the United States, enriches lives around the world by advancing scholarship in the humanities, social sciences, and natural sciences. Its activities are supported by the UC Press Foundation and by philanthropic contributions from individuals and institutions. For more information, visit www.ucpress.edu.

University of California Press
Oakland, California

Library of Congress Cataloging-in-Publication Data

Names: Cohen, Philip N., author.
Title: Enduring bonds : inequality, marriage, parenting, and everything else that makes families great and terrible / Philip N. Cohen.
Description: Oakland, California : University of California Press, [2018] | Includes bibliographical references and index.
Identifiers: LCCN 2017025976| ISBN 9780520292383 (cloth : alk. paper) | ISBN 9780520292390 (pbk. : alk. paper) | ISBN 9780520965959 (e-edition)
Subjects: LCSH: Families. | Equality.
Classification: LCC HQ503 .c64 2018 | DDC 306.85—dc23
LC record available at https://lccn.loc.gov/2017025976

26   25   24   23   22   21   20   19   18   17
10   9   8   7   6   5   4   3   2   1

Contents

Acknowledgments

All the essays here have been revised and updated from their original appearance on the blog. In many cases I found errors in the old posts or changed my mind about things. In addition, while updating and editing these, I often added new material that was never on the blog (such as the Mary name trend back to 1780). I haven't specified how the essays changed so as not to burden the text, but where there are conflicts I prefer the book version. I'm a little embarrassed at the prospect of people finding places where I now contradict myself or turned out to be wrong, but that's the price I pay for the great privilege of having conducted this work in public, with all the benefits that entails.

The data sources for the analyses in the book are in the footnotes, which sometimes point to blog posts for more detail. There isn't much complicated programming involved, but in a few cases I provide links to data and computer code for that as well. I made most of the figures using Microsoft Excel, which despite its annoying qualities seems to be the most efficient and versatile tool for data presentation that I happen to know how to use; I'm happy to share the underlying data files for any of these if I can find them, so feel free to ask.

I was lucky to write a blog during a time when academic blogs were gathering places for critics and like-minded readers alike. The essays that form the basis for this book benefited directly or indirectly from the exchanges that came out of that milieu. Some people regularly responded in the comments section (almost always a friendly and civil place, I'm happy to say), while many others discussed these ideas with me in other settings. At the risk of offending more people than I impress, I list some of the names that come to mind here. I hope they and many other readers will carry on these conversations, which have made my career, and my life, so interesting and rewarding for the last few years: Syed Ali, Esping Anderson, Andy Andrews, Karl Bakeman, Bill Bielby, Khiarra Bridges, Tristan Bridges, Neal Caren, Karen Carr, Megan Carroll, Carrie Clarady, Stephanie Coontz, Carolyn Cowan, Phil Cowan, Emily Danforth, Paula England, Myra Marx Ferree, Tina Fetner, Gary Gates, Claudia Geist, Jennifer Glass, Ted Greenstein, Jessica Hardie, Amy Harmon, Heidi Hartmann, Mike Hout, Matt Huffman, Michelle Janning, Jeehye Kang, Meredith Kleykamp, Rose Kreider, Beth Latshaw, JaeIn Lee, Jennifer Lee, Lucia Lykke, Scott Matthews, David Meyer, Joya Misra, Laura Beth Nielsen, Pam Oliver, CJ Pascoe, Lisa Pearce, Joanna Pepin, Andrew Perrin, Allison Pugh, Rashawn Ray, Vanesa Ribas, Barbara Risman, Virginia Rutter, Liana Sayer, Meg Austin Smith, Chris Uggen, Reeve Vanneman, Ashton Verdery, Lisa Wade, Joanie Weston, Kristi Williams, and Moriah Willow. I am also very appreciative of Naomi Schneider at the University of California Press for embracing this project and for her help in getting it done. Copyeditor Elisabeth Magnus did exacting and patient work on the prose, for which I'm grateful

I've been incredibly fortunate to have the family I do. I'm grateful to my parents, Avis and Marshall Cohen, as well as the larger family—consanguineous, affinal, and fictive—for making me, and this book, possible. I have tried to keep my wife, Judy Ruttenberg, and daughters, Charlotte and Ruby, out of the essays, but as I look back at this work, the presence of these truly wonderful people is deeply felt and immensely appreciated.

Introduction

I started writing my blog, *Family Inequality*, in 2009. My purpose was to engage with people around the social trends and events that were dramatically shifting the landscape in which I worked. These were stark: Economic inequality increased, with those at the top pulling away from everyone else and progress stagnating or worse in the middle. Marriage rates fell and the proportion of children born to parents who weren't married rose. And inequality in access to marriage ramped up, in particular the gap in marriage rates between rich and poor, and between Black and White. These three trends are all interconnected, and each became a part of the cultural and political debates of the day on everything from parenting styles and poverty rates to election demographics and the future of economic growth.

Then, in 2012, same-sex marriage erupted into academic sociology with the publication of an incendiary study claiming children were worse off if their parents were gay or lesbian—just as the issue was working its way toward the Supreme Court. This raised the possibility that social science, wielded by religious conservatives for political ends, would derail the very visible progress toward a possible breakthrough in equality for gay and lesbian couples. Most of us who had already been arguing about marriage and poverty and inequality were now drawn into the tumultuous dispute over what came to be known as marriage equality. In my case, I was arguing *for* marriage, or at least access to marriage, for gays and lesbians, as I was also arguing *against* reliance on marriage as a solution to our society's growing economic inequality. And the cultural warriors on the other side—the ones who were always complaining that the decline of marriage was eroding the social foundations of civilization itself—were now fighting to block the extension of marriage rights. In other words, it was a great time to be a family inequality blogger (plus, I had tenure).

The debate over marriage and inequality has tended to feed the worry that individualism, and the individual freedom it begat, has weakened social bonds and increased insecurity—and may ultimately increase inequality. In the clucking voice of the cultural conservative, this comes out something like this: Well, you wanted sexual freedom, with no constraints, and now you're surprised when you end up single, or sort of single, without economic security—and your children grow up to be rudderless cultural relativists, playing video games in your basement before eventually producing undisciplined children who put a drag on the prosperity created by previous generations.

On the other side, I and most academic social scientists usually argue that freedom in—and from—relationships is essential for fuller human development and that the marriages (or other relationships) that survive in such a context are better for everyone involved. When people don't have enough money to take care of themselves and their children, we should all chip in to help give them the security and stability that everyone needs to thrive. In that way freedom and equality don't have to be at odds, and everyone benefits.

Marriage equality took on an outsized role in this debate, partly because of what I like to call, somewhat dramatically, the Regnerus Affair, after the author of the infamous 2012 study, sociologist Mark Regnerus. To some, including Regnerus, gay marriage represents the ultimate individualist decadence—the kind of freedom-first approach that undermines the very concept of society. To others, marriage equality is the culmination of a civil rights struggle for equal protection under the law, the social recognition of family diversity, and the beginning of a society that embraces, respects, and supports families regardless of their structure and composition. The issue ultimately put on the table—at the center of the table—the question of gender itself, the existence or desirability or necessity of two gender categories in our families and between our individual selves. This confluence of conflicts is why the debate over marriage equality became so encompassing, raising strong emotions far beyond the relatively small proportion of people intimately affected by the legal battle. And that's why marriage equality ended up in the center of this book. The timeliness of the issue, the intensity of the cultural and political battles it set off, and the pertinence of the issues raised for broader questions related to gender and inequality all came together.

For academic social scientists, who were already engaged in a search for greater engagement with the public, the marriage equality debate was a case study and a rallying point. It raised many of the big questions at or near the surface of our work. What is the proper role of social science in political and legal debates? How do we express our moral and political (and even religious) selves without compromising the integrity of our work as researchers and academics? In short, how do we make ourselves relevant and useful without becoming partisan hacks? These questions took on a fiercer intensity after the election of Donald Trump (which occurred after most of this book was written), raising the specter of a post-truth society in which a fear-driven, nationalist politics supports an autocratic ruler who mocks science and its practitioners in the academy. The soul-searching and political struggles over these issues will no doubt require another volume.

ENDURING BONDS

As I sat down to compile the best essays from my blog, I saw that marriage equality tapped into the broader questions about inequality I had wrestled with for years. But it was just one core aspect of the multilayered social organism that is our system of inequality. And social bonds are a vital component in the cellular architecture of that organism.

Bonds can be good (like love) or bad (like slavery). So what are the bonds of family? Some of both. In the evolution of our species, the emotional bond between parent and child meant mothers took care of babies, which enabled us to keep developing outside the womb without having to feed and care for ourselves. That prolonged infancy meant our heads (and brains) could grow bigger, which we would eventually need to play Pokémon Go. So family bonds are great. But family bonds are also the building blocks of social hierarchies, of which families historically were the first, with the power of men over women and adults over children.

Put one way, we need bonds—or, maybe, discipline—to have freedom. (It's probably no coincidence that some people find they can achieve true emotional release only through the experience of sexual bondage.) That may be a banal observation about the human condition, but it's directly relevant to the problem of families and inequality. We want to encourage and develop and cherish the bonds we think are good but release the bonds that are harmful—and both types are highly salient in and around families.

In the 2015 Supreme Court decision *Obergefell v. Hodges,* which granted marriage rights to same-sex couples, Justice Anthony Kennedy described the historical emergence of "new dimensions of freedom" within marriage, marking "deep transformations" that "have strengthened, not weakened, the institution." He was referring to the extension of legal rights to women and the end of state bans on interracial marriage. On the theory that love is the strongest leash, Kennedy held that an institution governed by freedom and equality was stronger than one held together by coercion and dominance. That's an optimistic vision of freedom, but it's not an obvious view of institutions. What is a "strong" institution—one that persists over a long time, one that has a lot of members, or one that reflects the value we put on freely chosen relationships?

Kennedy wrote, "The nature of marriage is that, through its enduring bond, two persons together can find other freedoms, such as expression, intimacy, and spirituality." It took the late justice Antonin Scalia, a conservative Catholic, to point out that marriage isn't really about freedom. In his furious dissent, Scalia mocked the idea that people find "freedoms" in the "enduring bond" of marriage. "One would think Freedom of Intimacy is abridged rather than expanded by marriage," he scoffed. "Ask the nearest hippie." Scalia had a point. It may seem self-evident to us that "the right to personal choice regarding marriage is inherent in the concept of individual autonomy," as Kennedy wrote, but marriage does represent a self-imposed, contractual limit on individual autonomy. Still, Scalia need not have feared Kennedy's opinion as some sort of radical tract. When

Kennedy wrote that "marriage is a keystone of the Nation's social order," he extended the notion of enduring bonds to the societal level. He meant the good kind of bonds, but that's not a simple option to exercise. And did gay and lesbian activists fight for marriage rights so they could fortify the social order, which still in many ways marginalizes them? There are conflicting visions at work here. The enduring bonds of family are neither all good nor all bad.

FAMILY INEQUALITY

Of the nine hundred or so posts on my blog, I really only considered a few hundred for inclusion in this book, working with those that might fill a coherent set of categories around common themes. It's clear that my overriding concern was with the place of families in the system of inequality, with a recurring emphasis on the question of who gets what kind of family, and the consequences of that social ordering. I addressed that issue from all directions and distances and with different degrees of focus—always drawing on whatever skills and knowledge I happened to have handy, and inspired by whatever I was reading. These are the chapters that emerged.

The role of families in perpetuating inequality frequently drew me to questions about parenting: the observable or invisible practices that help shape children's personalities, resources, and relationships. Chapter 1 looks at the broad cultural sweep of parenting practices—such as the demise of the name Mary—as well as contemporary controversies over corporal punishment and religion. Of course, in the case of children, the parental bond is a key element of their security and a precondition for the eventual exercise of freedom and liberty. But such bonds also become weapons in the hands of abusive or exploitative parents. Further, families are just one element in the system of inequality, and nothing they do can overcome some more structural features of the system. So the essays on parenting tee up an exploration of family structure and inequality. Focusing on poverty and crime, chapter 2 pushes back on the idea that the rise of single mothers is the underlying cause of growing inequality and its consequences.

The focus on single mothers with respect to poverty and crime has led our national policy makers into an unhealthy obsession with promoting marriage as a solution to poverty, crime, and almost any other problem they can think of. This is not just an innocent mistake in interpreting social and demographic trends, however. Single mothers are the visible expression of the historical trend toward both gender equality and more diverse family structures, which have had the effect of decentering the married, man-woman, breadwinner-homemaker nuclear family. Chapter 3 puts marriage promotion and its promoters in the context of this historical change, branding them as retrograde defenders of what should be a bygone era of uniquely segregated and unequal gender relations. From a pose as supporters of the good kind of enduring bond—the loving, harmonious, supportive, married-parent family—they emerge as surprisingly mean-spirited, doing more shaming and blaming than assisting and uplifting (and their programs don't work).

Ironically, but not really, marriage promotion and marriage denial are bedfellows in our historical moment. Some of the most influential people who want to make poor parents get married also wanted to prevent gays and lesbians (and their children) from accessing this esteemed social and economic status. Chapter 4 is a retelling of the Regnerus Affair, the dumpster fire that burned in academia as political and legal debates over marriage equality were occurring nationwide. Besides airing a lot of academic dirty laundry, that episode helped expose the gender paranoia at the heart of the marriage promotion movement: the fear that modern society no longer needs gender itself, at least in its traditional binary expression.

The end of gender as we know it seems at odds with another trend, the apparent increase in gender differentiation in the cultural milieu of children, as seen in the tendency to divide toys and clothes, and entertainment, by gender. My sensitivity to this issue was heightened as a result of the prolonged debates over gender and marriage, and as my own daughters went through the Disney Princess ages this hypergendering became an irritant as well as, I have to admit, an entertaining diversion. So chapter 5 discusses the accentuation of gender differences with an emphasis on culture and parenting, including not just children's movies but also bathrooms, orthodonture, and color preferences.

Gender difference is a key cognitive element of gender inequality—if we don't create gender differences in our minds, and enforce them in our social behavior, then the inequalities associated with gender might lose traction and slip away. That also means that gender distinctions matter more when they reinforce the social hierarchy. Chapter 6 addresses gender inequality through the core issues of occupational segregation, economic inequality, and the division of labor. Chapter 7 is the parallel set of essays on the intersection of race and gender inequality. In both cases, there are thorny issues of definition and measurement, but we have a strong imperative to master enough of the facts to give us a knowledge base for addressing persistent inequality. This chapter includes case studies in inequality, on women's educational attainment, Detroit, and marriage—the essays where I thought my contribution turned out to be useful.

Finally, chapter 8 focuses on feminism and sexuality. I argue that US society (like every other society) is still a patriarchy—a case, I admit, that became a little easier to make after Trump's election. And I attempt to buttress the case for feminism, using that perspective to critique some of the common tropes of the propatriarchy intellectual establishment. These include sexual shaming and rape denial. The chapter concludes with a return to gender difference questions, which continue to bedevil feminism both theoretically and practically—as we see in the disputes over young women's vocal fry and uptalk and in gender-segregated sports, to name just a few examples.

Families are great, families are terrible, and families are everything in between. No simpler, more idealized summary will be as true as that overbroad nonconclusion. But whether our view is ultimately positive or negative, families emerge both as the linchpin of our system of inequality and as the best hope for many of its most vulnerable victims. For better and for worse, their bonds are enduring, in our individual lives and in the historical development of our modern societies. And understanding how that works can only help.

IN THE CLASSROOM

One of the great things about my job is I get to choose what subjects I teach, but for most of the past decade I felt it was important to keep the family sociology classroom experience in mind when I was blogging so that I could keep my writing focused and stay on task. And since I usually blog about whatever is right in front of me, a lot of this book takes off from what was happening in that classroom, and I've used a lot of this material in my own courses. If you are considering using this book to accompany a family course, here are some suggestions, put in terms of common themes or chapter headings. Chapter 1 is *introductory* material, especially relevant if you, like me, focus on modernity and its attendant identity questions. Chapter 2 may help with discussions of *social class* and economic inequality. Chapters 3 and 4 deal with *marriage* but also might contribute to conversations about *research methods*, research ethics, and the integration of research and policy work. I've used the material in chapters 5 and 6 to supplement my syllabus on *gender*, concerning both children (as in the case of gender socialization) and adults (especially when the subject is work and inequality). Chapter 7 should be useful for the section on *race*, especially with a focus on African Americans and demographic trends. Finally, chapter 8 may pair well with teaching about *sexuality*, particularly for those interested in discussing *feminism* in relation to sexuality. We who teach families need to stick together, so I hope this helps—and please let me know how it goes.

1 Modernity, Parenting, and Families

My research career began with an interest in modern inequality, and especially in how different kinds of inequality intersect (in the 1990s, this concern often went under a list that now seems quaintly short: "race, class, and gender"). My first project as an intern was to examine large demographic data sets from the US Census Bureau and figure out how many unmarried couples were living together.[1] That and a few other projects eventually made me a family demographer, but my interest in inequality persisted. I started pulling families and inequality together—and increasingly saw families as one of the key pieces of the intersecting inequality puzzle. To get into that requires more than the simple observation that children inherit the wealth or poverty of their parents—although that is a good deal of the point. It requires unearthing what happens within families, the gender and age and power issues that percolate behind the closed doors of the family household. And to see the overall effect of families on inequality, we need to tackle the less obvious—and hard to track—problem of who get to have the families they want, which (as the marriage equality debate taught us) turns out to be the crux of many matters.

In this chapter I start with several essays on what we now call "parenting," the uniquely modern practice of transforming the raw material of humanity into interlocking—even if disordered—pieces of the social order. Nothing in this process is as obvious as it seems, from the individual yet profoundly social decision of what to name a child through the immediate imperative to keep children safe. From sudden infant death syndrome to Santa, from vaccine exemptions to screen time, parenting is a complicated performance that both reflects and builds identities in the family, and between families. Inequality is not the only product of this performance, but it's one of the most important.

1. WHY DON'T PARENTS NAME THEIR DAUGHTERS MARY ANYMORE?

For the first time in the history of the United States of America, the name Mary fell out of the top hundred names given to newborn girls in 2009, according to data from the Social Security name database. This milestone in our cultural transformation apparently went unnoticed beyond the few readers of my blog. In the raw numbers, the number of Marys born as of 2016 was down 95 percent from 1961, the last year she was at #1—a drop from 47,645 that year to just 2,487 now.

Mary was the #1 name every year in the database from 1880—when Social Security records start—to 1961 (except for a five-year stint as second to Linda in 1947–52). Naming your daughter Mary was as traditional as girls wearing blue (the color associated with the Virgin Mary). In fact, however, we now know Mary has been falling in popularity since 1850, but hardly anyone noticed. In 1961, 2.3 percent of girls were given the name Mary, but in 1850 it was 13 percent. Going back further, the signers of the US Constitution in 1787 had forty-three wives, 21 percent of whom were named Mary (another 21 percent were named Elizabeth, but that name was never again as dominant).[2] I also checked sixty-seven wives of Confederate and Union generals and found that 28 percent were named Mary. Among regular people, a study of naming in the town of Hingham, Massachusetts, found that 12 percent of girls were named Mary around 1800 (Sarah was almost as popular before 1800).[3]

Now, thanks to a law that allows old federal records to become public after seventy-two years, and the diligent efforts of the IPUMS (Integrated

Figure 1. Percentage of girls in the United States given the name Mary, by year of birth: 1780–2015. Source: Author analysis of US Census data at IPUMS.org and Social Security Administration data at www.ssa.gov/oact/babynames/. From 1780 to 1880 the data are limited to those born in the United States.

Public Use Microdata Series) database at the University of Minnesota, we can analyze the names of individuals in the United States going back to 1850—and since some women in the 1850 Census were quite old I can look back as far as about 1780 to see what proportion of them were named Mary back then (figure 1).[4] Here is the resulting trend for Mary, expressed as a percentage of all girls born in the United States. By the time Mary fell from the #1 spot her dominance had already long since faded.

Naming patterns demonstrate how that which is most personal is profoundly shaped by social trends larger than ourselves. That's why, even with about two million girls born each year in the United States, the number named Mary is always within a few hundred of the previous year—and why the line in figure 1 is so smooth. In the tradition of treating statistical trends as horse races, I imagine that there is one person named

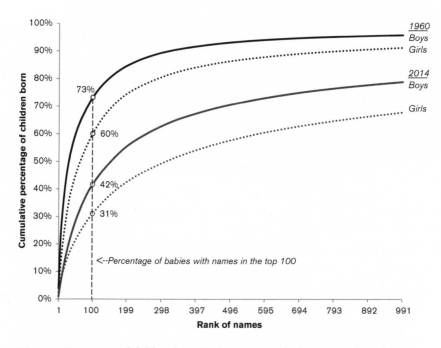

Figure 2. Percentage of children born, by frequency rank of names: 1960 and 2014, by gender. Source: Author analysis of Social Security Administration data at www.ssa .gov/oact/babynames/.

Mary, who is constantly falling behind: first behind Linda, then Lisa, Jennifer, Ashley, Jessica, and so on, all the way to Isabella and Sophia and Emma. That's what it looks like, but that's not how it happens—it's just an illusion created by the amazing regularity in human behavior, which produces an orderly succession of names. Somehow, the millions of individual decisions that parents make produce steady trends like this.[5]

The trend is powerful, but how it works is opaque. Something in "the culture" is applying pressure to millions of families in such a way that the already tiny proportion deciding to use Mary becomes smaller almost every year. The fact is: few people nowadays want to name girls Mary. Why?

It's not the fall of religion. Consider that, in 2014, there were 1.6 times as many girls named Nevaeh—*heaven* spelled backward. The rise (and, already, beginning of a fall) of Nevaeh, which only appeared on the list in 2001, is a tipoff to what's going on. It's the long-term increase in naming diversity. Compare 1960 with 2014 (figure 2). The top hundred girls' names were given to 60 percent of girls in 1960, but they now represent just half that: 31 percent. Emma, the #1 name is 2014, was given to just 1.1 percent of girls.

So how do we understand this transformation? It's not immigration or ethnic diversity, although these may play some role in recent decades. (Maria showed potential, rising as high as thirty-first place in the early 1970s, but now she's crashed as well, down to #115.) In fact, in the old days Mary was common among Blacks as well as Whites, and my own analysis of the census data shows that Mary was very common among the children of immigrants from Germany and eastern Europe as well as Ireland and the United Kingdom.

As I try to fit these facts to my broader analysis of family trends, I think the collapse of Mary is mostly about the emergence of a modern view of children. The modernization theory of name trends was advanced most famously by Stanley Lieberson in his book *A Matter of Taste*. He saw the rise of individualism in modern naming practices. "As the role of the extended family, religious rules, and other institutional pressures declines," he wrote, "choices are increasingly free to be matters of taste."[6] Mary— both a traditional American name and a symbol of religious Christianity— embodies this trend.

In the old days no one ever asked if the name Mary had "jumped the shark," because children's names weren't the subject of fashion. Now parents interested in the happening names consult the Social Security list, along with many others available all over, to help find just the right name. (Personally, I recommend a name that is not that popular— somewhere between 100 and 400—but that shows increasing popularity. That way your kid will be one of the older ones in a growing group of kids with the same name that look up to her—and you will look like a trendsetter.)

Two centuries ago, the vast majority of European Americans were not looking for a unique name, or a name that was coming into vogue, or a name that matched a popular cultural figure—or trying to avoid a name that had jumped the shark. They usually just named children after family members. Besides the sad fact that many children died at young ages—and that there were too many children to keep track of (the average White woman had seven children in 1800)—it just didn't seem to occur to people that children were priceless individuals. And naming wasn't a way to make a statement about character and identity.

By the twentieth century Americans had started to fixate on the uniqueness of each child (and they only had about two per family). Not only was difference valued, but individuality emerged as a project—starting with naming—of creating an identity. That doesn't mean everyone wants a unique name (though, unlike in the past, some people do try for that). It means that naming is a statement of the kind of person kids are to become. So people are influenced by a TV show or a hit song and names shoot upward as fads, or crash downward when an image crisis occurs. Minor name crazes are apparent in the data after the popularity of hit songs such as "Maggie" (Rod Stewart, 1971), "Brandy" (Looking Glass, 1972), and even "Rhiannon" (Fleetwood Mac, 1975). On the other hand, the movie *Forrest Gump* killed the name Forrest in 1994, the public coming out of Ellen DeGeneres as gay seems to have tanked Ellen in 1997, and the scandal named after Monica Lewinsky marked the beginning of the end of Monica in 1998.

After all this time, amazingly, it's quite possible Mary will come back. In 2014 she had her second year of not falling in the rankings, which could signal the start of a turnaround (my 2012 essay for the *Atlantic* on this topic may or may not have played a role here). But she can never come back as she once was—a default traditional name. If she does, it will be as a fashion trend, as happened most dramatically with Emma. Emma was #3 in 1880 but fell almost continuously until the mid-1970s—as low as 458th—before turning around for a meteoric rise to #1 in 2008 and 2014. Unlike Bertha, who was once a top contender before disappearing, Emma is the rare name that rose from the ashes as fashionably classic.

If Mary does come back, it will raise a vexing question: Is it better to be the default traditional name—the most popular during the centuries when naming was not a status-conscious choice—or the top name in a crowded, competitive field of fiercely contested alternatives? Either way, I doubt

Mary (or any other name) will have the kind of long-lasting dominance she once did.

2. "PARENTING" THROUGH THE (ONLY VERY RECENT) AGES

I've been thinking about what we can learn from language trends on families.

A while ago I read a column by the *Times*'s Lisa Belkin, in which she wrote about the supposed decline of overparenting and the rise of the hip new nonchalant parenting. It's a series of fads, she said: "After all, that is the way it is with parenting—which I bet was never used as a verb before the 20th century, when medicine reached the point where parents could assume their babies would survive." It bugged me at the time that the *Times* couldn't supply her with an intern—or a dictionary—to actually run down the term so that she didn't have to speculate on when it had first appeared. More importantly, though, modern medicine is only part of the story. You would have to suspect a constellation of factors, including falling fertility, increasing educational investments, more higher education for parents/mothers, the modernization of medical and psychological expertise, the secularization of science, and who knows what else.

Anyway, I like the idea that parenting as a concept is relatively new. And she was right. According to the *Oxford English Dictionary, parenting* ("the activity of being a parent; the rearing of a child or children") appeared in the *Washington Post* in 1918, in the phrase "the philosophy of perfect parenting." Figure 3 shows the Google trend for the word *parenting* in books in American English from 1960 to 2008.

Consistent with the cultural shift idea—fewer, healthier children and richer, more educated parents—*parenting* emerged with reference to its discrete qualities as a modern activity. (The *OED* reports that it appeared in Britannica's *Book of the Year* in 1959: "the supervision by parents of their children.") The academic database JSTOR has a use of the term from 1930, but that's in reference to biological procreation, not rearing. The first time it is used in the sense of "rearing" is in the *Social Service Review*

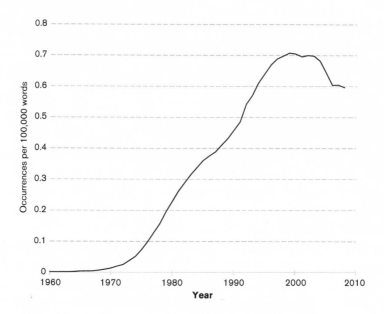

Figure 3. Uses of *parenting* in American English, 1960–2008.
Source: Author analysis of Google Ngrams database.

in 1952 in an article about foster care: "It is impossible in a changing world to expect to find a perfect or final solution to the difficult problem of sharing the parenting of children between child-care agencies and inadequate own parents."[7] It starts appearing routinely in the core journal *Marriage and Family Living* in 1953, as in this from 1954: "Sibling rivalry is one of the commonest evidences of poor parenting."[8]

Wait, really? Good kids with good parents don't have sibling rivalry? That should mean sibling rivalry has declined as a concern since parents' education increased and standards rose after, say, the 1940s. Except, of course, sibling rivalry wasn't discovered (or, at least, named) until the 1930s, as Google ngrams also show. The emergence of parenting has accompanied a host of attendant parenting deficits. The modern path of progress is littered with obstacles of its own creating.

As usual, the ratcheting up of standards (which may or may not be good for kids) starts among the well-off, and the more rigorous standards are then enforced upon those at lower levels in the social order, who are left to scrape together some cheap advice from the Internet or one of the thousands of how-to parenting books.

Individuality, Dated

Modern parenting is both faddish and individualistic—conformist in its ideals, which include uniquely tailoring the experience to the individual child. In the essay on naming girls Mary, I said that two centuries ago it just didn't occur to people that children were priceless individuals. But what is the evidence for this? After reading Stanley Lieberson's work on naming in the late nineteenth century, I turned to Viviana Zelizer's *Pricing the Priceless Child.* She tracks the shift in the cultural valuing of children to that period as well. Before that time orphans were either handy little workers or burdens to be shed, and mortality rates in orphanages were astronomical; after that, they (or some of them) were expensive objects of priceless value for infertile couples. Also in the late nineteenth century there were bursts of activity in the production of parenting advice and in the professionalization of elementary education.[9]

Somewhere in that reading I came across the phrase "child's individuality," and it seemed to flag the birth of modern childhood. Ngrams concurs, showing that the term first appeared in the 1860s and then rocketed up in usage frequency in the last two decades of that century.

A read through the citations from that period shows they are concentrated in the parenting advice and education fields. Here's an example from the advice literature in 1890: "A child is liable to be looked upon as if he were simply one child among many children, a specimen representative of childhood generally; but every child stands all by himself in the world as an individual, with his own personality and character, with his own thoughts and feelings, his own hopes and fears and possibilities, his own relations to his fellow-beings and to God."[10] And one from the education literature in 1886: "The child's individuality and freedom should be sacredly respected. All educational processes are to be based on a careful study, not only of child-nature in general, but also of the idiosyncrasies of the individual pupil."[11] This was the new, modern scientific attitude toward children, ushering in the century of "parenting."

3. HOW DO THEY DO IT?

How do families transmit inequality? This is an area where some of sociology's big ideas are being pursued, challenged, and tested through empirical studies—and where sociology is directly relevant to a pressing public issue: rising inequality.

Much of the current research on what poor versus middle-class families *do* that helps ensure their kids end up in a class position similar to their parents' focuses on "cultural capital."[12] In the theoretical language from Pierre Bourdieu, this goes back to "habitus," which is something like the internalization of social structures encountered through the life course, processed into a practical sense of acceptable action for the individual. It's that sense of entitlement, plus the skills to pull it off, that partly responds to, and partly drives, the reciprocal behavior of gatekeepers along the way to success (or its absence).

The most influential researcher on this question might be Annette Lareau, whose book *Unequal Childhoods* has become iconic.[13] But even the richest of these studies can't yet prove that the behavior they see causes the outcome we expect. As convincing as Lareau's evidence is that rich and poor parents do it differently, the data can't tell us that's why the rich kids end up richer (or healthier or happier) in the long run. This contributes to parents' anxiety.

Nowhere is the anxiety about successful parenting more acute than it is around the skills and "choices" of mothers. What is it that more educated mothers (or parents generally) do better, if anything, and does this result from their training or from knowing which books to buy and fads to follow—or are there other things about these homes, families, neighborhoods, friends, schools, and so on that account for this pattern?

Consider obesity. Preschool-aged children are more likely to be obese if they have unhealthy habits like watching too much TV, eating on irregular schedules, or not getting enough sleep. Maybe educated parents do better to prevent these things because of their know-how or other resources. But the same research that shows these factors matter also shows that mothers' education itself matters more—even when their effects are statistically controlled.[14]

To illustrate the strength of this relationship, I measured the association of mothers' education level and their children's obesity using a sample

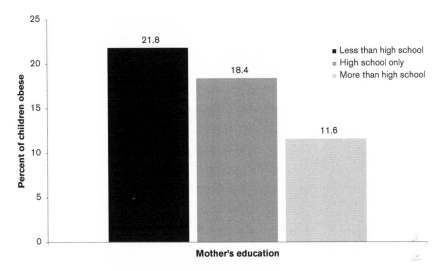

Figure 4. Mother's education and children's obesity rate. With statistical controls for age, sex, race/ethnicity, family structure, mother's age, and number of siblings (limited to children living with their mothers). Source: Author's analysis of the 2011– 12 National Survey of Children's Health, available by special request from the Data Resource Center for Child and Adolescent Health, childhealthdata.org/help /dataset.

of almost forty thousand children ages ten to seventeen who were part of the National Survey of Children's Health. In a statistical analysis that included the child's age, sex, race/ethnicity, family structure, number of siblings, and mother's education, the last variable had the largest effect. Children of mothers who didn't finish high school had obesity rates almost twice as high as those whose mothers had gone to college when the rest of the variables were controlled (figure 4).

Naturally, income is part of this educational advantage. And part of what rich people do that poor people can't is spend money on their kids. For example, married parents with two children and an income less than $57,000 per year spend on average $160,000 on each child from birth to age eighteen—on everything from diapers and food to extra bedrooms and summer camp. For families with incomes of $100,000 or more, that amount rises to $370,000.[15] If the difference between poor and rich parents is the ability to pay tuition at a fancy school, or the job contacts they get from similarly situated coworkers, then we don't need rocket social science to figure out what's happening. But the constant discussion of parenting practices and their effects on children draws us away from those simple mechanisms, as if the simplest explanation for class reproduction is unsatisfying. And the more we scrutinize the effects of parenting practices, the more parents drive themselves to distraction trying to keep up with the latest advice.

Privilege Gone Wrong

News about parenting practices that may help children achieve success fuels the practices that it reports on, in turn leading to more news stories on what the most conscientious parents are doing.[16] And this at least contributes to the decisions by some high-end working women to scale back or drop out of their careers. Once they are no longer employed, these overachievers apply their many skills to parenting, ratcheting up the pressure on everyone else.[17] Lately we have seen a new battleground in the parenting wars, closely related to social class: vaccinations.

One of the paradoxes of privileged parenting is that some richer parents feel so empowered and efficacious that they reject commoner solutions to children's problems. In a study of twenty-five mothers who rejected vaccines, Jennifer Reich described a group of mothers who saw themselves as professionals with parenting practices so superior that these would overpower the risk of infectious diseases—especially if the mothers could keep their children away from unclean *others* (I'm paraphrasing, of course).[18] The sociological irony is that through what they see as advantageous individualistic behavior rich parents are creating collective outcomes that may be extremely harmful.

In 2015 an epidemic of nonvaccination in California led to a strict new law clamping down on vaccine exemptions.[19] But before the law changed we got a great look at the pitfalls of intensive parenting. One key element of vaccine avoidance is that, although it's motivated by individualism, it's a practice of groups. And one way such groups are organized and maintained may be by interacting in and around schools—hot spots for parenting fads and identity performance.

When California posted its vaccination rate data, Kieran Healy did some great visualizations of rates across schools.[20] I followed his links to

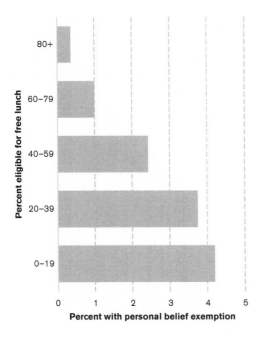

Figure 5. Kindergartners with vaccine personal belief exemptions, by school free-lunch eligibility rate. Private schools excluded because free-lunch data were unavailable.

the data and did some more descriptive work, adding more information on school type and poverty levels. Vaccine exemptions were listed as "Personal Belief Exemptions" (PBEs) in the data; these are the forms by which a parent at the time opted out of the immunization requirement for starting school. I counted up the PBE rate in kindergarten for just under seven thousand schools.[21]

It's hard to say what percentage of kids need to be immunized for different diseases to achieve the proper level of community ("herd") protection, so I arbitrarily calculated percentage of kids attending schools with more than 5 percent exempt. It's clear the problem of vaccine exemptions is concentrated in private and, especially, charter schools: just 11 percent of public school kindergartners were in schools with 5 percent or more PBEs, compared with 30 percent of private school kids and 36 percent of those in charter schools. So private and charter schools are clearly hotbeds of nonvaccination. But there is a more general social class pattern as well, as revealed by the free-lunch eligibility data (figure 5). The relationship between exemption rates and percentage of children eligible for free lunch is negative and very strong—the more poor kids there are, the fewer parents are demanding exemptions from vaccines.

Interestingly, although the relationship between poverty and exemptions is strong in both charter and regular public schools, it is *stronger* in the charter schools. That is, the difference in exemption rates between rich and poor charter schools is greater than it is in regular public schools. My guess is that charter schools do not per se promote vaccine exemption. But because they are more parent driven, or recruit certain types of parents, charter schools are more ideologically homogeneous. And because antivaccine ideology is concentrated among richer parents, charter schools provide them with a fertile ground in which to generate and transmit antivaccine ideas. That's why, although richer parents in general are driving vaccine denial, it's especially concentrated in charter schools. This seems consistent with the general echo-chamber nature of information sharing in cultural niches and the clustered, contagious nature of parenting fads.

The vaccine story seems to contradict the rich-parents-are-awesome idea, especially if you think rich people's parenting is great because more educated parents have more knowledge about what matters for kids. So it's an important caution for the general argument that social class status is passed from generation to generation because of the difference in parenting quality between richer and poorer parents. There is a mix of causal factors in the story of social class reproduction, including parenting decisions and more purely monetary benefits.

What is the best policy response to this situation? I would say public policy should help people be better parents but also reduce the gap in outcomes between children with better and worse parents. We already do that, of course—that's what schools are for—but we could do it better. If there is a social class gap in nutritional standards at home, for example, we provide good nutrition for all children at school. If poor parents don't have time and resources to provide sufficient child care and supervision, we can provide subsidies to make high-quality child care available to everyone. And so on. We can't mandate equal treatment of everyone at all times, but we can do a lot to mitigate the unequal consequences of parenting practices for children.

Figure 6. Children playing on seesaws at East Hill School in Ithaca, New York, circa 1970. Photo courtesy of the History Center in Tompkins County.

4. PARENTING SURVIVOR BIAS

Children's play used to be very dangerous. In 1910, about two hundred children were killed in the streets of New York City, most of them playing in the streets, doing work for their families, or just wandering around unattended. There were no public playgrounds in New York in 1910, but a few generations later parents were demanding safe places for their kids to play.[22]

Figure 6 shows the playground at my elementary school in Ithaca, New York. Those seesaws were great fun until the other kid got bored and hopped off while you were in the up position. I myself survived such a fall onto the broken-glass-strewn asphalt, with a nasty scrape to show for it (attended to by the school secretary; there was no "school nurse" back then). This kind of harsh experience made me the tough sociologist I am today. And what made me a wimp compared to 1910 kids made me gritty compared with 2010 kids. What does not kill us makes us stronger, goes the myth.

While some modern parents are trying to ease the way for the children's success, others are embracing the goal of training children to overcome adversity, to build up their *grit* (like the privileged parents who want to self-make their kids' immune systems by denying them vaccines). This concept was recently embraced by journalist Brigid Schulte in in her book *Overwhelmed* and trashed by education critic Alfie Kohn in *The Myth of the Spoiled Child*.[23] In addition to the confusion caused by receiving competing messages from experts, however, people's judgment is frequently corrupted by a common logical problem: survivor bias.

In a society that loves (to a fault) rags-to-riches stories, the neurosurgeon, motivational author, presidential candidate, and secretary of housing and urban development Ban Carson stands out as a man who rose from a poor Black family in Detroit to the pinnacle of professional success. One day on the campaign trail in 2016, Carson was retelling the mythical tale of how he was able to overcome being the kid nicknamed Dummy because his mother, who herself could barely read, required her children to read books.[24] She had turned their adversity into success, and Carson had emerged victorious.

"As a fifth-grade student, I was a horrible student," he told his Iowa audience. "Anybody here in fifth grade?" When a group of kids raised their hands, he asked, "Who's the worst student?" To his surprise, rather than just getting a chuckle, as he was accustomed to from adult audiences, Carson saw all the kids pointing at one of their own, a boy named Seth. The scene quickly went viral, making Carson look like a bully who had embarrassed an innocent, underperforming kid on a national stage. But Carson was serious. When his staff, doing quick damage control, brought Seth back to meet the candidate for a photo after the speech, Carson said to him, "You know what we're going to want for you, right? You're going to be a neurosurgeon, ok? But all you have to do, to turn it around, is *read*. I just started reading, I got to the point that it was my favorite thing in life. It didn't take long before I knew more than all those people who said I was dumb. So you do that, too, ok?"

This is an extreme example of survivor bias, identifying a single trait from an anomalous case and attributing the outcome to that quality. It's not surprising that the one child to rise from Carson's classroom to become a wealthy doctor read a lot, but that is not evidence that reading is the one ingredient necessary for success. The classic example of this is the hucksters who sell stock advice based on post hoc analysis of successful companies, recommending that people copy arbitrary bits of their practices.[25] Of course, reading is good, so this isn't bad advice. But it's still survivor bias because it's attributing a very unlikely outcome to a common trait—and turning that into single-minded advice: "Just read!" (I'll discuss the structural barriers to success for Black children in Detroit later, in chapter 7.)

When you apply survivor bias to something from your past that was really bad—that is, not just a single trait but a specific bad experience—you reproduce a common American meme: I am the person I am today because of the bad things that happened to me (implication: so stop complaining and get to work).

Take spanking. NFL player Adrian Peterson, caught beating his four-year-old son with a stick, said, "I have always believed that the way my parents disciplined me has a great deal to do with the success I have enjoyed as a man."[26] His logical error is the same at Carson's.

Consider a lifeboat with a dozen children. If just one boy survived, he would probably say, "I have always believed that my lifeboat experience has a great deal to do with the success I have enjoyed as a man." Who could blame him? That's the experience through which he sees everything that follows. And Americans might agree with his explanation, buying his books and paying to attend his motivational speeches. That's a survivor bias: the people who should be dragging down the average aren't there to weigh in.

Further, if you just look at a dozen famous neurosurgeons and find that every one of them read a lot as a child, that would seem like an open-and-shut case for reading. Or if you find a dozen professional football players who were beaten as kids. But without knowing how many kids experienced the same things and failed, you have no idea whether those experiences are generally useful at all. People who suffer and succeed often incorrectly attribute their success to what they suffered.

Spanking is so common and so widespread in the United States—especially among marginalized groups—that it's hard to say it caused anyone's success. In 2014, the General Social Survey found that 70 percent of Americans agreed with the statement "It is sometimes necessary to discipline a child with a good, hard spanking."[27] But when you break that down by race, gender, and the region people lived in when they were children, you find it rises as high as 88 percent among Black men who, like Peterson, are from the South (figure 7).

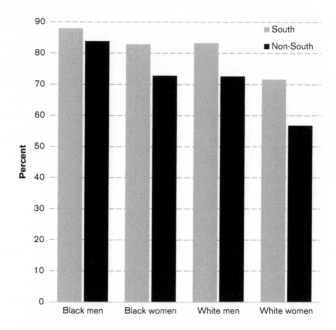

Figure 7. Percentage agreeing with the statement "It is sometimes necessary to discipline a child with a good, hard spanking": by race, gender, and region of residence at age sixteen. Source: Author analysis of the 2008–14 General Social Survey, available from the data archive at Survey Documentation and Analysis, sda.berkeley.edu/.

In the discussion of corporal punishment that surrounded the Peterson scandal, several Black commentators said harsh discipline was a matter of survival for Black children. *New York Times* columnist Charles Blow put it this way: "I understand the reasoning that undergirds much of this thinking about spanking: Better to feel the pain of being punished by someone in the home who loves you than by someone outside the home who doesn't."[28] And sociologist Michael Eric Dyson connected the practice directly to slavery and southern plantations: "Black parents beat their children to keep them from misbehaving in the eyes of whites who had the power to send black youth to their deaths for the slightest offense. Today, many black parents fear that a loose tongue or flash of temper could get their child killed by a trigger-happy cop. They would rather beat their offspring than bury them."[29]

With physical discipline nearly ubiquitous among southern Blacks a generation or more ago—and still pervasive today—it's probably impossible to determine whether today's Black adults benefited from the experience. (Overall, research shows that corporal punishment is more often harmful than helpful for children's subsequent development.)[30] But if spanking were a reasonable adaptation to racism and its attendant hardships, necessary for children to toughen up and learn to follow orders so they don't get killed by Whites, why would Black men support it more than Black women? Maybe Black men were disciplined more harshly when they were kids and therefore are more likely to see it as part of what helped them survive or succeed.

The people who think corporal punishment helps children because it helped them are not alone among the survivors of difficult childhoods. But that doesn't mean they're right.

Real Survivors

On top of the logical error of survival bias is a more subtle effect that is real: survival selection. It is real because the one lifeboat guy who lived was probably not randomly chosen to survive the ordeal—he was probably the healthiest in the first place, or maybe the meanest (shoving everyone off the boat and drinking their water). This makes his story, like Carson's and Peterson's, seem more credible, even though lifeboat populations have very high mortality and the lifeboat is not actually what made the survivor stronger. Harsh experiences may weed out weaker people, but that doesn't mean the harsh experience was actually good for the survivor. Avoiding the whole lifeboat experience is probably the best policy.

You can see this in another example, the "Black-White mortality crossover," a classic demographic puzzle I did some work on in graduate school.[31] Here's how it works. In the United States overall, Whites have a life expectancy 4.5 years longer than Blacks. At birth, they are projected to live to 78.7 versus 74.2 years respectively (all these numbers are for non-Hispanics). But at very advanced ages, Blacks have lower mortality rates than Whites in any given year; the crossover occurs at age 88 in the 2009 data (figure 8).

There are two explanations for this pattern. First, to live to old age in Black America you have to be tough. Infant mortality alone is 2.3 times

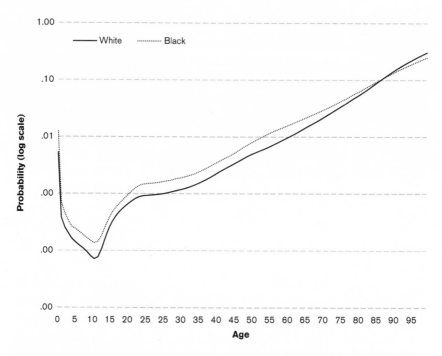

Figure 8. Probability of death, non-Hispanic Blacks and Whites by age, 2009.
Source: Author analysis of data from the National Center for Health Statistics.

higher for Black babies than for Whites, and the gap remains large through most of adulthood. This creates a survivor selection effect. Because of the greater risks to their health at younger ages, Blacks in America have had to run a survival gauntlet to get to old age. From birth, 89 percent of Whites can expect to live at least to age sixty, compared with only 82 percent of Blacks. The most hardy Black people are most likely to make it through, and as a result they are less prone to dying than the Whites who had a relative cakewalk to old age. The other reason is actually a data error: Blacks at older ages are more prone to exaggerating their ages, meaning some of those people over age eighty-eight aren't quite as old as they say (and birth records weren't that good for Blacks in 1920, especially in the South). Even a little rounding up is enough to skew the race differences at old ages, because the rates rise a lot with every year of age. This exaggeration is actually a cultural expression of the survivor effect—it shows that it's a badge of honor to have made it through that gauntlet.

The Black-White mortality crossover means that, although Whites live longer than Blacks overall, at older ages there are Black survivors who feel justifiably proud of their longevity (and might even attribute it to the hardships they experienced).

Making the best of a bad situation might be a good practice for survivors, and not a bad lesson to impart to our children, but in the end most bad experiences are actually bad.

5. SANTA'S MAGIC, CHILDREN'S WISDOM, AND INEQUALITY

Eric Kaplan, channeling Francis Pharcellus Church, writes in favor of Santa Claus in the *New York Times*. The Church argument, written in 1897, is that (a) you can't prove there is no Santa, so agnosticism is the strongest possible objection, and (b) Santa enriches our lives and promotes nonrationalized gift giving, "so we might as well believe in him."[32] It's a very common argument, identical to one employed against atheists in favor of belief in God, but more charming and whimsical when directed at killjoy Santa deniers.

All harmless fun and existential comfort food. But we have two problems that the Santa situation may exacerbate. The first is science denial, and the second is inequality. So consider this an attempted joyicide.

Science

From Pew Research comes this Christmas news: "In total, 65% of U.S. adults believe that all of these aspects of the Christmas story—the virgin birth, the journey of the magi, the angel's announcement to the shepherds and the manger story—reflect events that actually happened."[33] On some specific items, the scores were even higher. The poll found 73 percent of Americans believe that Jesus was born to a virgin mother—a belief shared even by 60 percent of college graduates. (Among Catholics agreement was 86 percent, and among Evangelical Protestants 96 percent.)

So the Santa situation is not an isolated question. We're talking about a population with a very strong tendency to express literal belief in fantastical accounts. This Christmas story may be the soft leading edge of a more hardcore Christian fundamentalism. For the past twenty years, the General Social Survey (GSS) has found that a third of American adults agree with the statement "The Bible is the actual word of God and is to be taken literally, word for word," versus two other options: "The Bible is the inspired word of God but not everything in it should be taken literally, word for word" and "The Bible is an ancient book of fables, legends, history, and moral precepts recorded by men." (The "actual word of God" people are less numerous than the Virgin Birth believers, but the two beliefs are related.)

Using the GSS for the years 2010–14, I analyzed people's social attitudes according to their view of the Bible (see figure 9). Controlling for their sex, age, race, and education, and the year of the survey, those with more literal interpretations of the Bible were much more likely than the rest of the population to

- Oppose marriage rights for gay men and lesbians
- Agree that "people worry too much about human progress harming the environment"
- Agree that "it is much better for everyone involved if the man is the achiever outside the home and the woman takes care of the home and family"

In addition, among non-Hispanic Whites, people believing in the literal truth of the Bible were more likely to rank Blacks as more lazy than hardworking and to believe that Blacks "just don't have the motivation or willpower to pull themselves up out of poverty."[34]

This isn't the direction I'd like to push our culture. Of course, teaching children to believe in Santa doesn't necessarily create "actual word of God" fundamentalists—but there's some relationship there.

Children's Ways of Knowing

In 1932 Margaret Mead challenged the notion that young children not only knew less, but knew differently, than adults, in a way that paralleled

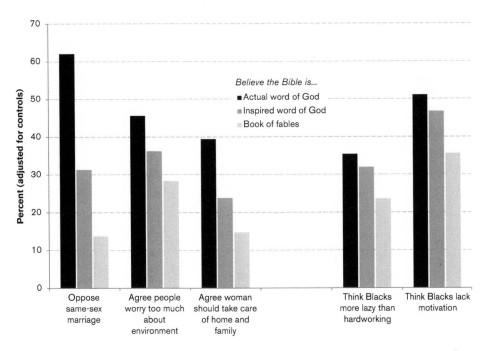

Figure 9. How social attitudes differ according to view of the Bible. Percentages shown are adjusted for age, sex, education, and race/ethnicity. Attitudes toward Blacks shown for non-Hispanic Whites only. Source: Author analysis of the 2010–14 General Social Survey available from the data archive at Survey Documentation and Analysis, sda.berkeley.edu/.

the evolution of society over time. Children were thought to have thought processes much like those of "savages," with animism in "primitive" societies being similar to the spontaneous thought of young children. This went along with the idea that believing in Santa was indicative of a state of innocence. In pursuit of empirical confirmation of the universality of childhood, Mead investigated the Manus tribe in Melanesia, who were pagans, to look for magical thinking in children: "animistic premise, anthropomorphic interpretation and faulty logic."[35]

Instead, she found "no evidence of spontaneous animistic thought in the uncontrolled sayings or games" of a few dozen children over five months of continuous observation. And while adults in the community attributed mysterious or random events to spirits and ghosts, children never did: "I found no instance of a child's personalizing a dog or a fish or a bird, of his personalizing the sun, the moon, the wind or stars. I found no evidence of a child's attributing chance events, such as the drifting away of a canoe, the loss of an object, an unexplained noise, a sudden gust of wind, a strange deep-sea turtle, a falling seed from a tree, etc., to super-naturalistic causes."[36]

On the other hand, adults blamed spirits for hurricanes hitting the houses of people who behaved badly, believed statues could talk, thought lost objects had been stolen by spirits, and said people who were insane were possessed by spirits. The grown men all thought they had personal ghosts looking out for them—with whom they communicated—but the children dismissed the reality of the ghosts that were assigned to them. They didn't play ghost games.

Does this mean magical thinking is not inherent in childhood? Mead wrote: "The Manus child is less spontaneously animistic and less traditionally animistic than is the Manus adult [*traditionally* here referring to the adoption of ritual superstitious behavior]. This result is a direct contradiction of findings in our own society, in which the child has been found to be more animistic, in both traditional and spontaneous fashions, than are his elders. When such a reversal is found in two contrasting societies, the explanation must be sought in terms of the culture; a purely psychological explanation is inadequate."[37]

Maybe people have the natural capacity for both animistic and realistic thinking, and societies differ in which capacity they nurture and develop through children's education and socialization. Mead speculated that the pattern she found had to do with the self-sufficiency required of Manus children. A Manus child, she wrote, must "make correct physical adjustments to his environment, so that his entire attention is focused upon cause and effect relationships, the neglect of which would result in immediate disaster. . . . Manus children are taught the properties of fire and water, taught to estimate distance, to allow for illusion when objects are seen under water, to allow for obstacles and judge possible clearage for canoes, etc., at the age of two or three."[38] Further, perhaps in contrast to our own industrialized society's complex technology, the simple technology of the Manus is understandable to children without the invocation of magic. And she observed that parents didn't tell the children imaginary stories, myths, and legends.

I should note here that I'm not saying we have to choose between religious fundamentalism and a society without art and literature. The question is about believing things that aren't true and can't be true. I'd like to think we can cultivate imagination without launching people down the path of blind credulity.

Modern Credulity

For evidence that culture produces credulity, consider the results of a study that showed most four-year-old children understood that Old Testament stories were not factual. Six-year-olds, however, tended to believe the stories were factual, *if* their impossible events were attributed to God rather than rewritten in secular terms (e.g., "Matthew and the Green Sea" instead of "Moses and the Red Sea").[39] Why? Belief in supernatural or superstitious things, contrary to what you might assume, requires a higher level of cognitive sophistication than does disbelief, which is why five-year-olds are more likely to believe in fairies than three-year-olds.[40] These studies suggest children have to be taught to believe in magic. (Adults use persuasion to do that, but teaching with rewards—like presents under a tree or money under a pillow—is of course more effective.)

Children can know things either from direct observation or experience or from being taught. So they can know dinosaurs are real if they believe books and teachers and museums, even if they can't observe them living (true reality detection). And they can know that Santa Claus and imaginary friends are not real if they believe either authorities or their own senses (true baloney detection). Similarly, children also have two kinds of reality-assessment errors: false positive and false negative. Believing in Santa Claus is false positive. Refusing to believe in dinosaurs is false negative. In figure 10, which I adapted from a paper by Jacqueline Woolley and Maliki Ghossainy, true judgment is in regular type, errors are in italics.[41]

We know a lot about kids' credulity (Santa Claus, tooth fairy, etc.). But according to Woolley and Ghossainy their skepticism has been neglected: "Development regarding beliefs about reality involves, in addition to decreased reliance on knowledge and experience, increased awareness of one's own knowledge and its limitations for assessing reality status. This realization that one's own knowledge is limited gradually inspires a

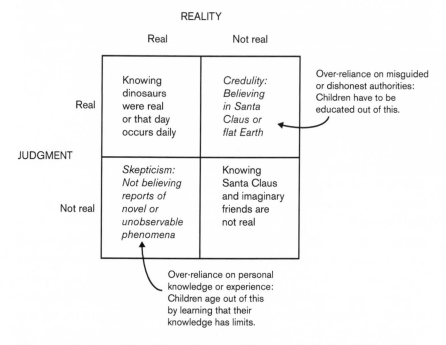

Figure 10. True knowledge, false positives, and false negatives in how children think.

waning reliance on it alone for making reality status decisions and a concomitant increase in the use of a wider range of strategies for assessing reality status, including, for example, seeking more information, assessing contextual cues, and evaluating the quality of the new information."[42]

The "realization that one's own knowledge is limited" is a vital development, ultimately necessary for being able to tell fact from fiction. But, sadly, it need not lead to real understanding: indeed, under some conditions, such as, apparently, those in the United States today, it often leads instead to reliance on misguided or dishonest authorities who compete with science to fill the void beyond what we can directly observe or deduce. Believing in Santa because we can't disprove his existence is a developmental dead end, a backward-looking reliance on authority for determining truth. But so is failure to believe in vaccines or evolution or climate change just because we can't see them working.

We have to learn how to avoid the italics boxes without giving up our love for things imaginary, and that seems impossible without education in both science and art.

Rationalizing Gifts

What is the essence of Santa, anyway? In Kaplan's *New York Times* essay it's all about nonrationalized giving, or giving for the sake of giving. The latest craze in Santa culture, however, says otherwise: Elf on the Shelf, which exploded on the Christmas scene after 2008, selling in the millions. In case you've missed it, the idea is to put a cute little elf somewhere on a shelf in the house. You tell your kids that it's watching them and that every night it goes back to the North Pole to report to Santa on their nice/ naughty ratio. While the kids are sleeping, you move it to another shelf in house, and the kids delight in finding it again each morning.

In other words, it's the latest in Michel Foucault's Panopticon development.[43] Consider the Elf on a Shelf aftermarket accessories, like the handy warning labels, which threaten children with "no toys" if they aren't on their "best behavior" from now on. Is this nonrationalized gift giving? Quite the opposite. In fact, rather than cultivating a whimsical love of magic, Elf on a Shelf is closer to a dystopian fantasy in which the conjured enforcers of arbitrary moral codes leap out of their fictional realm to impose harsh consequences in the real lives of innocent children.

Inequality

My developmental question regarding inequality is this: What is the relationship between belief in Santa and social class awareness over the early life course? How long after kids realize there is class inequality do they go on believing in Santa? This is where rationalization meets fantasy. Beyond worrying about how Santa rewards or punishes them individually, if children are to believe that Christmas gifts are doled out according to moral merit, than what are they to make of the obvious fact that rich kids get more than poor kids? Rich or poor, the message seems the same: children deserve what they get.

I can't demonstrate that believing in Santa causes children to believe that economic inequality is justified by character differences between social classes, or that Santa belief undermines future openness to science and logic. But those are hypotheses. Between the antiscience epidemic and the pervasive assumption that poor people deserve what they get, the whole Santa enterprise seems risky. Would it be so bad, so destructive to the wonder that is childhood, if instead of attributing gifts to supernatural beings we told children that we just buy them gifts because we love them unconditionally and want them—and all other children—to be happy?

If parenting practices matter for children—and they must—then family structure must matter as well; before we can ask what effects adult behavior have on children, we have to know which adults we're talking about in the first place. Debating the finer points of parenting may seem like a middle-class pursuit—and middle-class voices do dominate the endless public conversations of this kind—but of course parents at all income levels worry about what they can do to help their children be happy, healthy, and successful. And family structure imposes some crucial limits on their options—the topic to which we turn next.

2 Marriage, Single Mothers, and Poverty

A pillar of modern ideology is the belief that we're individual actors determining our own destinies and that any undesirable outcome should be blamed on, and punished as, the individual's failure. Our treatment of single parents may be the paradigmatic illustration of that belief. The "blame the victim" view of poverty begins with the decisions mothers make that are believed to cause their children's poverty—and only then extends to blaming the children themselves when (or even before) they become poor adults. So that's what this chapter is about: blaming poverty on single mothers, and, through the framework of modern individualism, disciplining the whole population.

1. WHAT DOES IT TAKE TO ELIMINATE POVERTY?

Recently, two Washington think tanks—the (barely) left-leaning Brookings Institution and the (very) right-leaning American Enterprise Institute (AEI)—brought together a panel of experts to produce a "consensus plan" to address poverty and the lack of social mobility in the United States. As has become common practice for think tanks, they released the report at a gath-

ering of reporters and writers, policy people, and other think tank opera-
tives known as a "launch event." Since Brookings and AEI are among the
most influential (and rich) think tanks in town, the event was held at the
National Press Club, and it featured a keynote speech by *New York Times*
columnist David Brooks.[1] All of this—the bipartisan panel, the press event,
the celebrity columnist—showed what a Big Issue poverty had become.

Watching the launch event video online, my frustration grew at the
portrayal of poverty as something beyond simple comprehension and
unreachable by mortal policy. It's just not. As I will explain, the whole
child poverty problem amounts to $62 billion per year. There are certainly
important details to be worked out in how to eliminate it, but the basic
idea is pretty clear—you give poor people money. We have plenty of it.

This conclusion was obvious, yet amazingly not remarked upon in the
first forty minutes of the launch event (which, I admit, is all I watched).
The opening presentation, by Ron Haskins, started with a simple chart of
official poverty rates, which I have reproduced in figure 11 using Census
Bureau data.

Haskins started by pointing to the line for poverty rates among the elderly, which he called "the nation's greatest success against poverty." He
added, "There is good research that shows that it's caused at least 90 percent by Social Security. So, government did it, and Social Security is the
reason we're able to be successful to reduce poverty among the elderly."

Then everyone at the event proceeded to ignore the obvious implication
of Haskins's statement: when you give people money, they aren't poor anymore. The most unintentionally hilarious such evasion was in the keynote
address by David Brooks. He said this, according to my unofficial
transcript:

> Poverty is a cloud problem and not a clock problem. This is a Karl Popper
> distinction. He said some problems are clock problems—you can take them
> apart into individual pieces and fix them. Some problems are cloud prob-
> lems. You can't take a cloud apart. It's a dynamic system that is always inter-
> spersed. And Popper said we have a tendency to try to take cloud problems
> and turn them into clock problems, because it's just easier for us to think
> about. But poverty is a cloud problem. . . . A problem like poverty is too com-
> plicated to be contained by any one political philosophy. . . . So we have to be
> humble, because it's so gloomy and so complicated and so cloud-like. . . .

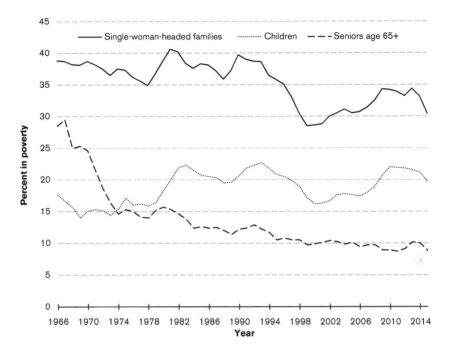

Figure 11. Poverty rates for children, seniors, and single-woman-headed families, 1966–2015. Source: US Census Bureau historical poverty tables, www.census .gov/data/tables/time-series/demo/income-poverty/historical-poverty-people .html.

Poverty is an and/and issue, because it takes a zillion things to address it, and some of those things are going to come from the left, and some are going to come from the right. . . . And if poverty is this mysterious, unknowable, negative spiral-loop that some people find themselves in, then surely the solution is to throw everything we think works at the problem simultaneously, and try in ways we will never understand, to have a positive virtuous cycle. And so there's not a lot of trade-offs, there's just a lot of throwing stuff in. And social science, which is so prevalent in this report, is so valuable in proving what works, but ultimately it has to bow down to human realities—to psychology, to emotion, to reality, and to just the way an emergent system works.

Poverty is only a "mysterious, unknowable, negative spiral-loop" if you specifically ignore the lack of money that is its proximate cause. The vast majority of poor people either can't work or do work that doesn't pay enough. They don't need character, they need cash. Sure, spend your whole life wondering about the mysteries of human variation—but could we agree to do that after taking care of people's basic needs?

I wonder if poverty among the elderly once seemed like a weird, amorphous, confusing problem. I doubt it. But it probably would have if we had assumed that the only way to solve elderly poverty was to change the personalities and behaviors of children to induce them to give their parents more money. Then we would have to worry about the market position of their children, the timing of their births, the complexity of their motivations and relationships, the vagaries of the market, and the folly of youth. Instead, we tax earnings and give the money to old people. Imagine that.

So, How About We Stop Moralizing and End Child Poverty?

How much would you pay to stop having to listen to rich people tell poor people how to run their families? If my calculations are correct, we can end child poverty for $62 billion per year. Is that a lot? No, it's not. It's $578 per nonpoor family—and I'll put it on a sliding scale for you. Details below.

David Brooks is not alone in his thinking. Americans tend to think of poverty as a giant, intractable problem, combining intergenerational dynamics, complex policy trade-offs, conflicting cultural values, and "personal responsibility" (not to mention genetics). For example, in her book *Generation Unbound,* Isabel Sawhill (also a Brookings analyst) says, "If we could return marriage rates to their 1970 level, the child poverty rate would be about 20 percent lower."[2] She's (wisely) not advocating that, because it's impossible, but think of it. Rolling back one of the major demographic trends of the last half century would be social reversal on an unprecedented scale—for a measly 20 percent reduction in poverty? Apple alone could eliminate 100 percent of US poverty for two years with the money under its couch cushions.[3]

In our system, the vast majority of poor people are in hard-to-employ categories. As Matt Bruenig recently wrote, 83 percent of poor people are either children, old people, people with disabilities, students, people taking care of family members, or people who can't find jobs. (Among the employed poor, most are poor because they are sharing their income with family members who can't work.) We are "a country that relies heavily on the market to distribute the national income," Bruenig writes.[4] That's true, but it's actually the market via the family. If these vulnerable groups are people who need someone else's labor to support them, at least temporarily, then the attitude written into our policies is that such support should come from their families. If your family can't do it—or you don't have a family—good luck. It doesn't have to be this way.

Look: children usually (fortunately) don't make money. Somehow income from someone else's labor has to pay for their homes, schools, medical care, and food. A lot of that money comes from (that is, through) the state (for rich and poor kids alike). But under our stingy welfare state, if their parents don't have decent jobs they wind up poor. The mind-set that sees our welfare system as an immutable object looks at this and says, "These kids are poor because of their parents; they shouldn't have had kids if they were poor." Wrong. They're poor because we insist on it.

In a commentary piece, Sawhill clarified that the main reason children of single mothers have a hard time is that they lack resources: "The effects on children of the increase in single parents is no longer much debated. They do less well in school, are less likely to graduate, and are more likely to be involved in crime, teen pregnancy, and other behaviors that make it harder to succeed in life. Not every child raised by a single parent will suffer from the experience, but, on average, a lone parent has fewer resources—both time and money—with which to raise a child. Poverty rates for single-parent families are five times those for married-parent families."[5] That's right. The children of single parents are more likely to be poor because they have fewer parents present, and the ones they do have make less money than other parents (they're women, they're often poor women, and they're often taking care of kids alone, so they're time- as well as cash-poor). And that has consequences for the children's future development and well-being.

But I would like to live in a society—in a neighborhood, a community—in which people without good jobs can still have children, while they're young, and have happy families. And I'm willing to pay my share of the cost of that. Are you? It's not as much as you think.

Here are the details. The poverty line is a dollar amount assigned to every family based on the number of adults and children living together.

Table 1.   How to eliminate child poverty at a cost of $61.6 billion.

Nonpoor deciles	Families (thousands)	Average total resources	Average surplus	Tax rate on surplus	Average tax per family	Total raised (thousands)
1	10,665	188,919	155,520	.018	2,799	29,856,002
2	10,007	101,948	73,693	.016	1,179	11,799,626
3	10,511	78,625	53,036	.014	742	7,804,523
4	10,723	64,819	40,390	.012	485	5,197,364
5	10,719	53,975	31,040	.010	310	3,327,199
6	10,899	45,193	23,346	.008	187	2,035,486
7	10,744	37,658	16,777	.006	101	1,081,563
8	10,605	30,977	11,231	.004	45	476,436
9	10,972	24,893	6,351	.002	13	139,364
10	10,943	18,390	2,013	.000	0	0
Total	106,789	$59,395	$40,874	.014	$578	$61,717,562

SOURCE: Author calculations from the March 2014 Current Population Survey via IPUMS.org.

NOTE: *Families* refers to Supplemental Poverty Measure Resource Units, which are families (or single people) presumed to share expenses and income. Surplus is the amount by which the family's total resources exceeds the poverty threshold. $61.6 billion is the total needed to raise every poor family with children above the threshold.

With the 2014 Current Population Survey data, I calculated how much each poor family was below their poverty threshold. Summed together, that is the amount we need to raise (each year) to end child poverty.

I'm just focusing on families with children for now. There are 6.5 million poor families with a child under eighteen, and on average they are $9,450 below the poverty line based on their family size and composition. So, to eliminate child poverty we need $61.6 billion per year.[6] Where are we going to get that kind of money? I distributed this cost across the nonpoor families, on a sliding scale, and put the results in table 1.

There are 107 million nonpoor families, which works out to about $578 per family per year to pay this bill and end the scourge of child poverty. Of course, $578 is a lot of money for some people, but on average the nonpoor families have incomes $40,874 more than their poverty threshold. To ease the pain, I created a simple sliding scale. I broke the nonpoor families into ten equal-size bins from rich to less rich, and slid the tax rate from 1.8

percent down to 0 percent (that way there's no penalty for moving just over the poverty line). So a family with total resources (cash income and other inflows) of about $54,000 would pay about $310 per year.

How hard would this program be to implement? We already have all the infrastructure in place to move income around; it's just a change in the tax code—you give tax refunds to people whose incomes are below the line and tax people whose incomes are above it. My proposed tax is applied only on the *surplus* for each family—that is, the resources they have (after taxes, work expenses, health care, and child care) over their poverty threshold. If we tax the surpluses of the richest 10 percent of nonpoor families at the virtually painless rate of just 1.8 percent—and everyone below them at an even lower rate—we end child poverty in the United States.

Some people say the pope should stick to religious matters and not speak about politics. Some people also say a social scientist should stick to scientific analysis and not make moral demands. You can ignore my moralizing, because I am no moral authority. But you should understand the fact that child poverty is a choice we make with our policies. Eliminating child poverty does not require restructuring American families, conducting mass contraception campaigns, or instilling a new ethos of shame to change the behavior of the poor.[7] It just costs a little money.

2. REDUCING POVERTY THROUGH MARRIAGE

The business of ignoring the simple solutions to poverty and pumping up the many mysteries underlying the problem involves careful scrutiny of poor people's personal lives, especially their family lives. One such approach is to assert that poor people have inherent (biological, genetic) flaws. Charles Murray, a senior researcher at the AEI, leads on this front, writing, for example:

> No major Republican politician is willing to say in public that some of the social problems we most deplore are rooted to some degree in personal deficiencies. Try to imagine a GOP presidential candidate saying in front of the cameras, "One reason that we still have poverty in the United States is that a lot of poor people are born lazy." You cannot imagine it because that kind of thing cannot be said. And yet this unimaginable statement merely implies

that when we know the complete genetic story, it will turn out that the population below the poverty line in the United States has a configuration of the relevant genetic makeup that is significantly different from the configuration of the population above the poverty line. This is not unimaginable. It is almost certainly true.[8]

Murray is right that mainstream politicians don't talk this way. Politicians focus instead on the flawed behavior of poor people, for which they may—in polite political discourse—be blamed. Republican politicians have lined up to offer marriage as a solution to poverty. Then-candidate for president Jeb Bush said, "The most effective anti-poverty program is a strong, two parent family."[9] That was also a theme for Florida Republican senator Marco Rubio in his presidential campaign. It's a popular message among conservatives (especially appealing to voters who are married and not poor). "The greatest tool to lift children and families from poverty is one that decreases the probability of child poverty by 82 percent," Rubio said. "But it isn't a government program. It's called marriage."[10]

That 82 percent statistic came from a Heritage Foundation operative named Robert Rector (who is the cartoon-villain embodiment of partisan hackery). Rector observed that the poverty rate for single parents with children was 37.1 percent, compared with 6.8 percent for married couples with children. He concluded, "Being raised in a married family reduced a child's probability of living in poverty by about 82 percent."[11]

That's it! The difference between 37.1 and 6.8 is 30.3, which is 82 percent of 37.1, so marriage reduces poverty 82 percent. You don't get to be the "intellectual godfather of welfare reform" (as Rector has been called) without knowing a thing or two about statistics—or by obsessing about the details of cause and effect.[12]

However, using Rector's simplistic logic, there is stiff competition for the "*greatest* tool for lifting people out of poverty." For one thing, what about increasing your income? Rubio could just as well have said, "The greatest tool for lifting people out of poverty is a *full-time job*, which decreases the probability of living in poverty by 85 percent." That's because the poverty rate for children who don't have a full-time, year-round employed parent is a whopping 58 percent, compared with only 8 percent for those kids who do—an 85 percent reduction in poverty risk.[13]

Unfortunately, when the political fact-checking website PolitiFact investigated Rubio's statement and my rebuttal, they let him go on a technicality, giving him a "mostly true" rating.[14] Rubio's error is not about policy details or math, though; it's about causality. If we made a law that only rich people could get married, the census data would give you a similar result—not because marriage caused wealth, but for the opposite reason.

That other part of Rubio's statement—"the greatest tool . . ."—is also wrong. Using a multivariate approach (statistically considering a number of factors at once), I can illustrate the relative greatness of three important poverty-reducing tools: marriage, employment, and education. Figure 12 shows the poverty rates for children with and without each of these parental conditions, estimated at the average values of each variable (in addition to age, sex, race, and ethnicity, which are not shown).

Each condition is associated with a lower probability of living in poverty for children. But notice two things. First, of the three tools, marriage is the least great once the other factors are considered—it's associated with the smallest reduction in poverty. And second, once the other factors are considered, the poverty reduction associated with marriage is much less impressive than it was in Rubio and Rector's formulation—the drop now is only from 15 percent to 9 percent. That's because poverty is reduced by income, and of these three factors marriage has the least direct effect on income. Employment is obviously greatest, and college increases income by allowing people to get better jobs; marriage works mostly by bringing another earner into the family, and also through a reverse-causality effect—people with greater income (or earning potential) are more likely to be married.

Telling people to get a job, or an education, if they don't want to be poor is no more or less helpful, or innovative as a policy, than telling them to get married. These are all things the vast majority of parents would do if they had their druthers—and things people who aren't poor will blame them for not doing if they fail.

And Blame They Do

Beyond the relentless affirmation of marriage's antipoverty value, one of the meanest right-wing statistical memes about poverty is the question,

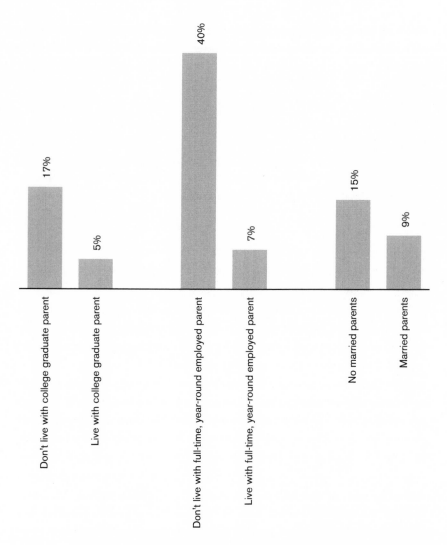

Figure 12. Predicted percentage of children poor, by parental conditions. Source: Author calculations from the 2015 March Current Population Survey via IPUMS.org. Children are ages zero to seventeen; estimates are shown at the mean of controls for child age, sex, race, and ethnicity.

"With all the money we've given them, why are the poor still poor?" I saw it in a commentary by Christine Kim, who wrote:

> Since the mid-1960s, government has spent more than $19.8 trillion (in 2011 dollars) in total on means-tested welfare programs. With 80 such federal programs, targeted government spending for low-income families—including on health, education, housing, and income supports—totaled nearly $930 billion in fiscal 2011 alone. If converted to cash, this sum would be four times what is needed to lift every poor family out of poverty. About half of this annual means-tested spending goes to families with children. If divided among the 14 million poorest families with children, each family would receive about $33,000. Why, then, have poverty rates remained so high for so long? Clearly, the solution to alleviating poverty is not more of the same.[15]

Ron Haskins of Brookings used the same numbers, rearranged slightly, to come to the same conclusion: money spent on means-tested programs is wasted because poor people refuse to get married (and get jobs).[16] This way of manipulating welfare state spending, like the marriage and poverty meme, seems also to have originated from Robert Rector at Heritage, who offered it in congressional testimony in 2012.[17]

This meme is—and I am choosing my words carefully—stupid and evil.

It's stupid because it ignores how poverty is calculated and how "means-tested" money is spent. If you took away Medicaid and housing support alone, the poverty line for a single mother with two children would have to be a lot higher—because poor people would have to spend more of their incomes on these necessities. About half of all that means-tested money is spent on medical care, mostly Medicaid. So, if you took away Medicaid (and Obamacare subsidies), how much would a single mother with two children need to survive? Health insurance alone would cost her more than $10,000 (and without an insurance subsidy the risk of catastrophic costs would be untenable).

Further, all those nonpoor families living on $33,000 or more in employment income are getting benefits, too, like tax-subsidized employer-provided healthcare, mortgage interest deductions, unemployment insurance, and retirement savings. If you took all that away and gave these nonpoor families $33,000 to live on, they wouldn't be nonpoor for long. So the argument is stupid.

It's also evil, because it says, "We've thrown so much money at poor people and it just doesn't work, so it's time for them to step up and contribute a little themselves." This ignores the reality that most poor people either can't work or are already working, just not for pay. The main thing Kim wants them to do is get married. She even says, "If single mothers simply were to wed the father of their child, their likelihood of living in poverty would fall by two-thirds" and adds that "contrary to myth the fathers are quite 'marriageable.'"

Her calculations for this are not shown, which is probably just as well. But the idea that the "benefits" of marriage—that is, the observed association between marriage and nonpoverty—would accrue to single mothers if they "simply" married their current partners is bonkers. The notion of a "marriage market" is not perfect, but there is something like a marriage queue that arranges people from most likely to least likely to marry. When you say, "Married people are better off than single people," a big part of what you're observing is that, on average, the richer, healthier, better-at-relationships people are at the front of that queue, more likely to marry and then to display what look like the benefits of marriage. Those at the back of the queue, who are less (if not totally) "unmarriageable," clearly aren't going to have those highly beneficial marriages if they "simply" marry the closest person. They don't have the assets. (I return to this problem in the next chapter.)

But back to evil. The idea that we've spent so much on poverty that it proves spending doesn't solve poverty is like saying, "We've spent $32 trillion on the military just since 1949, and we don't have complete world domination yet, so obviously war is not the answer." Oh, wait, I do agree with that (figure 13).

Why do we keep throwing money into war after war after war, watching the trillions add up with no measurable progress toward our stated goals? Because we don't spend money on the military and fight wars to fix the world, to "cure" it and prevent future wars. We do it to fatten defense contractors, tighten the labor market, prop up unpopular allies, and defend the country from the occasional threat. The defense industry doesn't have to defend the claim that the spending is a one-time thing to eliminate a problem. In the same way, giving poor people money—or in-kind

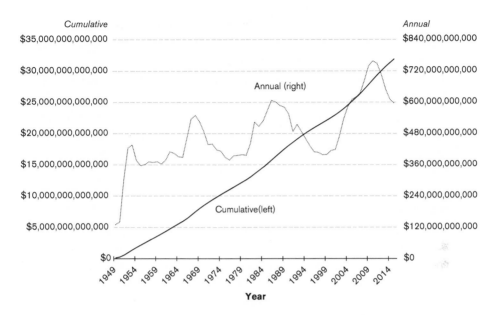

Figure 13. US military spending, 1949–2015 (constant $2014). Source: Stockholm International Peace Research Institute, www.sipri.org/.

benefits—to lift them out of poverty today, to help them survive, is not a solution to poverty, it's a treatment for poverty. If we had more decency we'd do more of it.

3. SINGLE MOTHERS AND CRIME

When single mothers aren't being held responsible for the problem of poverty, they're often being blamed for other social ills, including crime. The connection between family structure and crime has become harder and harder to make rationally, but that might not have made it less politically potent.

Consider Washington, D.C. From its peak in 1991 to the recent low point in 2012, the homicide rate in that city fell 83 percent. (Nationally during that time violent crime fell by about half.) That's the kind of stunning good news that ought to inspire a radical reevaluation, subjecting our assumptions and understandings about urban crime to new scrutiny and holding up our policies to the light of the new facts.

And yet, when we do discuss these positive trends, the "breakdown" of the family is usually not part of the story. That's surprising because it was a *big* part of the story twenty-five years ago, when D.C. was the murder capital of the country in the midst of a national crime wave. I think single mothers—especially those who were raising their kids back in the 1990s—deserve an apology from the conventional-wisdom purveyors of that time.

While the D.C. homicide rate was dropping 83 percent, the percentage of children living with single mothers hardly changed (falling just a few percentage points).[18] Looking at the plunge in murder, an Associated Press story in 2012 consulted experts and concluded that the success could be attributed to rising incomes, improved law enforcement technology and community relations, and better trauma care to save shooting victims (although the number of nonfatal assaults has fallen similarly).[19] If that's what caused the decline, why was the murder rate so high in 1991? If you go back to the press reports from the late 1980s and early 1990s, you would have heard a lot about family structure.

Here's a very early *Washington Post* story about D.C. and Baltimore, from 1985, raising the alarm about an apparent growing epidemic of amoral, violent, young Black men:

> Such incidents have raised new fears here and across the country about the growing instability of urban black family structure and the creation of an underclass of young men capable of killing for a warmup jacket or a pair of running shoes. Social scientists, law enforcement officials and community leaders share some of the same theories about the reasons for this kind of homicide among poor black youngsters. They point to the intense desire for material things amid deprivation, easy access to handguns, and the inability of parents—often young, unmarried mothers—to control or instill values in their children.[20]

In 1991, when Health and Human Services Secretary Louis W. Sullivan released a study on homicide trends, he declared:

> The collapse of the American family in the past few decades is historically unprecedented in the U.S., and possibly in the world. Nowhere is this trend

more apparent than in the black community. Some argue that the high rate of single parenthood has not adversely affected our children. But, sadly, the research does not bear them out. . . . Study after study has shown that children from single-parent families are five times more likely to be poor and twice as likely to drop out of school. . . . They are also more likely to be involved in criminal activity, to abuse drugs and alcohol, to suffer ill health, and to become trapped in welfare dependency.[21]

Sullivan's solution was a return to a "culture of character," in which, among other things, "children growing up without a father are a small minority." A 1994 article focusing on the increase in homicide among young people summarized it this way: "At the bottom of all this, people in every section of the juvenile justice system say, is a critical lack of parenting. . . . Federal officials estimate that 70 percent of children in juvenile court are from single-parent households. In the last 30 years, the proportion of single mothers has grown from one in 20 to one in four."[22]

Family structure and parenting were not the only explanations offered for the epidemic of murder. There was plenty written about crack cocaine and the drug war turf disputes, the availability of guns, and poverty and failing schools. But that single-parent theme was quite widespread. Maybe single mothers have since gotten better at instilling character in their would-be criminal sons—in which case they should also get more credit today.

What Is the Connection?

It's easy for a rational observer now to see that the links between single motherhood and crime were overblown. But in 1990 the connection seemed obvious. Looking at the national trends, by 1990 the proportion of families (with children) headed by single mothers was 2.5 times higher than it had been in 1960, and violent crime had increased by 4.5 times (figure 14). Who could doubt that the collapse of the traditional family was driving the explosion of violent crime?

However, by my reading of the research, although it is true that children of single mothers are more likely to commit crimes, other factors are more important. That must be the case, or we wouldn't see the overall US trends in crime and single-parent families split so dramatically starting in the 1990s.

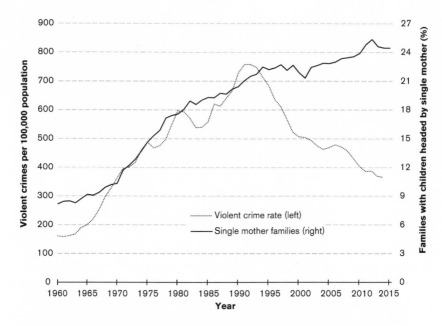

Figure 14. Single-mother families and violent crime rates, 1960–2015. Sources: Single-mother families from US Census Bureau, www.census.gov/topics/families /families-and-households.html; crime rates from FBI Uniform Crime Reports, www.fbi.gov/about-us/cjis/ucr/crime-in-the-u.s/2014/crime-in-the-u.s.-2014 /tables/table-1.

When I suggested we reevaluate the single-mother blame story in an essay on the *Atlantic* website, I faced an excited conservative backlash.[23] The consensus among them was that single parents do cause crime but that incarceration prevents crime. As incarceration increased, eventually it overcame the effect of family breakdown. In essence, they now blamed single mothers (and "deadbeat" dads) not only for crime but also for mass incarceration.

Maggie Gallagher, prominent leader in the movement to stop gay marriage, wrote: "The ending of the violent crime wave was a great policy achievement. It seems however to involve massively incarcerating millions of young men we have not succeeded in civilizing. There is never only one way to skin a cat. But I'm not sure our souls should rest too comfortably on the solution we found."[24] More concisely, *New York*

Times columnist Ross Douthat tweeted, "Fortunately, family breakdown doesn't create any problems that mass incarceration of young men can't solve." (Charles Murray called that tweet "Lovely. Menckenesque.")[25] Elizabeth Marquardt, who worked for a right-wing family website, chimed in, "Well for Pete's sake, one thing we now do is lock up a lot more of those fatherless boys and throw away the key. Which means less crime."[26] Then Brad Wilcox wrote a blog post under the title, "Who Needs an Intact Family? Jail Will Do Just Fine," suggesting that we might be "forced to choose between a stronger marriage culture and mass incarceration."[27]

Looking at two aggregate trends, as I have in figure 14, is never enough to tell a whole story of social change, of course. However, if two trends going together doesn't prove a causal relationship, the opposite is not quite as true—if two trends do *not* go together, the theory that one causes the other has a steeper hill to climb; other variables must be involved. Regardless of whether incarceration contributes to the decline in crime (and the strength of this association is debated), the theory that family structure drives the trend is in trouble. It is one thing to say that children who grow up with one parent present are more likely to commit violent crime. As a statistical association that is true, although the causal story is muddied by important confounds. But it is another—unjustified—thing to say that the crime wave of the 1980s and 1990s was substantially driven by the rise of single parents, which was a common assumption.

To seriously investigate this question, we need to get beyond the fact that children with unmarried parents are more likely eventually to commit crimes and ask how *much* of the violent crime problem is attributable to this relationship. Just as millions of poor people live in married-couple families—even as single parents are much more likely to be poor—many violent criminals grew up with married parents. Here's one stab at quantifying the relationship.

Stephen Demuth and Susan Brown wrote, in 2004, that identifying the causal effect of family structure itself on whether kids become violent is very difficult. You need to consider parental monitoring and supervision, the quality of the relationship between parents and children, and the level of conflict in the home, as well as poverty, education, family transitions, housing, neighborhood factors, and so on.[28] However, they offered some numbers we can use to roughly estimate the relationship between single parenting and violent crime.

Using a large, national survey, they added up the self-reported violent acts of students in grades 7 to 12 in 1995. The kids were asked how many times in the last year they (1) "hurt someone badly enough to need bandages or care from a doctor or nurse," (2) "use or threaten to use a weapon to get something from someone," and (3) "take part in a fight where a group of your friends is against another group." They didn't ask the specific number of times but rather asked kids to report "0 (never), 1 (once or twice), 2 (three or four times), or 3 (five or more times)." I used those reports to create a ballpark estimate of the number of violent incidents.

That gives us enough to get a sense of what was going on in 1995, near the peak of the crime wave. The idea was just to see the magnitude of the family structure difference and the relative contribution to violence of kids in each group. By my rough reckoning (inexact because the survey didn't literally count every violent act), children of single mothers committed an average of 1.9 violent acts per year, compared with 1.2 violent acts for kids whose parents were married. That's a pretty big difference. (Children living with single fathers were the most violent, incidentally, at 2.3 acts per year.)

In this sample, 26 percent of children lived with parents. On the basis of the amount of violence committed by each kid, and the relative size of the groups, I calculate that those 26 percent of kids living with single parents committed 35 percent of the violent acts. That is definitely more than their share, but it's not close to most of the total. Note that there are a host of real reasons, not taken into account here, why children with single parents commit more violence. The calculation is just to estimate the size of the difference we are trying to understand.

To take still another swing at this, I looked at the family backgrounds of people in prison. In her critique of my essay, conservative writer Kay Hymowitz cited a study from 1987 that found 70 percent of juveniles in custody didn't grow up with both parents, and another from Wisconsin 1994 that found 87 percent.[29] But Hymowitz missed the large, national study the Bureau of Justice Statistics does on inmates, which includes family background information. With a few calculations, I figured out from their 2004 survey that 55 percent of state and federal prisoners did not "live most of the time while growing up" with both parents.[30] That is still a majority of prisoners, but it's clearly not the whole crime problem.

That 2004 survey also showed that three-quarters of state and federal inmates had previously been sentenced to prison or probation. So maybe the biggest cause of crime is incarceration. That sounds circular, but it's not crazy when you realize that, contrary to the quote from Elizabeth Marquardt above, mass incarceration isn't usually about "throwing away the key." Most prisoners get out. In 2010, for example, about seven hundred thousand went in, and seven hundred thousand came out—so it's very reasonable to ask whether incarceration affects people's propensity to commit acts of violence in the future.[31]

In light of all this, what do we make of the association between single parenthood and crime, anyway? The prisoner survey also showed that the folks in prison had experienced high rates of poverty, homelessness, substance abuse, physical abuse, and the incarceration of other family members. In that light, if only 55 percent of this population is from homes without married parents, that's not a very strong case for an independent effect of family structure—the single parenthood was just part of a suite of conditions and problems compounding each other. In fact, this is consistent with other research showing that family structure per se does not drive children's violent delinquency; instead, the violent acts of children of single parents are more likely caused by problems of family attachment, negative peer interactions, and neighborhood conditions that lead to violence.[32]

In sum, I have no trouble believing that the decline of married-couple living arrangements contributed to the rise in violent crime rates since the 1960s. And we have to be able to consider that without assigning blame to these parents. Single-parent families have lots of challenges and short-ages—mostly of money and time—that make it harder for them, on average, to keep their kids in line. (And, of course, one of the causes of single parenthood is the rise of incarceration.) In the absence of adequate support from the state, the labor market, or other family members to help them get by, it's not surprising that the problems they experience include a higher risk of violence. But there are many other conditions and problems contributing to violence and crime that we could address short of rearranging people's family structure (which, as we'll see in the next chapter, is highly impractical anyway). And in the end I see nothing to justify the apocalyptic end-of-civilization associations between single mothers and crime that were commonly served up in the 1990s—and that apparently are still appealing to many of today's family conservatives.

The corollary of single-mother blame is marriage promotion. This is the policy that many liberals and conservatives have come to agree on, at least in principle—trying to find a way to get more poor people married. Proponents have spent a lot of money and a lot of time, and have poured a lot of shame and scorn on single parents, but their efforts have yet to yield any change in the downward trend in marriage rates. So why do they persist? They have their reasons, as we'll see in the next chapter.

3 Marriage Promotion

The federal marriage promotion policy was officially launched with the 1996 welfare reform, although it had long historical antecedents. In the end it will surely be recorded as another abuse of the weak for political purposes, producing no benefit for the targets of the policy while shoring up the ideological and political commitment and constituencies of its proponents. But in this case the movement—which is what marriage promoters consider themselves—included a large research and policy-producing establishment, reformers with PhDs and foundation expense accounts, who had personal as well as philosophical investments in the cause. It has been a disaster—achieving nothing, costing a lot—but somehow these protagonists have managed to survive unscathed and unchastened.

1. WE CAN'T BUILD OUR SOCIAL SYSTEM AROUND MARRIAGE ANYMORE

Twenty years ago, the conservative Hoover Institution published a symposium titled "Can Government Save the Family?" A who's-who list of that decade's culture warriors—including Dan Quayle, James Dobson, John

Engler, John Ashcroft, and David Blankenhorn—was asked, "What can government do, if anything, to make sure that the overwhelming majority of American children grow up with a mother and father?"[1]

There wasn't much disagreement on the panel: end welfare payments for single mothers, stop no-fault divorce, remove tax penalties for marriage—and fix "the culture." From this list the only victory they got was welfare reform, which drove some single mothers into the workplace and increased the immiseration of many single-parent families but didn't affect the trajectory of marriage and single motherhood. So the collapse of marriage continues apace. Since 1980, for every state in almost every decade the percentage of women who are married has fallen. That is, in 200 cases of state changes in marriage rates since 1980, 198 show declines (the exceptions are Utah in the 1990s and Vermont in the 2010s).[2]

But the "marriage movement" lives on. In fact, its message has changed remarkably little. In that 1996 symposium, Dan Quayle wrote: "We also desperately need help from nongovernment institutions like the media and the entertainment community. They have a tremendous influence on our culture and they should join in when it comes to strengthening families." Sixteen years later, in its "State of Our Unions" report, the National Marriage Project included a ten-point list of familiar demands, including this point #8: "Our nation's leaders, including the president, must engage Hollywood in a conversation about popular culture ideas about marriage and family formation, including constructive critiques and positive ideas for changes in media depictions of marriage and fatherhood."[3] Most recently, the 2015 "consensus" report on poverty and mobility to which I referred in chapter 2 again urged a public information campaign to promote marriage.[4] (In my class last year, one Black student described a billboard in her neighborhood promoting marriage that stood for years, gradually fading throughout her childhood, showing a happy formal wedding photo.)

So little reflection on such a bad track record—it's enough to make you think they're not actually serious about increasing the marriage rate. Advocates like to talk about turning it around, bringing back a "marriage culture." But is there a precedent for this, or a reason to expect it might happen? Not that I can see, in the United States or anywhere else. Figure 15 shows the trend in the marriage rate since 1940, with some possible

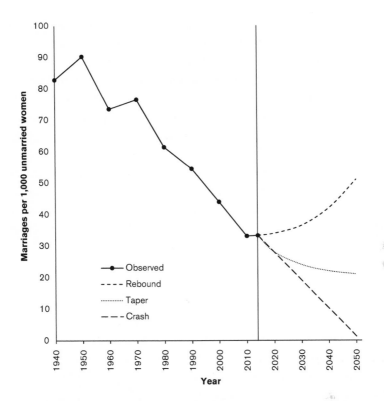

Figure 15. Refined marriage rate, 1940–2014 (with scenarios to 2050). Sources: National Center for Health Statistics (1940–60), www.cdc .gov/nchs/data/vsus/vsrates1940_60.pdf, Table 107; National Center for Family and Marriage Research (1970–2000), www.bgsu.edu /content/dam/BGSU/college-of-arts-and-sciences/NCFMR /documents/FP/FP-13-11.pdf; author analysis of American Community Survey data from IPUMS.org (2010–14); author imagination (2015–50).

scenarios to 2050. (This is the refined rate, or the number of new marriages relative to the number of unmarried women.)

Unsurprisingly, 1950 was peak marriage, a year in which 90 out of every 1,000 unmarried women got married (or 9 percent of all eligible women). From that year the decline was quite steep; it was almost straight down after 1970—an unprecedented drop of more than 50 percent in those four decades. Note that figure 15 leaves out individual-year fluctuations to give us a bird's-eye view of the historical trend. But I left in the fluctuation from 2010 to 2014; that may simply reflect a catch-up from marriages that were delayed by the Great Recession (which began in 2008), or it might be the beginning of change in the trend. In any event, the long-term drop is unlike anything we've ever seen.

This decline in marriage is also global. Official statistics for Europe show that 89 percent of the population live in countries that have seen declining marriage rates every decade since the 1970s. Marriage is also declining in most of the world, from Pakistan and Russia to Mexico, Brazil, and Japan.[5] It is true that the giant countries—China and India—both have near-universal marriage, but even there, as in most rich and poor countries, marriage age is creeping up.[6] And most concerning to would-be marriage promoters, there are as yet *no cases* of major developed countries reversing this trend.

Something has to give. The line in figure 15 labeled "Crash" shows what will happen if the US marriage rate keeps declining at the average rate seen between 1950 and 2014—it hits zero just after 2050. Of course, major demographic trends usually don't just smash into 0 or 100 percent, so I don't expect that. Alternatively, as the marriage movement folks hope, the trend might rebound. I show a hypothetical rebound, which is really the most optimistic twist imaginable—a reversal the scale of which has never been seen in history. Even that unrealistically optimistic scenario would only get marriage rates back up to their mid-1990s level by 2050—and remember that in the mid-1990s the sky-is-falling community was already pretty sure civilization was headed for a dismal demise. The more realistic future is some kind of taper, which I have also added to the figure. In that scenario, which is optimistic about marriage but not ridiculously so, we eventually learn to live with a marriage rate as low or lower than what we have now. And we can do that.

How Much Marriage?

The people promoting marriage never specify—or even seriously consider—how much marriage they want, which is how you can distinguish them from social scientists. They simply treat every potential increase in marriage as good and every downtick as a sign of the deepening crisis. They describe marriage at the societal level as a *thing*—so you can speak of "strengthening marriage," which just means having more of it. But maybe marriage as a system would work better—creating more stable, more beneficial, more egalitarian social relationships—if the practice were less than universal, if it occupied something less than our whole adult lives. I don't know what the best level is, but I do know that the optimal point would depend on other social conditions; there might be a world where 100 percent or 0 percent marriage was ideal, but I assume that in our world it must be somewhere in between, and that it's a moving target.

It's obvious that marriage is most universal in poorer societies, and also those with less gender equality. Consider the broadest pattern. Among 125 countries with available data, there is a strong correlation between the percentage of women married and gender inequality (using a composite UN measure that takes into account maternal deaths and teen births, and the gaps in political representation, education, and employment). Those with more marriage are less gender equal (figure 16).

Return to the two largest developing countries in the world, India and China, which are labeled in figure 16, together representing more than a third of the world population. The figure shows an interesting contrast. Both are considered middle-income countries by the World Bank, but China's average income is about 4.5 times greater. In India the average age at marriage for women is low (about twenty) and 98 percent of women in their early thirties are married; the country ranks 130th in the world in gender equality. Indian men are twice as likely as women to have a high school education, and three times as likely to be in the labor force; just 12 percent of the national parliament is female. China's women are just as likely to marry by their early thirties, but they marry at about age twenty-four on average, a crucial difference. This is related to China's long-term investments in education for girls as well as boys, its promotion of women's labor force participation, and its much lower fertility rate. As a result, Chinese women are much more equal to men than are India's, and the country ranks fortieth in gender inequality.[7] Early, universal marriage is a key barrier to gender equality.

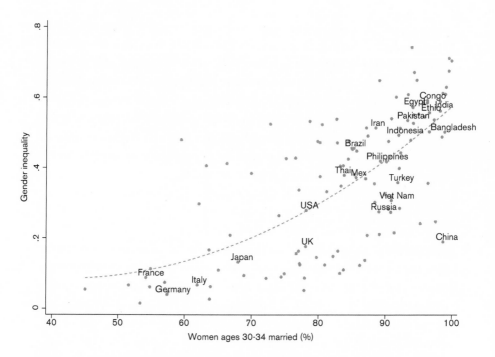

Figure 16. Marriage and gender inequality in 125 countries. Data for 2000 or later, as compiled in 2008. Sources: Marriage data from United Nations Population Division; gender inequality from United Nations Development Programme, Human Development Reports.

Considered with the evidence of falling marriage rates over time, this global pattern suggests that the decline in marriage—people spending a smaller portion of their lives married, on average—is part of a larger global transition toward gender equality. Of course, gender equality is just one socially desirable goal. My point is that if we always assume more marriage is good and less is bad, we can't seriously consider the potential trade-offs. There are good marriages (characterized by cooperation, love, intimacy, and stability for children), and bad marriages (with exploitation, rape and violence, child abuse, misery, and alienation), as well as good and bad outcomes for people who aren't married. The number of marriages is not on its own a good indicator of social well-being generally, or family well-being specifically.

Live with It

In the face of these ambiguities, and the apparent impossibility of trying to redirect the ship of marriage, we have to do what we already know we have to do: reduce the disadvantages accruing to those who aren't married, or whose parents aren't married. If we take the longer view, we know this is the right approach. In the past two centuries we've largely replaced such once-vital family functions as food production, health care, education, and elder care with a combination of state and market functions. Consequently—despite results that are, to put it mildly, uneven—our collective well-being has improved rather than diminished even as families have lost much of their material hold on modern life.

This doesn't mean family stability is unconnected with well-being. In fact, the two are reinforcing. In their book *Doing the Best I Can,* sociologists Kathryn Edin and Timothy Nelson argue that policies to improve the economic security of poor people and their children also tend to improve the stability of their relationships.[8] That fits with the comprehensive policy analysis done by Shawn Fremstad and Melissa Boteach, who recommend pairing economic policies such as employment and wage support with social services including reproductive health care and couples counseling. They argue convincingly that the resulting economic and social security for those with relatively low incomes could result in more stable families as well.[9] Note that more family stability does not always mean a higher marriage rate—although it might—but rather a greater level of control over family life, and less stress and tumult in children's lives. In addition to more marriage, family stability might include better, more supportive relationships with nonresident parents, more stable cohabiting relationships, and less hardship in single-parent families.

What we can't count on is marriage itself as the linchpin in our system of care. We can't build our social welfare system around the assumption that everyone does or should get married if they or their children want to be adequately cared for. That's what it means when pensions are based on a spouse's earnings, when people are dependent on employers to provide sick leave or family leave, and when high-quality preschool is unaffordable for most people. So let marriage be truly voluntary, and maybe more people will even end up married. Which is fine.

2. MARRIAGE (NOT) PROMOTED

Increasing marriage is a long-standing goal of federal welfare policy. The first lines of the 1996 welfare reform law, which famously ended welfare as we knew it, were these:

> The Congress makes the following findings:
>
> (1) Marriage is the foundation of a successful society.
>
> (2) Marriage is an essential institution of a successful society which promotes the interests of children.
>
> (3) Promotion of responsible fatherhood and motherhood is integral to successful child rearing and the well-being of children.[10]

In any other rich country, this might seem like an odd opening for legislation enabling a program to provide assistance to poor families, especially single-parent families. But here, marriage is king—at least when it comes to moralistic political rhetoric. The title of the act, "Personal Responsibility and Work Opportunity Reconciliation," clearly signals what it is *not* about: providing material assistance to people with inadequate income to support their families.

In the service of this ideological assertion about the importance of marriage—that is, one that could not be empirically tested—the federal government proceeded to spend more than a billion dollars promoting marriage among the poor, money that came from the federal welfare program and went out through the Healthy Marriage Initiative and the Responsible Fatherhood Initiative, which were greatly expanded during the Bush administration. When President Bush was promoting the Healthy Marriage Initiative in 2004, the Heritage Foundation's Robert Rector and Melissa Pardue were delighted, their optimism unbridled:

> The President's Healthy Marriage Initiative is a future-oriented, preventive policy. It will foster better life-planning skills—encouraging couples to develop loving, committed marriages before bringing children into the world, as opposed to having children before trust and commitment between the parents has been established. The marriage program will encourage couples to reexamine and improve their relationships and plan wisely for the future, rather than stumbling blindly into a childbirth for which neither

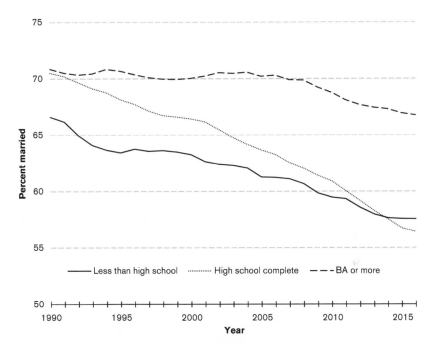

Figure 17. Percentage married, ages twenty-five to fifty-four, by education level, 1990–2016. Three-year moving averages. Source: Author analysis of Current Population Survey data via IPUMS.org.

parent may be prepared. The program will also provide marriage-skills education to married couples to improve their relationships and to reduce the probability of divorce.[11]

The real-life sad spectacles produced by the policy have included, for example, requiring lesbians (when they weren't even allowed to marry) and mothers with no partners to attend marriage education classes.[12] But it hasn't worked. And since the new policies took effect, marriage rates have fallen *fastest* for those with a high school education or less—the people most affected by the policy (figure 17). So as a policy it's not working.

In addition to the broad trends, we have solid, scientific program evaluations that look directly at the hundreds of millions of dollars spent and rigorously tests the programs' impact on people who actually participated in them. The US Department of Health and Human Services, which runs the programs, paid for rigorous research to evaluate them. The early reports were not good.[13] Unfortunately for the programs, the subsequent results unequivocally showed total failure.

(Not) Building Strong Families

The first major evaluation of federal marriage promotion was an eight-city study of more than 5,100 couples in the Building Strong Families (BSF) program. They used an "intent to treat" research design in which new-parent couples (unmarried or just married) who applied for the support program were randomly either given services or not. The experimental group got things like relationship skills education, a family support coordinator, and referrals to supportive services. The participants were an at-risk bunch—half African American, two-thirds not high school graduates, half with a child from a prior relationship, and earning, as a couple, on average about $20,000. After about fifteen months, the study followed up.[14]

This is the main finding: Nothing. There was no observable difference—not a *small* difference, not *almost* a difference, but *no* difference—in the percentage of program couples that were still together, cohabiting, or married, compared with the control group couples.

The Oklahoma City branch of the program, known as Family Expectations, did report that enrolled, unmarried couples had better "relationship quality" after fifteen months and had more positive attitudes toward marriage in principle—but they were still no more likely to be married than the control group.[15] On the other hand, the BSF report showed that there were *negative* effects at the Baltimore program site, where program couples were less likely to be romantically involved, were less supportive and affectionate, and had more assaults, worse coparenting relationships, and lower levels of father involvement.

But maybe it just took longer to show positive effects? No. The thirty-six-month evaluation was no more encouraging.[16] The comparison between those participating and those who applied but were randomly denied services showed no difference in relationship quality, relationship status, or, most important, marriage rate. Researchers found that fathers in the treatment group were actually less likely to spend time with their children thirty-six months later. On the other hand, children whose parents were in the treatment group were slightly less likely to have behavioral problems. It would be shocking indeed if a giant program with millions of dollars couldn't do anything of value for couples that volunteered to participate. But the fact that they produced no results on the key program goal of increasing marriage was devastating. Or it would have been if the marriage promoters were motivated by evidence.

(Not) Supporting Healthy Marriage

The BSF program was not focused on married couples. A separate program, Supporting Healthy Marriage (SHM), provided marriage education to low-income *married* couples with (or expecting) children. In their evaluation, more than six thousand couples in eight locations were randomly assigned to receive the training or not.[17] Those in the program group had a four- to five-month series of workshops, followed by educational and social events to reinforce the curriculum. "Longer than most marriage education services and based on structured curricula shown to be effective with middle-income couples, the workshops were designed to help couples enhance the quality of their relationships by teaching strategies for managing conflict, communicating effectively, increasing supportive behaviors, and building closeness and friendship. Workshops also wove in strategies for managing stressful circumstances commonly faced by lower-income families (such as job loss, financial stress, or housing instability), and they encouraged couples to build positive support networks in their communities."

This was a high-quality program with a good quality evaluation. And participation rates were good, with the average couple participating in twenty-seven hours of services and activities. But the treatment and control groups followed the exact same trajectory. At twelve months, 90 percent of both groups were still married or in a committed relationship, and after thirty months the figure was 81.5 percent (exactly!) for both groups. The study team also broke down the very diverse population but could not find a race/ethnic or income group that showed noteworthy different results. A complete failure.

But wait. There were some small improvements in subjectively measured psychological indicators. How small? For relationship quality, the effect of the program was .13 standard deviations, equivalent to moving 15 percent of the couples 1 point on a 7-point scale from "completely unhappy" to "completely happy." So that's something. Further, after thirty months, 43 percent of the program couples thought their marriage was "in trouble" (according to either partner) compared with 47 percent of the control group. That was an effect size of .09 standard deviations. So that's something, too. Many other indicators showed no effect. However, I discount even these small effects, since it seems plausible that program participants just learned to say better things about their marriages. Without something beyond a purely subjective report—for example, domestic violence reports or kids' test scores—I wouldn't be convinced even if these results weren't so weak.

In weighing the results, consider the cost: in round numbers, $9,100 per couple, not including evaluation or start-up costs. That would be $29 million for half of the 6,298 couples. The program staff and evaluators should have thanked the poor families who involuntarily gave up that money from the welfare budget in the service of the marriage promotion agenda. We know that cash would have come in handy—so thanks, welfare!

The mild-mannered researchers, realizing (one can only hope) that their work on this boondoggle was coming to an end, concluded, "It is worthwhile considering whether this amount of money could be spent in ways that bring about more substantial effects on families and children." One idea would be to just give the poor couples $9,000.

Boulevard of Broken Program Evaluation Dreams

Some of the people trying to bolster these programs—researchers, it must be said, who are themselves supported by the programs—have produced almost comically bad research. Here I'll briefly describe one such effort.

The program evaluation studies were directed at the people who participated in model programs. But the marriage promotion effort has been deep and wide, spreading money all around the country. By one informal estimate, relationship education and fatherhood programs have reached about a million people.[18] And what about the wider social impact—the people who see the billboards, whose friends are in programs, who get pamphlets or encouraging (or coercive) messages? In an article in the journal *Family Relations*, Alan Hawkins, Paul Amato, and Andrea Kinghorn attempted to show that the marriage promotion money had beneficial effects at the population level.[19]

They statistically compared state marriage promotion funding levels to the percentage of the population that was married and divorced, the number of children living with two parents or one parent, the nonmarital birth rate, and the poverty and near-poverty rates for the years 2000–2010. This kind of study offers an almost endless supply of subjective, post hoc decisions for researchers to make in their search for some relationship that passes the official cutoff for "statistical significance." Here's an example of one such choice these researchers made to find beneficial effects (no easy task, apparently): arbitrarily dividing the years covered into two separate periods. Here is their rationale: "We hypothesized that any HMI [Healthy Marriage Initiative] effects were weaker (or nonexistent) early in the decade (when funding levels were uniformly low) and stronger in the second half of the decade (when funding levels were at their peak)."

This is wrong. If funding levels were low and there was no effect in the early period, and then funding levels rose and effects emerged in the later period, then the analysis for all years should show that funding had an effect; that is the point of the analysis. This decision does not pass the smell test. Having determined that this decision would help them show that marriage promotion was good, they went on to report their beneficial effects, which were "significant" if you allowed them a 90 percent confidence (rather than the customary 95 percent, which is kosher under some house rules).

However, then they admitted their effects were significant only with Washington, D.C., included. Our nonstate capital city is a handy wiggle-room device for researchers studying state-level patterns; you can justify including it because it's a real place, or you can justify excluding it because it's not really a state. It turns out that the District of Columbia had per capita marriage promotion funding levels about nine times the average. With an improving family well-being profile during the period under study, this single case (out of fifty-one) could have a large statistical effect on the overall pattern. Statistical outliers are like the levers you learned about in physics—the further they are from the average, the more they can move the pile. To deal with this extreme outlier, they first cut the independent variable in half for D.C., bringing it down to about 4.4 times the mean and a third higher than the next most-extreme state, Oklahoma (itself pretty extreme). That change alone cut the number of significant effects on their outcomes down from six to three.

Then, performing a tragic *coup de grâce* on their own paper, they removed D.C. from the analysis altogether, and nothing was left. They didn't quite see it that way, however: "But with the District of Columbia excluded from the data, all of the results were reduced to nonsignificance. Once again, most of the regression coefficients in this final analysis were comparable to those in Table 2 in direction and magnitude, but they were rendered nonsignificant by a further increase in the size of the standard errors."

Really. These kinds of shenanigans give social scientists a bad name. (Everything that is nonsignificant is that way because of the [relative] size of the standard errors—that's what *nonsignificant* means.) And what does "comparable in direction and magnitude" mean, exactly? This is the kind of statement one hopes the peer reviewers or editors would check closely. For example, with D.C. removed, the effect of marriage promotion on two-parent families fell 44 percent, and the effect on the poor/near-poor fell 78 percent. That's "comparable" in the sense that they can be compared, but not in the sense that they are similar. Again, the authors helpfully explain that "the lack of significance can be explained by the larger standard errors." That's just another way of saying their model was ridiculously dependent on D.C. being in the sample and that removing it left them with nothing.[20]

Oh well. Anyway, please keep giving the programs money, and us money for studying them: "In sum, the evidence from a variety of studies with different approaches targeting different populations suggests a potential for positive demographic change resulting from funding of [Marriage and Relationship Education] programs, but considerable uncertainty still remains. Given this uncertainty, more research is needed to determine whether these programs are accomplishing their goals and worthy of continued support."

So if, after hundreds of millions of dollars, the programs don't work, at least maybe the researchers can get some more money out of it. The lead author, Alan Hawkins, has received about $120,000 in funding from various marriage promotion sources.

In the face of this unanimously bad news, the marriage promoters have taken to referring to the research as producing "mixed" results. These are some common rebuttals they have learned to offer, with my responses:

- *We shouldn't expect government programs to work. Just look at Head Start.* Of course, lots of programs fail. And, specifically, some studies have failed to show that kids whose parents were offered Head Start programs do better in the long run than those whose parents were not. But Head Start is offering a service to parents who want it, a service that most of them would buy on their own if it were not offered free. Head Start might fail at lifting children out of poverty while successfully providing a valuable, need-based service to low-income families.

- *Rich people get marriage counseling, so why shouldn't poor people?* As you can imagine, I am all for giving poor people all the free goods and services they can carry. Just make it totally voluntary, don't do it to change their behavior to fit your moral standards, and don't pay for it by taking cash out of the pockets of poor families. I fully support marriage counseling for people who want it, but this is not the policy platform to get that done.

- *These small, subjectively measured benefits are actually very important and were really the point anyway.* No, the point was to promote marriage, from the welfare law itself. If the point was to make poor people happier, Congress never would have approved it.

- *We have to keep trying. We need more programs and more research.* If you want to promote marriage, here's a research plan: have a third group in the study—in addition to the program and control group—who get cash equivalent to the cost of the service. See how well the cash group does, because that's the outcome you need to surpass to prove this policy a success.

The bottom line is that after the first $1 billion of welfare money, the federal program has not one proven healthy marriage to show for it.

3. TURNS OUT MARRIAGE AND INCOME INEQUALITY GO PRETTY WELL TOGETHER

As popular attention has turned to the issue of economic inequality, the forces of marriage promotion have seized on the idea that changing family structure—the decline of marriage—is part of the problem. And a small part of why income inequality has increased is that we have more families with one low income and more families with two high incomes.[21] So it's true that if we could go back to the days when every high-earning man married a low-earning woman, income inequality would be somewhat lower. And wouldn't that be progress!

However, there are two problems with hitching the marriage promotion wagon to this fact. The first is that the most dramatic increase in economic inequality has been the result of more and more concentration of very high incomes and vast wealth. This is the main story told in the blockbuster book about rising inequality by Thomas Piketty, *Capital in the Twenty-First Century*. One implication is that taxing the very rich would do a lot more to reduce inequality than things like raising the minimum wage (important as that is to do) or getting poor people to marry each other. The other problem is logical. Just because the decline of marriage has contributed to rising inequality does not necessarily mean that increasing marriage rates now would reduce inequality. Or at least not very much.

Two think tank marriage promoters, Bob Lerman and Brad Wilcox, recently made their case this way: "Had marriage rates not declined substantially among parents, many more families would have attained middle-class incomes, and the inequality across families would have increased at a slower rate."[22] It is true that falling marriage historically did contribute to rising inequality because of increasing selectivity in marriage, so that richer people were getting and staying married more, and increasing social class endogamy, so that there were more two-high-income families lording over more one-low-income families. And all of that has been exacerbated by widening underlying inequality, with high-end incomes generally pulling away from low-end incomes, relatively unchecked by income redistribution.

One obvious solution is to take money away from married high-income people and give it to single low-income people. With all the benefits that married people get—many of them through no special effort of their own, but rather as a result of their social status at birth, race, health, good looks, legal perks, or lucky breaks—it seems reasonable to tax marriage, like a windfall profits tax, or an inheritance tax, or a progressive income tax. But if you're squeamish about taxing a behavior that is "good" like marriage, you might prefer just taxing wealth a little more, which would accomplish much the same thing. This elegant solution would decrease inequality, increase well-being for poor people, and equalize life chances for children. In other words, it's politically out of the question.

What about the less reasonable but more often mentioned solution—more marriage—that Wilcox and Lerman promote? Maybe then low-income single people could become high-income married people. But, failing that (and they would fail at that), they would at least become low-income *married* people. The family science right-wing establishment says to poor single people: "See how well married people are doing? Get married and you'll be like them." To their rich donors and political allies, they say, "Make *them* earn their benefits by demonstrating their moral fiber and manning up, like *us*." Welfare reform attempted this and successfully forced many single mothers into the labor force for the cause of character development—but it failed in its goal of marrying them off.

So more marriage is the plan, and the marriage movement has set a course that leads inexorably to success (for them): either by successfully raising marriage rates among the poor (extremely unlikely) or by justifying the continued denial of basic welfare to the poor and shoring up the political case against economic redistribution (extremely likely).

Why should we think that today's unmarried people would get the same benefits from marriage that currently married people do? If marriage is becoming increasingly selective—that is, it's increasingly the most well off who are getting and staying married—then you can't assume that the benefits observed among actually married people would be reaped by those who have so far been left out (or have opted out) of the increasingly stringent marriage selection process. They may not have the assets that lead to marriage benefits: skills, wealth, social networks, and so on.

Wilcox and Lerman say that family income would have risen more—and there would be less inequality—if more people were married, because the incomes of married couples rose faster than average. They show that at the median, that is, in the middle of the income distribution, the income of married-parent families has grown faster than the income of single-parent families. The fact that single-parent families are mostly below the median contributes to growing inequality and a stagnant overall median. They think this shows that more families would have had growing incomes if they had been married.

Figure 18. Married-parent family income at the tenth, fiftieth, and ninetieth percentiles, 1979–2016. Income is adjusted for inflation; includes different-sex married-parent families in their own households, in which the husband is age twenty-five or older. Source: Author analysis of Current Population Survey data via IPUMS.org.

Going beyond the median to compare the top and bottom of the income distribution will help us see not just growing inequality but also why getting poor people to marry won't help them as much as Wilcox and Lerman say it would. Let's look at the ninetieth and tenth percentiles, as well as the median, among married-parent families. Figure 18 shows that the income of the married-parent family's ninetieth percentile has risen 50 percent since 1979, while that of the median has risen 24 percent. But the tenth percentile's income has fallen 4 percent. So if poor single people finally start getting married, which married parents are they going to look like?

The chart shows dramatically increasing inequality among married-parent families. The high end of the married-parent income distribution is where the big gains are, and these are not the parents that the marriage promoters are talking about. Pouring more married couples into the bottom of this distribution—which is what marriage promotion would do, even if it were successful at increasing marriage—isn't likely to fix the problem of inequality.

4. MARRIAGE PROMOTION AND THE MYTH OF TEEN PREGNANCY

A number of prominent liberals and conservatives have publicly agreed that marriage promotion is a good policy to help reduce poverty. For example, *New York Times* columnist Nicholas Kristof cited "the importance of two-parent families" as one of the issues where Republicans have "proved right."[23] Journalist Ruth Graham, writing in the *Boston Globe,* quoted sociologist Andrew Cherlin summing up the shifting mood: "It's true that there's a line some liberal sociologists won't cross, that line of accepting marriage as the best arrangement. . . . But I think there are a growing number of sociologists who would concede that in the world we live in today, marriage seems like the best way to give kids a stable family life."[24] I was quoted as the dissenting sociologist, not because I'm against marriage but because, as Graham paraphrased me, "simply prodding the currently unmarried into matrimony will not magically make them more stable, healthy, and wealthy."

Although, as we have seen, the evidence in favor of marriage promotion policies is not there, the marriage promoters are still holding onto the idea of a cultural revival, and in recent years they have taken to using as an example the supposed success of the cultural intervention to reduce teen pregnancy in order to show how we might increase marriage and reduce nonmarital birth rates. This has been a common refrain from Brad Wilcox, quoted here by Graham: "As evidence of his optimism, Wilcox points to teen pregnancy, which has dropped by more than 50 percent since the early 1990s. 'Most people assumed you couldn't do much around something related to sex and pregnancy and parenthood,' he said. 'Then a consensus emerged across right and left, and that consensus was supported by public policy and social norms. . . . We were able to move the dial.'"

This is the same conclusion drawn in the "consensus" poverty report I discussed earlier.[25] I think that interpretation is not just wrong but the opposite of right.

I don't know of any evidence that cultural intervention affected teen birth rates. Cultural *intervention* effects are not the same as wider cultural effects—of course, cultural change is part of the trend in marriage and birth timing. For example, a popular economics paper showed reductions in teen birth rates in places where *16 and Pregnant* was more popular, but even if that show was influential the finding is not evidence that the campaign to reduce teen pregnancy worked.[26] Yes, there was a campaign to end teen pregnancy, and teen pregnancy declined. I think the trend might have happened for the same set of reasons the campaign happened in the first place—the same reasons for the decline in marriage and the shift toward later marriage. The campaign was one expression of shifting norms toward women's independence, educational investment, and delayed family formation. When culture changes, it will be apparent in things like the *16 and Pregnant* effect.

Teen Pregnancy Doesn't Exist

If you had never heard of "teen pregnancy," you would see the decline in births among teenagers as what it is: part of the general historic trend toward later births and later marriage. If you look at birth rates for all ages, there is a consistent shift toward older ages: few births at young ages, more at older ages (figure 19).

Nothing special seems to be happening with teens. As teen births fall, for example, births for women over age thirty-five have risen the fastest—these are not the same women, but they are part of the same trend, having babies later. And it's not limited to this country; teen birth rates are falling around the world. The global teen birth rate fell 29 percent from 1994 to 2014. It is true that teen births fell faster in the United States in the last twenty years than they did in most other rich countries, but that was from a much higher starting point. As of 2014, teen birth rates in the United States remain 22 percent higher than in the rich countries of the world (as defined by the World Bank), and more than 2.2 times higher than the average in the countries of the European Union.[27]

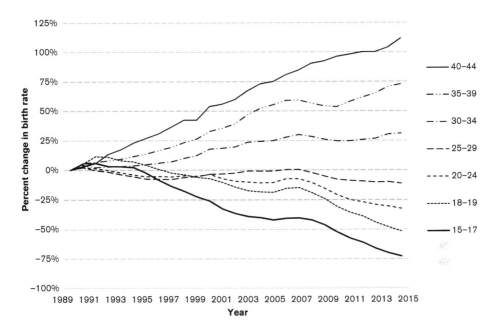

Figure 19. Percentage change in birth rates, by age, 1989–2015. Source: Author analysis of data from the National Center for Health Statistics (Martin et al. 2017).

The campaign to reduce teen births succeeded in doing what was happening already. This is not a model for marriage promotion.

To summarize:

- Teen births as a separate category are a myth; there are just births to people under age twenty.
- Teen births have fallen as people increasingly delay childbearing and marriage. Falling teen births are part of the global historical trend on marriage: rising age at marriage, declining marriage rates.
- The campaign to prevent teen births coincided with the trends already under way. Any suggestion that this could be a model for promoting marriage—that is, a policy that goes against the historical tide on marriage—is without basis.
- There remains no evidence at all to support any policy intervention to promote marriage.

This is why I think the idea that declining teen births are an example of how a policy for "cultural" intervention can reverse the historical tide is wrong.

5. THE MARRIAGE MOVEMENT HAS FAILED (LONG LIVE THE MARRIAGE MOVEMENT)

I opened this chapter with a 1990s-era symposium on promoting marriage. Their one success was the 1996 welfare reform, which stripped poor families of a welfare entitlement, tied cash benefits to work requirements, and wrote marriage promotion into the welfare law. They failed at promoting marriage. But the struggle for marriage on the cultural front remains a morale booster in right-wing circles and still attracts foundation money. It's therefore an undead campaign. Although lifeless, it can still cause harm. One of the senior statesmen of marriage promotion is David Blankenhorn, and I present his case here in some detail to help illuminate the evolution of the movement.

Blankenhorn's Lost Long Decade

Blankenhorn likes to collect signatories for statements of bold blandness, conservative feel-goodism dressed up as high-minded moments of clarity and reason under the mantle of his Institute for American Values (IAV). A 2000 pamphlet entitled *The Marriage Movement: A Statement of Principles* lined people up behind the declaration of "something new: a grassroots movement to strengthen marriage" and pledged to "turn the tide on marriage" in the 2000s.[28] It also embraced the notion that "a healthy marriage culture benefits every citizen in the United States," including, oddly, "gay or straight" Americans, whose right to marry Blankenhorn spent the next decade or so viciously opposing.

In the decade that followed, the "marriage movement" was a disastrous failure on its own terms as marriage rates plummeted. For Blankenhorn, the nadir may have been his 2010 humiliation by federal judge Vaughn Walker in California's Proposition 8 case, *Perry v. Schwarzenegger.*[29] The would-be intellectual leader of a cultural revival, and the author of several high-minded books, Blankenhorn was disqualified as an expert in the losing cause, having provided, according to the court, "inadmissible opinion testimony that should be given essentially no weight." Under scrutiny, it was clear that his expertise was limited to making moralistic proclamations.

At the time of his Proposition 8 disqualification, Blankenhorn and then-ally Maggie Gallagher were also part of the team assembled by the Heritage Foundation to motivate a research program showing the harms caused to children by same-sex couples (which is the subject of the next chapter). As with the general goal of "turning the tide on marriage," this too was a spectacular failure, as the research was discounted or dismissed by one court after another, including ultimately the Supreme Court, when Justice Anthony Kennedy rebuked them for conspiring to deny family stability and recognition to the children of gay and lesbian couples.

But achieving one's stated goals is not the measure of success in right-wing foundation land, where billionaires heat their tax shelters with burning cash and millionaires exchange bloated salaries in the service of ideological reproduction. The bottom line is always the same—protect the wealth of the very rich, and distract the public with inflammatory divisiveness. The social issues are mostly details—marriage, "thrift," religion, guns, and so on—although these are occasionally genuinely seized upon by a confused crusader for one random cause or another. And of course, at whatever effective tax rate they're avoiding, the money they're burning is yours.

Anyway, fortunately for Blankenhorn (and his staff, including his wife, Raina), the United States had a devastating financial collapse in 2008. Early funding from the Templeton Foundation positioned him to take advantage of the crisis, eventually leveraging the disaster to waste something like $9 million of right-wing foundation money on the issue of "thrift."[30] Foundations like Templeton and Bradley decided to pollute the public square with the idea that what we really need to fix is Americans' culture of personal saving. The reforms IAV proposed included promoting small loans, opposing gambling, and teaching children good behavior— and of course marriage. As far as I can tell, the result was some books and pamphlets. (You probably missed their 2012 blockbuster pamphlet, *An American Declaration on Government and Gambling*, produced on behalf of a failing organization run by a right-wing church organization under the name Stop Predatory Gambling, whose board includes Barrett Duke;

they were shellacked on the Massachusetts antigaming ballot measure in November 2014.) In the thrift era, times were good: funding from Bradley and Templeton brought the IAV's total revenues up to a 2010 peak of $5.7 million, its highest level in a decade. David and Raina's combined annual salaries rose above $400,000. But when those grants ran out, they took a 25 percent pay cut.

After the California humiliation, Blankenhorn—with his then deputy, Elizabeth Marquardt—attempted a soft pivot on gay marriage.[31] In 2012 the two of them spoke out against a ballot measure in North Carolina that would have banned same-sex civil unions as well as marriage, saying it went "too far" in the direction of bigotry, instead of merely barring gays and lesbians from equal status in marriage.[32] (Voters approved the measure anyway, but it was later found unconstitutional.) That led to yet another declaration, "A Call for a New Conversation on Marriage," which launched with seventy-five signatories in early 2013.[33] They called marriage "society's most pro-child institution" (versus unspecific contenders). Presumably because they were still billing Templeton for the thrift work, they also called marriage and thrift "the two great engines of the American middle class since the nation's founding." They wrote: "The new conversation does not presuppose or require agreement on gay marriage, but it does ask a new question. The current question is: 'Should gays marry?' The new question is: 'Who among us, gay or straight, wants to strengthen marriage?'"

With shifts in public opinion and the courts in favor of gay marriage, the marriage movement was unraveling. Maggie Gallagher, who claims to have cowritten the 2000 Statement of Principles, was furious.[34] Not only had Blankenhorn dropped opposition to gay marriage, he had stopped referring to the gender of spouses in his descriptions of the awesome benefits of marriage; for Gallagher, shifting the conversation from the importance of both a mother and a father to the value of "two parents" was a brutal betrayal. The issue was not marriage, in other words, but gender (a point we'll dig into in the next chapter).

Unlike Blankenhorn, Gallagher and her National Organization for Marriage had a track record of political victories with American voters, winning ballot measures against gay marriage in some states. Whether Blankenhorn is in the long run successful in his attempt to outflank his former comrades and reboost his flagging income remains to be seen. Whether he will be successful in changing "the culture" is already clear.

Agenda, Rewarmed

The impetus for this essay is a Blankenhorn treatise titled "Marriage Opportunity: The Moment for National Action," which, when republished in *Washington Monthly,* was retitled to the more topical but deeply ridiculous "Can Gay Wedlock Break Political Gridlock?"[35]

In 2000, according to Blankenhorn, the story of marriage decline had been about cultural change, caused by "increases in intimacy expectations, greater social approval of alternatives to marriage, the greater economic independence of women, 'no-fault' divorce reform, the rise in social insurance programs that make individuals less dependent on families, the expansion of market and consumer mores into family life, and lesser social supports and pressures to get and stay married from family, friends, professionals, churches, business, and government."

The problem then was young people "translating attitudes into action" and rushing into cohabitation. The new document admits that "for millions of middle- and lower-class Americans, marriage is increasingly beyond reach" and says we need to "reduc[e] legal, social, and economic barriers to marriage." In 2000 there was no mention of barriers, only of cultural decay. The new embrace of "marriage opportunity" is part of an attempt to co-opt progressive support and "give birth to a new pro-marriage coalition that transcends the old divisions."

> As it becomes increasingly clear that aspirations to family formation are being stymied by wage stagnation and disappointing job prospects among working-class and less-educated men, conservatives are coming to realize that they need to be concerned about economic and labor market bottlenecks that reduce men's employability, damage their marriageability, and help drive the cycle of family decline. To be sure, important non-economic factors are also at work. But the increasingly dire situation of less-skilled men in the marriage market and in the labor market implies that no amount of moral suasion can, by itself, restore a marriage culture among the less privileged. Improving the economic prospects of the less educated, especially men, is vital.

This concession is a testament to the effectiveness of the political agitation around economic inequality after the shock of the economic crisis (and foreshadowing the Bernie Sanders presidential campaign). But because the marriage promoters still believe that declining marriage causes social collapse, the "fraying of our common culture," it seems unlikely that they will be able to generate a truly unifying coalition.

The dire state of our union need not follow from declining marriage. Under a decent welfare state, which equalized resources, mitigated risks, and created shared responsibility for children's well-being—in other words, created conditions more like the ones rich single parents can achieve today—we could survive this cultural shift. The lesson of economic hardship and insecurity undermining marriage isn't that we need to fix those things so that people can be married—it's that we need to fix those things so that people can move through the stages of their lives with a sense of confidence and self-efficacy.

Blankenhorn has not abandoned his old scaremongering and Chicken-Little-ism about marriage. For children, single parenthood is "trapping them in a multigenerational cycle of poverty or family instability"; for adults, singledom is sapping their productivity; for communities, low marriage rates are "depriving them of role models and support networks." Then there's the pseudoreligious mumbo-jumbo that got Blankenhorn's testimony thrown out of the California case, unfalsifiable pronouncements that amount to "Marriage is super special!": "Marriage draws its strength from broadly shared assumptions and values. Its unmatched power to bind families together, over time and through hardship, stems from its standing as a social norm, not just a legal status. It needs the social legitimacy and broad cultural buy-in that come, in America, from being a realistic aspiration of the many, not just a privilege of the few."

Blankenhorn loses me at the idea that there is a thing called "marriage" that has a level of "strength" and "needs" of its own. By the time he gets to "The two-parent married family [is] a touchstone of America's economic and moral vitality," sociological readers may be scratching their heads and mumbling something about Talcott Parsons and the 1950s. One thing that is clear is the consequence of marriage promotion as a policy: it wasted more than a billion dollars of poor families' welfare money for nothing.

Co-opting Gay Marriage

The "grassroots movement to strengthen marriage," which Blankenhorn claimed credit for in 2000, has failed. Demographically the results are in. Politically, too. Gay marriage won as the gays-are-bad-for-kids research was discredited and exposed as a conspiracy of bigots. (It's no wonder that Blankenhorn pleads, "It is not necessary for anyone to recant old positions, confess sins, or re-litigate old debates.") This drubbing by the forces of history leaves Blankenhorn and Co. struggling to conceal the bitter and defensive underbelly to their upbeat populism. To dress up their umbrage in magnanimity, they offer a smarmy, conditional embrace to gay men and lesbians—one they hope will put progressives generally in a bind: "Liberals fighting for social justice and economic opportunity are now called by the logic of their values to help extend the advantages of marriage to low- and middle-income couples who seek it for themselves, much as they fought to help gay Americans attain the right to marry. . . . Gays and lesbians who are winning marriage for themselves can also help to lead the nation as a whole to a new embrace of marriage's promise."

Two things about this. First, gay men and lesbians are not a political party. Some are "promarriage" and some aren't, even though almost all support the *right* to marriage. Some will join the marriage movement that once shunned and demonized them, and some will be progressive. Second, when have "liberals fighting for social justice and economic opportunity" ever *opposed* "extend[ing] the advantages of marriage to low- and middle-income couples who seek it for themselves"? What "logic of their values" requires a change on this issue? I would like to extend to poor people the advantages of not being poor.

In the absence of providing the obvious—and uncomplicated—support necessary for poor families to rise to a level of subsistence and security adequate to establish a basic command over their own futures, political or cultural intervention on the marriage front is deeply patronizing and morally offensive. Despite a welcome recognition of existing economic constraints, Blankenhorn's "new pro-marriage coalition that transcends the old divisions" ultimately extends the existing practice of shaming poor people for not being married to also shame progressives for not joining in that festival of moral disapprobation.

6. GETTING SERIOUS ABOUT PROMOTING
MARRIAGE TO END POVERTY

What if you really thought that we needed more marriage and that the way to get there was to change "the culture"? If reducing poverty or inequality was your goal, you would have to look at the marriage attitudes of rich Whites.

Matt Bruenig wrote: "After rigging the institutions to capture the majority of the national income and basically all of the national wealth, segregating themselves residentially, intermarrying almost solely in their rich enclaves, and even sealing off their schools from being accessed by the unwashed masses, these rich social conservatives turn around and implore others to marry people that they wouldn't touch with a ten foot pole, people they can't even bring themselves to make even the most minimal of community with."[36] In response, economist Sandy Darity tweeted: "I proposed that a marriage antipoverty strategy should have rich white men marry poor black women."[37] I don't want to put the onus for ending poverty just on promarriage pundits. Instead, as Darity suggests, we should think in terms of broader policy.

Marriage promotion is mostly about convincing (educating, coaching, coercing) poor people to marry other poor people. That follows from the "culture matters" perspective on marriage decline advocated by some social scientists as an explanation for declining marriage rates. For example, in a *New Yorker* profile of Harvard sociologist Orlando Patterson, Kelefa Sanneh writes: "[Harvard sociologist William Julius] Wilson argued that declining professional prospects made some black men less marriageable. Patterson thinks that declining marriage rates had more to do with the increased availability of contraception and abortion, which eroded cultural norms that had once compelled men to marry the women they impregnated."[38]

Whether the proximate cause is men's reduced economic prospects or changing norms, the fact is that if poor people changed their attitudes (norms, culture) about marriage—if they put more priority on the importance of marriage and worried less about the economic qualities of the match—there would be more marriage. And, marriage promoters say, this would reduce poverty, inequality, violence, and abuse.

An obvious problem with this whole enterprise is that the marriage boosters assume that the first marriage they generate through marriage promotion will be as economically beneficial to the participants as the average existing marriage observed in the population. But, as I note earlier in this chapter, if one of the reasons for nonmarriage is poor economic status, then it follows that the new marriages generated will on average be much less beneficial economically than the average marriage. And of course the policy doesn't even work, so this is really all very generous speculation.

If They Really Wanted to Change "the Culture"

For the decades that marriage promoters, from Dan Quayle and Bill Cosby to Jeb Bush and Marco Rubio, have been complaining that "the culture" isn't promarriage enough, they have focused on the attitudes and behaviors of the poor. The Blankenhorn treatise I discussed earlier speaks of the need to "restore a marriage culture among the less privileged."[39]

But although it's true that poor people (especially poor Black people) have seen a faster drop in marriage rates, pooling their incomes can only do so much to reduce poverty. If you really want marriage to reduce poverty, and you really think policy can change "the culture" to make more marriages, then what you really need is (as Darity said) some rich (mostly) White men to marry some poor (disproportionately) Black women.

Why not? Is it really more far-fetched to imagine you could change rich White men's attitudes toward poor Black women than it is to suppose you could "restore a marriage culture" among the poor? Maybe one reason policies to increase marriage among the poor haven't worked is that the economic benefits aren't great enough. If you were the kind of person who goes in for this sort of policy (which, again, *I am not*), you'd have to assume poor people would be more receptive to the idea of marrying rich people. So the problem must be that rich people don't want to marry them.

How difficult can this be? Just to put some numbers to the idea, I did the following simple exercise. Take all the poor single mothers and match them up with rich single men.

How many rich single men do you need? With this definition, I count 3.5 million poor single mothers (unmarried women living in their own

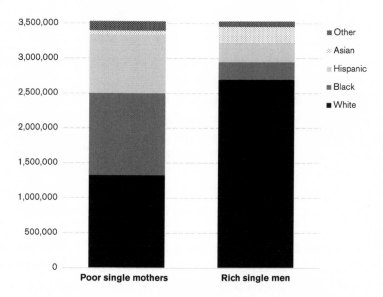

Figure 20. Poor single mothers and rich single men. Poor single mothers are unmarried householders living with their own children, below the federal poverty line. Rich single men are unmarried men with incomes of $80,000 per year or greater; both groups are ages eighteen and over. Source: Author calculations from the 2013 American Community Survey via IPUMS.org.

households with their own children, with family incomes below the federal poverty line). I started with the richest single man and went down the income ladder till I had enough to solve the single-mother poverty problem. It turns out you only have to go down to $80,000 per year in income. Figure 20 shows the matching, with the race/ethnicity of the two groups shown so you can see the composition of the two groups.

If the problem is that poor women are too economically choosy to marry the poor men in their lives, then we could easily lift these 3.5 million single mothers—and the 7.1 million children in their families—out of poverty simply by changing the antimarriage views of these selfish, rich, single men. Of course, we'd have to reduce racist attitudes also, but not entirely—only a third of the non-Black rich single men would need to open their minds to the possibility of marrying a Black woman. You would have to be creative with the incentives for these men, including consciousness-raising and parenting classes, as well as, for example, Starbucks gift cards and subscriptions to the *Economist.*

Hardly anyone really thinks you can socially engineer—through shame or tax incentives—the marital behavior of entire populations. So an idea like convincing rich men to marry poor women probably wouldn't really take off. But it couldn't be less effective than what the marriage promoters have achieved with the last billion dollars they spent.

Fighting losing battles—as the marriage promotion movement has done—doesn't always mean losing the war. In another area of policy, for example, Jeffrey Reiman has described US criminal justice policy as a "pyrrhic defeat," that is, a policy that succeeds at an unstated goal (demonizing the poor) by failing to achieve its stated goal (stopping crime).[40] This doesn't imply a deliberate conspiracy; rather, the effort yields enough of a certain kind of success to perpetuate itself. (It helps to have a religious or other source of zeal to get over the hard times without losing morale.) Like marriage promotion, the fight against marriage equality may have had some of this quality. Despite failing at its stated goals, the efforts may have yielded benefits for the individuals and organizations involved. And as the next chapter shows, the two campaigns often involved the same actors.

4 Marriage Equality in Social Science and the Courts

A press release from the publisher circulated on June 7, 2012. The tone was dramatic, promising to "challenge established views about the development of children raised by gay or lesbian parents." The journal, *Social Science Research,* would offer "compelling new evidence that numerous differences in social and emotional well-being do exist between young adults raised by women who have had a lesbian relationship and those who have grown up in a nuclear family."

Within a day, as journalists worked on their stories to meet the journal's embargo deadline, sociologists were circulating copies of the paper, by University of Texas sociologist Mark Regnerus. And the initial round of articles featured a dose of skepticism from researchers. The *New York Times* opened with reference to "bitter debate among partisans on gay marriage," as "gay-rights groups attacked the study, financed by conservative foundations, as biased and poorly done even before its publication."[1]

The story in *Time*, by Belinda Luscombe (quoting me and others), captured most of the red flags in the study that we would debate over the next few years: the right-wing funding, the dated nature of the accounts provided by young adults (describing their childhoods decades earlier), the histories of family disruption inherent in the cases of children whose parents were described as lesbian or gay, and the virtual absence of children in the study who were actually *raised by* lesbian or gay couples (as opposed to having parents who simply had a same-sex affair or briefly lived with a same-sex partner).

The study compares "any parent who ever 'had a relationship' with someone of the same sex to those who lived with both married biological parents from birth to age 18," I told Luscombe. "It is not about people who were 'raised by' lesbians or gay men."[2]

I didn't recognize it at first, but as the controversy unfolded I began to see this as a new front in the same war in which marriage promotion was just one battle: the struggle to preserve the gender binary itself—perhaps the final, core pillar of patriarchy.

The battle over same-sex marriage—which was not yet popularly known as *marriage equality*—was already raging in 2012.[3] But it intensified as activists on both sides raced to seize upon the broader implications of the issue, and a Supreme Court showdown seemed inevitable. On one side was the bitter and oddly mean-spirited attempt to preserve the "traditional" family—the married man-woman family, in which the two spouses play different yet complementary roles tied to the essential nature of their gender identities, and in which boys and girls are properly raised to replicate these inherent gender differences. On the other side—in a coalition demanding much more than simply marriage rights for gays and lesbians (as important as that issue was)—were the arrayed forces for tolerance, diversity, and equality in all things related to gender and sexuality and for the possibility of forming new families (or no families) without sacrificing the social support and community esteem that comes from conformity to accepted norms of family life.

By the end of what we might call the Regnerus Affair, we would know that his paper was the outcome of a concerted political campaign, waged by a coalition of activists and funded by right-wing foundations dedicated to preventing marriage equality, in which Mark Regnerus (and his collaborator, University of Virginia sociologist W. Bradford Wilcox) were essentially moles who easily penetrated the weak defenses of liberal academic social science and planted the research under a false facade of peer review in order to sway public opinion and the courts. But I didn't know all that in June of 2012; it came out in dribs and drabs on sociology blogs and activist websites, at once generating and testing our ability to respond in the face of political conflict and threats to our disciplinary integrity.

The first thing I noticed that put the Regnerus paper in a different category—not just conservative-leaning research but potentially the sharp end of something larger—was the conservative funders, the Witherspoon Institute and the Bradley Foundation. These were acknowledged in the paper and featured in the early news reports, with the *New York Times* story quoting Regnerus saying he had to turn to conservative foundations because "government agencies 'don't want to touch this stuff.'" In fact, the government was already touching "this stuff" in a very large way. At that time the National Institutes of Health was already $1 billion into the National Children's Study, a massive federal study of one hundred thousand children from birth to age twenty-one that aimed to include complete data on family structure, health, and behavioral outcomes (although it was later canceled because of poor planning and management).[4] Further, government agencies from the Centers for Disease Control to the Census Bureau were engaged in major studies on how to improve measurement and collection of data about sexual orientation and same-sex couples—all of which would make studying gay and lesbian families a routine part of social science.[5]

In his media promotion of the study, Regnerus contrasted his conservative funders with the Ford Foundation, remarking that "every academic study is paid for by someone. I've seen excellent studies funded by all sorts of interest groups."[6] But the Witherspoon Institute and especially the Bradley Foundation are not just any special interest groups. Bradley, one of the largest foundations in the country, sees itself as a "righteous combatant in an ideological war," directing its millions with "single-minded focus" toward conservative causes, according to Jane Meyer, the *New Yorker* writer and author of *Dark Money: The Hidden History of the Billionaires behind the Rise of the Radical Right*.[7]

Beyond the funding, the time line of the paper, as reported by the journal, also set off early alarm bells. The article was submitted to the journal twenty days before the data collection was even complete, and it was revised and accepted within six weeks of the submission. Swift acceptance is not inherently unethical, but it is highly unusual for that journal (or any traditional peer-reviewed journal), enough so to draw attention. And submitting a paper before the data are complete without disclosing that fact is simply unethical.

Finally, there was the immediate promotion of the article by antiequality advocates. In fact, the paper was cited (and not in a cursory way) in an activist brief against same-sex marriage the *day after* the study was published online.[8] The brief was for the *Golinski* case, which challenged the federal Defense of Marriage Act (DOMA), then being heard by a federal appeals court.[9] Despite Regnerus's denials, he was obviously coordinating with the opponents of marriage equality.

WHAT REGNERUS DID WRONG

With these obvious red flags, the paper attracted heightened scrutiny—which it deserved. And then Regnerus and his supporters overplayed their hand, misrepresenting the study and its implications. The press release had quoted Regnerus saying that "children appear most apt to succeed well as adults when they spend their entire childhood with their married mother and father." And the release described the respondents as "children raised in eight different family structures," although the study had virtually no children actually raised by gay or lesbian couples, instead grouping together all those whose parents (by the child's report) had ever had a same-sex romance. The court brief submitted by the conservative pediatricians group also falsely described the study as focusing on children "raised by same-sex couples."

In a piece at *Slate*, Regnerus used the results to argue that "the household instability that the [study] reveals is just too common among same-sex couples to take the social gamble of spending significant political and economic capital to esteem and support this new (but tiny) family form while Americans continue to flee the stable, two-parent biological married model, the far more common and accomplished workhorse of the American household, and still—according to the data, at least—the safest place for a kid."[10]

To look in more detail at the study design, Regnerus collected survey responses from young adults who described their family structure growing up, and then he divided them into different groups (see figure 21). In

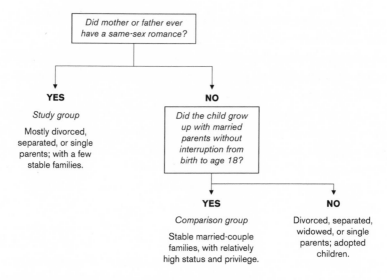

Figure 21. Outline of the Regnerus paper research design.

one group were all those who said either of their parents had ever had a same-sex romantic relationship. The other group—who said neither parent had ever had such a relationship—he divided again, setting aside all those who were adopted, or whose parents had ever divorced, separated, or been widowed. Then he compared what he called the "gay father/lesbian mother" group to the always-married parent group. The finding: those in the former category were more likely to report having a variety of economic, behavioral, and emotional problems. Two design problems rendered the study unfit for drawing meaningful conclusions. First, the parents who had ever had a same-sex relationship were a widely diverse group that shared not only sexual orientation but, more importantly, a history of family instability. Although a tiny number of them had raised their children as long-term, committed partners, the vast majority were single or divorced parents. Any difference that might be the result of parents' sexual orientation was confounded with the differences between those in long-term stable marriages versus those in disrupted families.

Second, the study did not take into account many background factors known to have dramatic effects on child well-being. For example, it is a sad fact that those from wealthy backgrounds are (on average) more likely to get and stay married (to each other) and more likely to have children who grow up to be rich and successful. Totally apart from sexual orientation, any study of how family background affects adult outcomes needs to take such material factors into account. The Regnerus study could not do that adequately. The research was derailed by its obsessive focus on sexual orientation—over more tangible factors that do affect children's well-being. That is why Regnerus lumped all gay and lesbian parents together, rather than differentiating families on the basis of parenting practices, family stability, or access to resources such as wealth and social status. (There were also other serious flaws with study, which I return to below.)

For children to grow up happy and successful, loved and secure, parenting does matter—a parent or parents who love, care for, and develop a positive relationship with their children. Also vitally important are access to financial resources, community support, good schooling, housing, health care, and basic security. When families have these assets, they are very likely to have positive outcomes regardless of the gender of their parents. This is what researchers and child welfare organizations mean when they say the sexual orientation of parents should not be a determining factor in children's adoption, placement, or support. In fact, the major American medical academies and associations—pediatricians, psychiatrists, psychologists, social workers—all support the adoption and parenting rights of gay and lesbian couples.

SOCIOLOGY RESPONDS

By June 29, Gary Gates, a longtime demographer of the lesbian, gay, bisexual, and transgender population, had assembled two hundred signatories for a "researchers respond" letter, which I published on my blog (it was later published by *Social Science Research*).[11] In addition to the substantive critique, the letter called out "the academic integrity of the peer review process"—which was to become a central issue later, when more details emerged.

Momentum built over the summer of 2012 for an effort to head off the study before it might sway the impending court decisions on same-sex marriage. Sociologists spoke out against it in the *Huffington Post* and on sociology blogs like *Scatterplot, OrgTheory*, and *Social (In)Queery*.[12] On the other side, one group of conservative scholars spoke out in Regnerus's defense on a Baylor University website, and in an impassioned defense, Regnerus's dissertation chair, Christian Smith, writing in the *Chronicle of Higher Education*, referred to Regnerus's treatment as an auto-da-fé.[13]

The time to intervene legally seemed short, as lower courts began citing the Regnerus study in marriage equality cases. In the *Golinski* case, the American Psychological Association led a group including the American Medical Association and the American Academy of Pediatrics that criticized the study and its misrepresentation in the courts.[14] But the American Sociological Association (ASA), with its lack of organization infrastructure for political intervention, was slower to respond. To push the association, I and a number of other sociologists brought the issue to our sections (subgroups within the association focused on particular research topics) in preparation for the August meeting of the ASA. At the time I was in the leadership of the Family Section, to which I brought a proposal asking ASA to intervene in the pending court cases to counter the Regnerus study.

The chair of the Family Section at the time was Paul Amato, a professor at Penn State University and a consultant on the Regnerus study—but he nevertheless supported the resolution. (Amato also had a secret: he had been one of the anonymous peer reviewers who approved the paper for *Social Science Research*.) The ASA campaign was successful in leading to an amicus brief from the association, under the research direction of Wendy Manning, which was finally published in February 2013.[15] Manning, a top-notch sociologist with a nonideologue reputation, struck the right balance in evaluating the evidence and drawing justifiable conclusions. On the issue of same-sex parenting and children's well-being, she wrote, we have the closest thing possible to a scholarly consensus: "When the social science evidence is exhaustively examined—which the ASA has done—the facts demonstrate that children fare just as well when raised by same-sex parents . . . Unsubstantiated fears regarding same-sex child rearing do not overcome these facts and do not justify upholding DOMA and Proposition 8 [which banned same-sex marriage in California]."

In response to the firestorm, *SSR* editor James Wright commissioned an internal audit of the publication process, written by Darren Sherkat, a fervent critic of right-wing religious sociologists who was also on the editorial board of the journal. Sherkat's report said the Regnerus paper should not have been published, as "scholars who should have known better failed to recuse themselves from the review process." In an interview Sherkat called the study "bullshit."[16] With the controversy spreading beyond academia, and the apparent unification of mainstream sociology against someone deemed heretic, conservatives rallied. Regnerus was lionized in a *Weekly Standard* cover story titled "Revenge of the Sociologists: The Perils of Politically Incorrect Academic Research"—with a cover cartoon showing him in a medieval torture chamber.[17]

The knives were indeed out for Regnerus. And it wasn't just scholarly debate over the technicalities of the research. Leftwardly inclined sociologists like me were naturally motivated to intervene because we thought the research was bad *and* we didn't like the effects it might have on civil rights, social equality, and the hoped-for demise of the traditional social order.

The tension was elevated by the interaction between the more staid academic critics and the less decorous social activists, who worked in closer contact—and at higher velocity—than either group was accustomed to. Any sociologist remotely connected to the issue was deluged with e-mails from gay rights activists, who relied on the academic criticism to validate their attacks on the research, in the same way that Regnerus and his coconspirators used their academic credentials to lend legitimacy to their cause. Thus, when a sociologist criticized the Regnerus paper, Scott Rose—a gay rights activist who was everywhere during this incident— wrote at the New Civil Rights Movement website, "Prominent Sociologist Delivers Devastating Professional Evaluation." Some of Rose's sensational accounts also viciously singled out the various actors for personal attacks, with headlines such as "Regnerus Editor James Wright a Worse Scumbag than Imagined." For low-profile professors immersed in the slow process of academic research and publication, the harsh spotlight and fast pace were disorienting. Worse, for some, was that Rose filed a charge of scientific misconduct against Regnerus at the University of Texas, which prompted a formal inquiry (the university decided the ethics charges weren't worth pursuing).[18] Academics of all persuasions shuddered.

Besides raising the profile of the scandal and its volume, the activists dug up vital information. While Rose was pressing his case, investigative journalist Sofia Resnick, working with the *American Independent*, filed public records requests with the University of Texas (where Regnerus was a state employee). It took months to overcome the university's legal objections, but by February 2013 Resnick started to publish Regnerus's e-mails and other documents.[19] Academics were shocked to see a peer's personal paper trail publicly dumped online (and gmail addresses started proliferating among professors at public universities), but the revelations were riveting and ultimately justified.

What had at first looked like a bad piece of research by a political hack was eventually revealed to be an actual conspiracy involving the biggest conservative think tank in the country (the Heritage Foundation), the giant Bradley Foundation, and a network of influential right-wing culture-war activists. The public records and the later disclosures demanded in high-profile court cases ended up exposing the conspiracy.

THE "COALITION"

Beyond the salaciousness of the academic scandal, the documents told a story of how Christian conservatives used big private money to produce research in service of their political goals and how the seemingly puny defenses of the academic establishment could easily be overrun by well-organized, well-funded interest groups. For the context of this book, this is also an important example of how activists and ideologues mobilized resources for the project of opposing marriage equality as part of their larger vision of defending gender differentiation itself.

The backstory began in late 2010, when the Heritage Foundation hosted a private meeting of social scientists and activists opposed to gay marriage to develop research strategies for the legal battles ahead. At the meeting, according to accounts given later, were Witherspoon Institute leader Luis Tellez, National Organization for Marriage head Maggie Gallagher, David Blankenhorn from the Institute for American Values (IAV), Wilcox and Regnerus, economists David Allen and Joe Price, and several others. Witherspoon is a right-wing think tank housed at Princeton University that, like IAV and the National Marriage Project (headed by

Wilcox) bundles foundation money and uses it to fund message-driving research. Heritage paid for the travel expenses.[20]

This would all become important information discrediting the expert testimony of Regnerus and others in later trials, because it showed the political motivations behind their research, which Regnerus had originally denied.[21] One result of the document dump was the exposure of Wilcox, whose name was not openly linked to the study. Wilcox had downplayed his role as "one of about a dozen paid academic consultants," but the documents showed he was a key collaborator on the original conception, design, and fund-raising, and had led the planning for disseminating the results in the media. He was director of the Witherspoon Institute's Program on Marriage, Family, and Democracy, which funded the study.

The Regnerus e-mails showed Tellez in the fall of 2010, on Wilcox's behalf, looking for an institutional home for the study. As they negotiated the terms for Regnerus taking on the job, Tellez wrote: "It would be great to have this before major decisions of the Supreme Court but that is secondary to the need to do this and do it well . . . I would like you to take ownership and think of how you want it done . . . rather than someone like me dictating parameters . . . but of course, here to help."

It's clear that Tellez, Wilcox, and Regnerus were sure they would find that children raised by gay and lesbian parents fared worse than those in what they smugly called "gold standard" (straight-married) families. When they were unable to get anything like the large sample they hoped for (grown children raised by same-sex couples are still rare), they adjusted the design in ways that further guaranteed that result. To get a larger sample, they grouped all respondents whose parents had ever had a romantic same-sex relationship, whether or not there was a long-term same-sex parenting relationship, thus combining a tiny number of children from stable gay and lesbian families with a much larger group from disrupted (as well as disproportionately poor and minority) families. Motivated to produce the result they were already planning for, they showed no hesitation in redrawing the conclusion they had started with—even though it was not supported by the evidence they had actually collected.

Regnerus got approval from Wilcox—on behalf of Witherspoon—for the plan he intended to bring to the director of the Population Research Center at the University of Texas. Wilcox approved the plan point by point, including what Regnerus described as the need to "get more feedback from Luis and Maggie [Gallagher]" and "the coalition meeting, the data collection, etc.)." That phrase "coalition meeting" would haunt Regnerus later, when he was accused of covering up the political nature of the project. But at the time, having Regnerus front the study was excellent for the project because he delivered the legitimacy and resources of a research center at a major university. The coalition was buying a seal of academic objectivity.[22]

With his planning grant from Witherspoon, Regnerus set off assembling a team. A series of e-mails shows him attempting to recruit academic consultants, offering professors a few thousand dollars and a paid trip to a meeting in return for their input and the right to list them as consultants. In the messages Regnerus described his role as "more managerial than intellectual" and said he wanted to assemble a team of "ideologically diverse scholars who are serious about doing good science on this important subject." To offset the conservative taint of the funders, he stressed, "This is *not* some right-wing conspiracy." And he promised future efforts to raise money from "GLBTQ orgs and donors"—support that never materialized.

Meanwhile, Tellez *was* working to raise more money for the study from the Bradley Foundation, which would eventually contribute $90,000. On April 5, Tellez wrote to Bradley vice-president Dan Schmidt, requesting money "to examine whether young adults raised by same-sex parents fare as well as those raised in different familial settings. This is a question that must now be answered—in a scientifically serious way—by those who are in favor of traditional marriage. . . . Our first goal is to seek the truth, whatever that may turn out to be. Nevertheless, we are confident that the traditional understanding of marriage will be vindicated by this study as long as it is done honestly and well."

The e-mail reports Regnerus sent Tellez throughout 2011 included details of Wilcox's suggestions for media planning, including a list of journalists Wilcox thought would be sympathetic—all before any of the data were even collected. Later, Wilcox suggested they go to a "big press gathering" run by Michael Cromartie, vice-president of the Ethics and Public Policy Center, which describes itself as "Washington, D.C.'s premier institute dedicated to applying the Judeo-Christian moral tradition to critical issues of public policy." The junket promised "great access to top media players." (Wilcox subsequently took a position at the American Enterprise Institute.)

In addition to a media strategy, Wilcox was working his networks to find an academic journal that would publish their report. In one message Wilcox mentioned the idea of submitting it to *Social Science Research* because the editor, James Wright, was a good friend of a late conservative colleague. Wilcox also pointed out that Wright "likes Paul Amato," whom they had secured as a consultant on the project. "Keep in mind," Wilcox wrote, "that even getting a report from UT [with] Paul Amato on board is a huge achievement."

Amato was arguably the most prominent sociologist involved. A distinguished professor with an endowed chair at Penn State, he was on his way to a term as president of the National Council on Family Relations, the leading professional association for family scholars, and he was elected chair of the Family Section of the ASA. When he agreed to sign on as a consultant for the study, he accepted his normal rate of $150 per hour, plus travel for himself (and his wife) to Austin for a meeting on the project.

That was the backdrop when Regnerus wrote to editor James Wright, suggesting Amato as a reviewer for the paper (a practice many journals encourage, either formally or informally, to help them find suitable, and willing, experts for peer review). Regnerus also sent a flattering e-mail to Amato: "I'd hope that if you're asked to review it, you would consider doing so. I think you're one of the fairest, level-headed scholars out there in this domain." When Wright did ask Amato to review, Amato disclosed the consulting relationship but the two agreed he could be impartial. (I don't fault Amato much for all this, incidentally, as his actions were within the realm of normal practices—and I appreciate that he shared with me his recollection of events.)[23]

Perhaps it was reasonable to have Amato as one reviewer among several, although his opinion should have been discounted as not entirely independent. Shockingly unreasonable, however, was Wright's decision to use Wilcox himself as one of the reviewers—and Wilcox agreeing to do it. In fact, e-mails released under subsequent public records requests (in Florida, where Wright was also a state employee) showed that Wright was coordinating with Regnerus and Wilcox to get the paper published in *SSR* on the rushed timetable preferred by the coalition.[24]

In his response to Wright's formal request to review the Regnerus paper—the paper that came from a project Wilcox initiated, raised money for, helped design, managed media relations for, and then sent to Wright—Wilcox wrote:

> Dear Jim:
> I'm happy to do this. Just want to let you know that I serve on the advisory board for this project—as does Kelly Raley [another UT sociologist] and others on the *SSR* board.
>
> Ok?
>
> Brad

Wright agreed. As I later told *Inside Higher Ed,* instead of "seriously reviewing the paper, [Wright] essentially whispered into an echo chamber of backers and consultants, 'We should publish this, right?'"[25]

In the end, two academic insiders with faculty positions, Wilcox and Regnerus—enabled by various PhD allies, credulous consultants, the journal editor, and his reviewers—were the conduits for a million dollars' worth of foundation-driven anti–gay marriage propaganda, disguised in legitimacy-laced peer review and served up to activists, courts, and legislators around the country through a sophisticated media campaign.

REPLICATION RESULTS

To the credit of Regnerus, he made the data from the New Family Structures Survey publicly available after publishing his own paper. Once we had access, my colleague Neal Caren quickly identified a number of errors in the paper and errors in the raw data—the kind of thing that happens in data collection, which reasonable researchers correct before publishing. For example, nine of the survey's respondents reported having been arrested before the age of four.[26] More thorough analyses conducted later, however, revealed much deeper flaws.

The first was by Simon Cheng and Brian Powell, who exposed Regnerus's data as ridiculously flawed and his methods incompetent. Most startlingly, more than half of the people he coded as having a "lesbian mother" or "gay father" had *never* lived with the same-sex partner, and 10 percent had never even lived with the supposedly gay or lesbian *parent*. One of the supposed children of a gay man also claimed he was seven foot, eight inches tall, weighed eighty-eight pounds, was married eight times and had eight children. Such evidence of people making up outrageous answers—without the data collectors noticing—undermines all confidence in the reports of other outcomes those same individuals mentioned, such as childhood sexual abuse.[27]

In a different paper, Michael Rosenfeld (one of the experts who had declined the invitation to serve as a Regnerus consultant) revisited the data and showed exactly how Regnerus's way of categorizing people according to a single item—whether either of their parents ever had a same-sex relationship—ended up lumping together a very disparate group that had one other thing in common: family instability. For example, Rosenfeld highlighted a young woman who had been born into a home with both biological parents but whose father had moved out when she was five, back when she was twelve, and out again when she was fourteen. Because the young woman remembered her mother ever having a same-sex relationship (with a woman who had never lived in the family home), she was categorized as having a "lesbian mother," and her hardships later in life were attributed to that fact.[28] Beyond a simple data error, this showed that Regnerus's myopic focus on sexual orientation distorted his entire analysis.

If not for the high political stakes, this might have been a relatively inconsequential case of bad research being corrected by subsequent replication: the process of science at work. But the coalition—with the backing of powerful ideological actors—pushed the case into the courts, where the legitimacy and reliability of the research became a legal, and political, matter.

COURT CASES CLOSED

Regnerus and the coalition he fronted achieved the remarkable feat of producing and promoting research that reached all the way into the halls of the Supreme Court, thanks ultimately to the sympathetic conservative ear of the late justice Antonin Scalia. That success is a testament to their organizing efforts and to the currency of their ideas in right-wing circles. In the end, however, they lost. Whether that was because of strategic errors, because their evidence was so weak, because the political winds had shifted so dramatically, or just because Supreme Court Justice Anthony Kennedy supports gay rights, we can't know.

Going into the courts, Regnerus and some of his academic colleagues fell back on the defensive argument that gay marriage should be banned because no one had proved it *not* harmful.[29] This was the line Regnerus and other conservative scholars took in an amicus brief submitted by in 2013 for the Supreme Court case over California's Proposition 8 and DOMA: "With so many significant outstanding questions about whether children develop as well in same-sex households as in opposite-sex households, it remains prudent for government to continue to recognize marriage as a union of a man and a woman, thereby promoting what is known to be an ideal environment for raising children."[30] When it comes to families, from this perspective, tradition is presumed benign and change is cause for suspicion and concern. It is a historical perspective that draws much more heavily from religion than from research.[31]

In her examination of Regnerus, acting as an expert witness in the 2014 Michigan case that became part of the definitive *Obergefell* decision, ACLU attorney Leslie Cooper seemed to agree that without large, high-quality studies we don't know all the consequences of redefining marriage. "So," Cooper asked, "if a nationally representative, large-scale longitudinal study is never done because it's too expensive, is it your opinion that same-sex people should never be allowed to marry?" Regnerus had no answer to that, but he complained, "Let's get out there and get some more [data] before we make wide-scale changes in an institution that has served us since time immemorial."[32]

If the law were run by sociologists, "time immemorial" would be disqualifying in a trial. But it was a desperate long shot by that point, anyway, as Supreme Court swing voter Justice Anthony Kennedy had already shown his reaction to this argument in the *Windsor* case a few months earlier. Justice Scalia did introduce the child well-being issue himself from the bench, during the 2013 Supreme Court oral arguments (the Proposition 8 and DOMA cases were argued the same day, which led to the *Windsor* decision). Arguing that there is "considerable disagreement among sociologists as to what the consequences of raising a child in a single-sex family, whether that is harmful to the child or not," Scalia offered the uncertainty argument. "I take no position on whether it's harmful or not," he said. "But it is certainly true that there's no scientific answer to that question at this point in time."[33]

It was to be the losing argument. Justice Anthony Kennedy responded: "There's substance to the point that sociological information is new. We have five years of information to weigh against 2,000 years of history or more. On the other hand, there is an immediate legal injury or legal—what could be a legal injury, and that's the voice of these children. There are some 40,000 children in California . . . that live with same-sex parents, and they want their parents to have full recognition and full status. The voice of those children is important in this case, don't you think?"

That was the crux of the *Windsor* decision that Kennedy would go on to author, and it laid the groundwork for his subsequent *Obergefell* decision, which made same-sex marriage a national right. In the interim, Regnerus and a dwindling number of increasingly fanatical-seeming academics attempted to stop the inevitable (Wilcox disappeared from public view in the marriage equality debate), but it was a mopping-up operation. In the *Windsor* case, neither Kennedy nor Scalia and Samuel Alito, in their dissents, invoked the argument that the children of gay and lesbian couples suffer harm as a result of their family structure. Even if there are lingering doubts about whether gay and lesbian families—on average—are "ideal" or not, the Court implicitly ruled that such concerns don't rise to the level needed to overcome the harms caused to gay and lesbian married couples and their children.

In the *Windsor* decision, Justice Kennedy declared that denying federal recognition to married couples creates a system of "second-class marriages" for no other reason than to "impose inequality," that it "humiliates tens of thousands of children now being raised by same-sex couples," and "makes it even more difficult for the children to understand the integrity and closeness of their own family and its concord with other families in their community and in their daily lives." Once the debate shifted to whether the government has justification to take away something of value from a distinct group, the burden was on the opponents of gay marriage to show some justification for it. And they couldn't.

In the Michigan case, Judge Bernard Friedman, in evaluating the expert testimony, eventually concluded there was "no logical connection between banning same-sex marriage and providing children with an 'optimal environment' or achieving 'optimal outcomes.'" And he added: "The Court finds Regnerus's testimony entirely unbelievable and not worthy of serious consideration."[34]

SAVING PRIVATE GENDER

Why do religious conservatives care so much about gay marriage? After *Obergefell*, the family right fell into what *New Yorker* writer Jeffrey Toobin called a "religiously themed retreat into victimology."[35] Among the 2016 Republican presidential candidates, Texas senator Ted Cruz said the decision caused "some of the darkest 24 hours in our nation's history," and Mike Huckabee declared, "Jesus wept."[36] Among the Christian right's intelligentsia, the view was no less dire. Patrick Deneen, a professor of constitutional studies at Notre Dame, was apocalyptic:

> While many have pointed to the 1973 decision of *Roe v. Wade* as an obvious historical analogue for the *Obergefell* decision, to my mind, the insistence that *all must conform* to the new, official definition of marriage that no civilization has ever endorsed until yesterday seems to be more aptly compared to life under Communism. . . . The "monopoly of violence" possessed by the State is now a main weapon in perpetuating this lie, and will be used mercilessly and without cessation against those who persist on pointing out that it seeks to perpetuate a lie.[37]

I may be naive, but I don't worry much that gay marriage will lead to the violent persecution of Christians in America.

Some Catholics and Evangelicals share the view that unrepentant gay men and lesbians will spend eternity in hell (one of them was the economist Douglas Allen, who testified to that effect in the Michigan trial).[38] That's obviously very serious in itself. But the opposition to gay marriage is broader than that. Framing the debate over same-sex marriage rights as a question of "marriage equality" was great civil rights politics, and it also was fundamentally true. But one of the reasons it worked so well may be that it made an end run around (some of the) true concerns of the conservative opposition. Beneath the homophobia and animus toward gays and lesbians, the opponents of same-sex marriage were ultimately motivated by a desire to defend the binary gender distinction itself, in all realms. Homosexuality is just one challenge to the binary gender regime that once was unquestioned and now seems suddenly frail; feminism and gender desegregation generally are the larger social forces pushing in that direction, and marriage equality is just one relatively small—but highly significant, symbolically—part of that wave of change.

In their legal efforts, the antiequality social scientists always returned to the gender difference of parents as their main concern. For example, Regnerus and others wrote in the brief I quoted from above: "Opposite-sex parenting allows children to benefit from distinctive maternal and paternal contributions."[39] In the obtuse, semicoherent manner typical of his off-the-cuff remarks, Regnerus explained in a 2014 Christian radio interview how opposition to same-sex marriage fits within the war to protect gender differentiation:

> I tend to think the way things are rolling at the moment, it's not just as if same-sex marriage fell out of the sky, and was on our plate. It was paved, right? The road to there was paved in part by all sorts of poor laws around opposite-sex marriage, right? And the giving away of what we might call the sort of functional definition of marriage, visions of complementarity. We have bought, hook, line, and sinker, the idea that essentially men and women are interchangeable in our marriages. And it's hard to get away from that, but I think we're going to have to.[40]

This approach is especially strong in modern Catholicism, which has adapted "complementarity" to co-opt science into ideology, in the "natural law" framework, to oppose family change as well as gender equality. In this view, gay marriage is an assault on everyone—even those who have nothing to do with gay-married couples—because it writes gender neutrality into law. It may be no accident that the remaining social science opposition to marriage equality comes largely from individuals who (like Regnerus and Wilcox) identify as Catholic and that the most successful mass movement against marriage equality may have been in France, an overwhelmingly Catholic country.

Pope Francis has spoken forcefully of the importance of defending the family, to oppose those who would "cancel out sexual difference."[41] He said: "The family is based on marriage, an act of freely given and faithful love between a man and a woman. It is love that seals their union and teaches them to accept one another as a gift. . . . We regret that other forms of cohabitation have been placed on the same level as this union, while the concept, consecrated in the biblical tradition, of paternity and maternity as the distinct vocation of man and woman in marriage is being banished from the public conscience."[42]

Regnerus was an uncredited contributor to a video series on sex differences and against same-sex marriage, called the Catholic *Humanum*.[43] In the final installment of the series, they celebrate the movement against marriage equality in France. Tugdual Derville, an activist from La Manif pour Tous, says: "To say, as the law was pretending, that men and women are interchangeable in education and even procreation, undermined a fundamental benchmark rooted in one's identity." The French movement's goal was the protection of gender differentiation, to stop a law that would "erase sexual differentiation and complementarity from the law and jeopardize the foundation of human identity: sexual difference and the resulting structure of parentage." The movement was defeated, and same-sex marriage became legal in France in 2013. But the French activists were more successful than the Americans at making the same-sex marriage debate about gender differentiation generally.

In the *Humanum* videos, there is a recurring theme of slow-motion images of men and women riding mopeds together, with the man sitting in front and both beaming. Girls are told they are beautiful, boys are told they are extraordinary and they can save the world. A woman in the video says desire comes from difference: "And so, for those who say there are no more differences, they are contributing to eliminating sexual desire, and they are simply reducing the desire to procreate." Thus gay marriage literally threatens the existence of the human race.[44] If those are the stakes—burning in hell *and* the end of humanity—then we should not be surprised at the passions and commitment of the activists involved. And we should be glad they were not successful in their efforts to stop the extension of civil rights to gays and lesbians.

The Regnerus Affair provides the link between the marriage promotion movement and the defense of gender itself. It was the political expression, from within academia, of a broader cultural defense of traditional gender, a position they perceive as increasingly under attack. In the next chapter I move to some of the many ways that gender differentiation thrives, and is maybe even deepening, in our culture today.

5 Doing Dimorphism

In the last chapter we saw the social science side of the ugly fight to block marriage equality. As it became clear they were losing, the Religious Right made objections of an increasingly martyr-like character, deploying the specter of anti-Christian persecution to paint themselves as the victims of modern amorality run amok. And after they lost, they turned to legislative efforts to protect the rights of religious people who remain opposed to gay marriage. But why such drama, when the issue directly affects such a small number of people—people who were already gay anyway? In the end I came to see it as a defense of gender difference itself and a reaction to the modern erosion of the presumed natural order of binary gender. That helps explain the emotional force of the debate. Gender is a core aspect of identity, and the gender order is a fundamental piece of traditional power structures, which are certainly not limited to religion.

In this chapter I dig into the cultural construction of gender difference, with examples from entertainment, relationships, and parenting. It turns out it doesn't take a right-wing conspiracy to erect, and defend, the many monuments to gender difference that surround us. Entertainment and popular culture, interpersonal relationships, and the countless choices and actions of parents—all these are sites of gender production. The gender order that we produce through these and other processes is built around a binary vision, a vision of "complementarity," and an exaggerated view of sexual dimorphism in our species. In this chapter I can't explain why this happens, but I can describe some of how it happens and can point toward some of the potential consequences.

1. GENDER WARS AND THE DEFENSE OF DIFFERENCE

Gender differentiation ties into a recurring theme in sociology: the institutional production of cultural naturalness. People have ways of making social differences—and inequalities—seem natural by ubiquitously reinforcing separation and promoting categorical identities. Marriage equality struck a nerve partly because it contributes to the feeling that Barbara Risman calls "gender vertigo," a loss of balance in reaction to the weakening of gender categories (she thinks this is essential and good; traditionalists disagree).[1]

Gender vertigo also contributed to the spike in conflict over transgender visibility and rights that followed legal marriage reform. As transgender visibility increased, equality advocates pushed forward local laws to protect transgender people from discrimination, and the backlash was fierce. The most prominent of these clashes in early 2016 was in North Carolina, when the state government overturned a Charlotte ordinance that allowed transgender people to use bathrooms according to their gender identity even if they had not taken the steps necessary to change the gender on their birth certificates. In other words, Charlotte would have protected the right of transgender men to use men's rooms, and transgender women to use women's rooms, regardless of their legal status. In March, the state blocked the Charlotte law (as well as any similar laws elsewhere in the state), on the false premise of protecting "privacy" in bathrooms.[2]

Protectors of the gender order have focused in these debates on keeping people with penises out of bathrooms for females. As Kristen Schilt and Laurel Westbrook wrote, "This exclusive focus on 'males' suggests that it is genitals—not gender identity and expression—that are driving what we term 'gender panics'—moments where people react to a challenge to the gender binary by frantically asserting its naturalness."[3]

It's no accident that gender's enforcers have drawn a line in the sand at bathrooms. These social spaces hold a prime place in the production of gender difference, as Erving Goffman observed in the 1970s: "The *functioning* of sex-differentiated organs is involved, but there is nothing in this functioning that *biologically* recommends segregation; *that* arrangement is totally a cultural matter. And what one has is a case of institutional reflexivity: toilet segregation is presented as a natural consequence of the difference between the sex-classes, when in fact it is rather a means of honoring, if not producing, this difference."[4]

I opposed the antiequality agenda personally on moral and political grounds, naturally (I can count on two hands the American academic sociologists who spoke out against marriage equality). But my scientific opinion is that the concern is misplaced. In some broad ways, of course, gender differences have eroded—for example, as women have gained political rights and access to gainful employment and as sexuality has become uncoupled from reproduction. On the rare occasions when they choose to, men can be nurses, preschool teachers, and even stay-at-home parents. More people don't marry, or don't have children. And some people live their lives gay. You might call all that a convergence of gender roles, or a weakening of gender difference.

But gender differentiation is alive and well, and its survival doesn't appear to require the reinforcement of conservative political activists. In fact, despite such advances as spotty transgender protection, in some respects the gender binary is bouncing back after a brief surge of androgyny in popular culture around 1970 (which Jo Paoletti traces in her fascinating book *Sex and Unisex*).[5] A visit to the Sociological Images Pinterest board on "pointlessly gendered products" underscores this point, displaying everything from Goldfish crackers and Q-Tips to toolkits and even Bibles that are contemporary conduits for needless gender-specific marketing campaigns.[6] In the Google ngrams database of English language usage, I found that appearances of the phrases "toys for boys" and "toys for girls" have each tripled in frequency relative to the phrase "toys for children" since 1960.[7]

In addition to separate physical spaces and consumer products, we are used to simplistic depictions of male and female body differences, as in the ubiquitous bathroom sign icons.[8] In children's fiction, male and female characters are sometimes depicted as different species, or as members of species that have much greater dimorphism than do humans. For example, my six-year-old daughter brought home a charming book called *The New Nest*, which told the story of a male and a female house sparrow setting up their home for the chicks. The illustrations add to the already ample dimorphism of the species in question by putting a necktie on the male and a string of pearls on the female.[9]

These are convenient fictions, literary exaggerations that smooth the way for more troubling social processes. They are part of what sociologist Lisa Wade calls an obsession with gender differences, which constantly highlights any difference we can find, and invents plenty we can't really find, to tell the story of "opposite" sexes instead of the modestly dimorphic bodies we actually inhabit.[10]

In a typical example, consider an often-cited study of infant perception. Researchers compared infant "looking time" at a mobile ("physical-mechanical object") versus a researcher's face ("social object") and reported that girls looked at the face longer while boys looked at the mobile longer.[11] The results, they concluded, "clearly demonstrate that sex differences are in part biological in origin." There are substantive criticisms of the study itself, but even if we take its results at face value, its deployment in support of the Men-Mars/Women-Venus narrative was completely out of proportion to the actual differences it reported. Using the means and standard deviations in the paper (and assuming normal distributions, for purposes of illustration), I produced figure 22, showing the distribution of looking times for male and female infants at the dangling mobile object.

There is a real difference in those distributions, but nothing like what you would need to reasonably refer to the sexes as "opposites," even if these patterns do precede socialization. The practical difference is small.[12] Now, if you could show me that infants who stare at the mobiles for fifty seconds are more likely to be engineers when they grow up than the ones who stare at them for forty seconds (regardless of their gender) then I would be impressed. But absent that (and no one has done that), I wouldn't give these amorphous differences at birth much weight in the explanation of actual segregation and differentiation among adults, which remains a pervasive source of gender inequality. And most of the body differences between men and women aren't necessary or sufficient to explain the

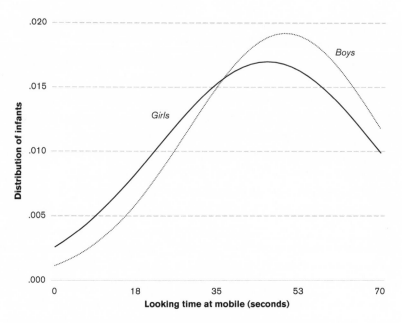

Figure 22. Male and female infant looking times at a dangling mobile.
Source: Author estimates from data in Connellan et al. (2000).

differences in social position that are much more widespread (and consequential).

Disney's Romantic Difference

As a sociologist who is also a parent of daughters, I've had plenty of time to contemplate the content of Disney kids' movies, especially those in the princess genre.[13] Beneath the plotlines and dialogue, I was always impressed by a pervasive aesthetic trait in the genre that provides a powerful connection to my concerns over gender differentiation: anatomical dimorphism, or the differences between males and females in body size and type.[14]

Once I noticed the extreme dimorphism in these movies—the differences between men and women growing to outlandish proportions—I couldn't take my eyes off them. In the blockbuster *Frozen* (which has been heralded for its less sexist plotline about sister power), there it was, in the dramatic moment when the princess's tiny hand falls into the prince's normal one. Her eyes widen—and suddenly her eyeballs are wider than her wrists. Giant eyes and tiny hands always symbolize femininity in Disney-movie land.

Consider another Disney princess movie with a decidedly female-empowering plot: *Brave*, which (before *The Hunger Games*) seems to have spurred millions of young girls to pursue careers in archery. The story is not about the romantic interests of the princess; rather, it focuses on how she rejects her parents' matchmaking. So far, so good. But what then of the bizarre depiction of her parents' bodies? They are ostensibly the same species (human), but his body is outsized relative to hers. Although the height difference between them is not extreme, his hands and neck are more than three-times wider than hers. The same distinction is apparent between the parents of Hiccup in *How to Train Your Dragon 2*, Stoick the Vast and Valka. During the romantic moment they share, her wrist appears to be about one-third the size of his (and her tiny fingers have to be bizarrely stretched to interlace with his). These ostensibly human characters are in some ways more like gorillas—among whom males and females are similar in height but males typically weigh more than twice as much as females—than like humans.

Disney has moved beyond the old-fashioned problem of passive princesses and purposeful princes, maybe most decidedly in *Mulan*, in which the "princess" is actually a soldier who becomes a princess only when she marries a general (and that's not until the awful sequel, actually). In *Tangled* (a retelling of Rapunzel), the female lead starts out as a damsel in distress but ends up with plenty of action sequences. And it's not all about falling in love. Still, the sexual dimorphism in *Tangled* is exaggerated. Despite relatively normal overall body size, at key moments in the romantic narrative Disney blows up certain differences. At the first sign of romantic contact, her eyes grow to twice the size of his. And when their hands meet, suddenly hers are those of a tiny child while his belong to a gentle giant, more than twice her size. (In fact, for a moment his wrist is the size of her waist.) In short, what looks like animated normality—anchoring fantasy in a cocoon of reality—contains its own fantastical exaggeration.

The patriarchal norm of bigger, stronger men paired up with smaller, weaker women is a staple of contemporary gender socialization. When

I ask my students, they almost universally express this preference for their own relationships, and the taller women complain of dating disadvantages. It turns out that hand size is the most dramatic difference in these children's movies, especially in the romantic scenes. (The male gnome's hands are three times bigger than the female's in *Gnomeo and Juliet*, for example, even though their bodies are similarly sized.) The nonanimated version of this obsession was dramatized to uproarious effect in the episode of *Seinfeld* in which the "man hands" of Jerry's girlfriend doom their budding relationship. That series celebrated the little things that mean a lot, and in this case hand size was the apparently minor quality that undermined the female character's essential femininity. In fact, the climactic restaurant scene, in which she tears into a lobster with her bare hands, required a hand double—hands that large are rarely seen among women. But in animation the gloves are off—and Disney is free to create characters with differences in hand size that dwarf normal sex differences.

Overall, US men today outweigh women by a ratio of 1.2 to 1, or 190 versus 157 pounds at the median.[15] But hand size is more genetic and less affected by lifestyle, especially at the wrist. And how big are the hand-size differences, really? First I found a variety of studies on topics ranging from carpal tunnel syndrome to judo mastery, with average wrist diameters for women about 10 or 15 percent smaller than men's. Then my search led me to an excellent anthropometric survey of US Army personnel from 1988.[16] In that sample of almost four thousand people, chosen to match the age, gender, and race/ethnic composition of the army, the average wrist diameters were 15.1 cm for women and 17.4 cm for men. On the basis of their detailed tables, I made figure 23 to show the distributions.

The average difference between men's and women's wrists in this army sample was 2.3 cm, or a ratio of 1.15 to 1. However, if you took the smallest-wristed woman (12.9 cm) and the largest-wristed man (20.4 cm), you could get a difference of 7.5 cm, or a ratio of 1.6 to 1. This is a case of a modest difference at the mean with relatively little overlap in the distributions: that is, most men's wrists were larger, but the difference was not large. Without being able to hack into the Disney animation computers with a tape measure I can't compare them directly, but from the pictures it looks as if the couples they depict often have differences greater than the

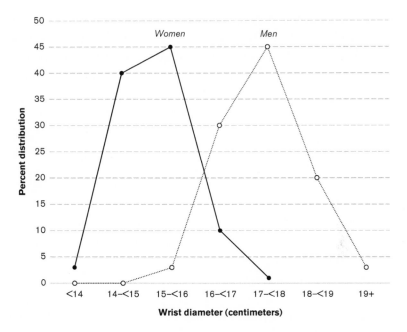

Figure 23. Wrist circumference distribution of active duty army men and women. Source: Author calculations from US Army data in Gordon et al. (1988).

most extreme differences found in the population—especially when love is on the line.

Go back to Disney's 1997 version of the mythological *Hercules*. In this story, of course, Hercules is a demigod, not a normal human. But he's also all man. In the movie, Hades says to Megara, "I need someone who can—handle him as a man," which she does. And since they involve him in such matters of the human flesh (and heart), that means their measurements are fair game for this analysis of dimorphism. (If he's really a different species, maybe Disney shouldn't feature him kissing a girl in a children's movie.) I did some simple measurements from one pretty straight shot in the movie (see the lower left of figure 24) and compared it to the US Army sample. Since it's a romantic moment, of course, the body differences are exaggerated more than in other scenes. Hercules is obviously extremely strong, and this woman is on the petite side, so I compared their

Figure 24. Dimorphic bodies. Hand scenes from animated movies. Clockwise from top left: *Frozen, Tangled, Gnomeo and Juliet, How to Train Your Dragon 2,* and *Hercules.*

measurements to those of the biggest man versus the smallest woman on each dimension in the entire army sample. On necks, the biggest man-woman ratio in the army sample is 1.7 to 1; Hercules and Meg come in at 2.3 to 1. On biceps it's 2.1 to 1 in the army and 2.8 to 1 in *Hercules,* and on wrists Hercules is 2.3 times larger, compared with a widest spread of 1.6 to 1 in the army. This is a long way of saying what's obvious in the movie: children will probably never see a real human couple with such grotesquely exaggerated body-size differences.

What Difference Does It Make?

Classic sexism is still a problem, of course. Consider the *Smurfs* movies, from Columbia Pictures (2011 and 2013), with toy support from McDonald's. The Happy Meal box I got announced, "Smurfs are named after their individual talents: there's Farmer, Painter and Baker. . . . Know your talent and find your Smurf name!" My daughters both got male

Smurf character toys, which struck me as interesting because the counter person had asked us if the meals were for boys or girls. Then I looked up the character list and realized they were all male except Smurfette, whose "individual talent" apparently is being female. (At that point, if it hadn't been for all the fat and salt and sugar in my meal, I might have stopped enjoying it.) This is a movie that, with its sequel, grossed almost a billion dollars. It's old-fashioned sexism, deriving from the story's midcentury European origins, in which boys or men are generic people—with their unique qualities and abilities—while girls and women are identified by their femininity.[17] In Smurfette's case, she was actually the creation of the evil Gargamel, who invented her to sow chaos among the all-male Smurf society. (His recipe for femininity included coquetry, crocodile tears, lies, gluttony, pride, envy, sentimentality, and cunning.) The males are Papa, Grouchy, Clumsy, Vanity, Narrator, Brainy, Handy, Gutsy, Hefty, Panicky, Farmer, Greedy, Party Planner, Jokey, Smooth, Baker, Passive-Aggressive, Clueless, Social, and Crazy. There is no boy Smurf whose identifying quality is his gender, of course, because he would seem ridiculously limited and boring as a character.

Contemporary animated film makers—especially Disney, but not just them—have taken a lot of flak for perpetrating sexist stereotypes like this. In our competitive child-rearing culture, parents want their children's entertainment to be not just fun but also instrumental in their development, including encouraging girls to be modern achievers instead of premodern princesses (that is, wives). And Hollywood is sensitive to the criticism over this kind of thing. Disney has moved toward female characters for whom gender is not the only identifiable attribute. That's laudable. So why should I focus on the extreme body differences? My writings on movie dimorphism are among my most popular, but they also cause some readers extreme aggravation, as people can't believe I get so worked up over unrealistic depictions of people in *cartoons* (a word they often repeat in all caps). But I'm not suing or picketing Disney, I'm just trying to learn something about mainstream culture from this work and its reception. Of course, on average real men's bodies are in fact bigger, and more muscular, than women's. And animation is an art form not limited by the boundaries of reality, which is what makes it great. But the exaggerations in these children's movies are extreme, they almost always promote the same image of big men and tiny women, and they are especially dramatic in romantic situations.

And this is not a timeless or universal feature of Western fiction or art. In the case of Hercules, we can actually compare the Disney depiction to ancient renditions of the demigod and his mistress. From fourth-century mosaics to Alessandro Turchi's seventeenth-century painting, the demigod is portrayed relative to Megara in much more normal human proportions than those seen in the Disney movie. Artists and entertainers choose whether to highlight the differences between male and female people. Whether and how they emphasize and act on the different qualities of men and women tells us something about their cultural milieu.

Artists have been pairing men's and women's bodies for millennia, and the sex differences have not usually been as dramatic as those seen in contemporary children's movies. As alternatives, consider classic works of art such as Michelangelo's famous rendition of Adam and Eve from the ceiling of the Sistine Chapel, completed in 1512, in which Eve's robust physique is comparable to Adam's (Michelangelo used male models for both male and female figures). Or look at old *American Gothic*, by Grant Wood, from 1930, depicting a rural couple in front of their church. Their bodily similarity is striking.

Return for a minute to the complaints about my overreaction to Disney's dimorphism problem. Among the hundreds of comments, this one represents a common complaint: "Cartoons aren't meant to accurately portray people, EVER. They are meant to exaggerate features, so that they are more prominent and eye catching. So feminine features are made more feminine, and masculine features are made more masculine. . . . The less realistic the proportions, the more endearing and charming we find the character. The closer to realistic they are, the creepier/blander they can become."[18]

A quick perusal of animated movies reveals that Disney is certainly not alone in emphasizing the larger size of males in general, and specific body parts in particular. But there are successful counterexamples as well—charming characters who are not so realistic as to be boring but who are also not extremely differentiated by sex. Tellingly, perhaps, these are usually in platonic pairings, old movies, or foreign movies. Look at *Kiki's*

Delivery Service, from Japanese director Hayao Miyazaki (1989); the charming couple—whose relationship is charged but remains G-rated—have very similar bodies and faces. In Disney's 1937 version of *Snow White,* the heroine was paired with a Prince Charming whose wrists were barely bigger than hers, and her normal waist looks giant by today's standards. In nonhuman pairings, Disney's 1970 *Aristocats* featured cats with exaggeratedly feminine and masculine personalities, but not extreme body-size difference. And, when you think about it, despite his larger wrists and neck, the bodies of Charlie Brown and Lucy were also very similar.

The extreme exaggeration of body size difference is contemporary, and oddly focused on romantic depictions in stories for children. Is it relevant to our current debates over gender difference? We still face skepticism about how much men can warmly nurture their children or work as nurses. Women in positions of leadership face extra scrutiny. And of course we all assume males and females belong in separate bathrooms. Unless we see that men and women have physical, emotional, and cognitive qualities in common as well, we will continue to hold suspect single parents, same-sex couples, and people in nontraditional roles.

The normal image is not simply natural; it's a product of the interaction between the natural world and our cultural ways. When the stories of our childhood set a standard that exaggerates gender differences and makes them seem natural—built into our very bone structures—they offer a limited vision of our human potential. When, as we saw in the previous chapter, Mark Regnerus defends the "vision of complementarity" between men and women and insists that children need a male and a female parent, he's afraid that if men and women were too similar we wouldn't need to pair them up in order to have complete families or sexual relationships. He needs a cultural image to anchor that obsession with difference—and Disney gives it to him.

In romantic attraction and mate selection, this thinking helps set up the ideal in which women *should* be smaller than men, the result of which is the pairing of couples according to taller man, shorter woman much more than would occur by chance. To illustrate this, I examined the height differences of married men and women in the Panel Study of Income Dynamics.[19] Because men are taller than women on average—the median for husbands

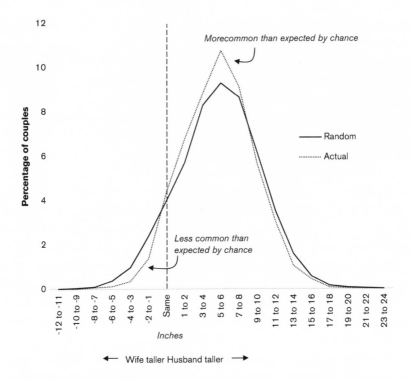

Figure 25. Height difference between husbands and wives, actual and randomized. Source: Author analysis of 2009 data from the Panel Study of Income Dynamics, described in Cohen (2014b).

in the sample is five foot eleven, compared with five foot five for wives—we expect most couples to have a taller man. But when you compare the actual distribution of height differences to the gap you would get if they married at random, you can see that couples sort themselves into that sweet spot of the four- to seven-inches-taller man and tend to avoid even those few taller-woman pairings you would get by chance (figure 25).

The prevalence of taller-man pairs increases the odds that any given couple we (or our children) observe or interact with will include a man who is taller and stronger than his partner. This is only a little removed from the notion that men and women should work in different—and, in fact, unequal—occupations, as well as other social expressions of gender difference. That's why I'm not letting this go.

2. PINK AND BLUE

When researchers are already convinced of the naturalness of gender difference, they will search high and low for confirming evidence. And their subsequent exaggerations affect people on the front lines of the gender divide: parents, who are insecure enough already. One of the persistent modern fixations with regard to gender and childhood is on color preference.[20]

Our society is brimming with stories of children who spontaneously conform to gender stereotypes—boys who prefer vehicles and violence, girls who lean toward dolls and dress-up—through no apparent effort on the part of parents. (Proud parents whose children don't conform are a vocal contingent but a distinct minority.) Pink and blue often feature in these stories, an area in which the pressure for conformity appears very strong, especially for boys. And some scientists have been happy to give the proud parents reason to believe their gender-typical children are deeply normal, which means the pink-blue divide has some biological or evolutionary basis.

By one evolutionary theory, "female brains should be specialized for gathering-related tasks," which "facilitate the identification of ripe, yellow fruit or edible red leaves embedded in green foliage." Or perhaps the preference evolved "because infant faces compared to adult ones are reddish-pink, and red or pink may signal approach behaviors that enhance infant survival."[21] One problem with these theories comes from research showing that color preference is only modestly different in very young children (age two or so), with a lot of overlap, and that difference widens with age in the subsequent year, which suggests a distinction of more social origin.[22] But that doesn't stop some people, even those studying *adult* color preferences, from speculating on their evolutionary origin: "Without ruling out any possibility at this point," write two researchers who surveyed American college students on their favorite colors, "we are inclined to suspect the involvement of neurohormonal factors. Studies of rats have found average sex differences in the number of neurons comprising various parts of the visual cortex. Also, gender differences have been found in rat preferences for the amount of sweetness in drinking water. One experiment demonstrated that the sex differences in rat preferences for sweetness was eliminated by depriving males of male-typical testosterone levels in utero. Perhaps, prenatal exposure to testosterone and other sex hormones operates in a similar way to 'bias' preferences for certain colors in humans."[23]

Such fanciful accounts build on common misconceptions about gendering children. One is that it has always been this way—with boys and girls so different naturally that products and parenting practices have always differentiated them. This is easily disproved in the history of clothing, which shows that American parents mostly dressed their young boys and girls the same until about a century ago. In fact, boys and girls were often indistinguishable, which was considered charming, as evident in a 1905 *Ladies' Home Journal* contest in which readers were asked to guess the sex of the babies. That's the same *Ladies' Home Journal* that infamously offered this advice in June 1918: "The generally accepted rule is pink for the boy and blue for the girl. The reason is that pink being a more decided and stronger color is more suitable for the boy, while blue, which is more delicate and dainty, is prettier for the girl."

Jo Paoletti, who tells this history, believes the evidence does not actually support a complete cultural reversal of the pink and blue rules. Rather, the early twentieth-century rules were very weak, and mass-marketed color clothing for children was a new phenomenon (one that manufacturers were eager to encourage, so parents wouldn't save money by simply dressing their children in hand-me-downs).[24] So rather than a specific rule, what matters is having a rule at all, and that's a modern cultural creation.

The rules of gender differentiation affect parents as well as children, in ways that we don't yet fully appreciate. To scratch the surface of that issue, I did a little research to see if today's strongly gendered parenting might change the adults who live in the color-coded worlds of their children. In the process, I also was looking for a simple way to test whether color preferences changed in adulthood (implying they're not simply genetic), and the gender of children seemed like a good, mostly random experiment to test that.

My online survey of 749 parents found that, as expected, mothers were much more likely to identify pink and purple as their preferred colors, with fathers preferring blue and green. But then I compared parents whose children were boys only, girls only, and a mix of boys and girls. The result was most clear for women: those whose children were boys had more "female" preferences—more pink and less blue. For men, having either boys only or girls only increased their odds of preferring blue.[25] The implication is that the gender socialization process, which is so strongly linked to parenting ideas and practices, does not end in childhood.

3. BRACED FOR BEAUTY

In contrast to the popular (not just conservative) perception that our culture is actually eliminating gender distinctions, as feminism tears down the natural differences that make gender work, and despite some barrier-crossing, we do more to gender-differentiate ourselves now than we did during the heyday of the 1970s unisex fashion craze. Jo Paoletti's collection of unisex clothing ads is eye-opening in today's climate, in which it is assumed that boys and girls will dress differently.[26] The gender differentiation of childhood today may be stronger than it has ever been.

And it's not just clothing and activities—it's our bodies themselves. We know that women are more likely to surgically alter their bodies than men are, consistent with the greater pressure on women to be beautiful. Women account for 90 percent of cosmetic surgery and 91 percent of non-surgical cosmetic procedures (such as Botox and chemical peels), according to the American Society for Aesthetic Plastic Surgery. But beyond simply beauty, both women and men favor surgeries that bring their bodies into gender compliance. After surgeries related to aging and fat, breast augmentation for women and breast reduction for men are the leading cosmetic surgeries.[27]

Sociologists like to say that gender identities are socially constructed. That just means that what it is, and what it means, to be male or female are at least partly the outcome of social interaction between people—visible through the rules, attitudes, media, or ideals in the social world. And that process sometimes involves constructing people's bodies physically as well. In today's high-intensity parenting, in which gender plays a big part, this includes constructing—or at least tinkering with—the bodies of children. For children, braces are a common form of body reshaping that plays an underappreciated role in differentiating girls from boys.

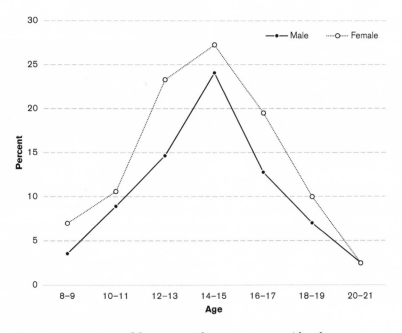

Figure 26. Percentage of those ages eight to twenty-one with at least one orthodontist visit in 2014, by age and sex. Source: Author analysis of Medical Expenditure Panel Survey data, available at meps.ahrq.gov /mepsweb/.

I started with a Google image search for "braces," and in the first one hundred images showing faces about ninety were girls. Why so many girls braced for beauty? Is this just another manifestation of the greater tendency to value appearance for girls and women more than for boys and men? The short answer is yes. It turns out that girls get braces more, even though girls' teeth are no more crooked or misplaced than boys'. And because braces are expensive, this is also tied up with social class, so that richer people are more likely to get their kids' teeth straightened—and as a result richer girls are more likely to meet (and set) beauty standards.

Hard numbers on how many kids actually get braces were oddly hard to come by. I could find no study that directly measured this for the United States. However, the federal government's Medical Expenditure Panel Survey asks people about their (and their children's) medical practice visits on an annual basis. This allowed me to check the rates of orthodontic visits by age and gender. By my calculations, 14 percent of females ages eight to twenty-one visited an orthodontist at least once in 2014, compared with 10 percent of males. The gap is largest in the age range twelve to thirteen, when 23 percent of girls compared with 15 percent of boys visited an orthodontist (figure 26). It seems that girls are wearing most of dental hardware.

Why? It's not just the parents. US girls generally are more anxious about the appearance of their bodies than boys are.[28] A study of about 1,500 Michigan public school children found that although boys and girls had equal treatment needs (orthodontists have developed sophisticated tools for measuring this "need," which everyone agrees is usually aesthetic), girls' attitudes about their own teeth were quite different from boys'.[29] Among these eight- to eleven-year-olds, girls were much more likely (10 percent vs. 6 percent) to say they there were not happy with their teeth, and 55 percent of girls versus 38 percent of boys said they wanted braces.

Girls are held to a higher beauty standard and feel the pressure—from media, peers, or parents—to get their teeth straightened. They want braces, and for good reason, as the famous and fabulous all have straight white teeth. Unfortunately, this subjects them to needless, expensive medical procedures and reinforces the overvaluing of appearance. It also shows one way that parents invest more in their girls, perhaps thinking they need to prepare them for successful careers and relationships by spending more on their looks. As is the case with lots of cosmetic procedures, people from wealthier families generally are less likely to need braces for more than cosmetic reasons but more likely to get them.[30] Add this to the gender pattern, and what emerges is a system in which richer girls (voluntarily or not) and their parents set the standard for beauty—and then reap the rewards (as well as harms) of reaching it.

Gender differentiation is a fascinating scientific subject. It's also an ideological ideal, a cultural creation, a political project, and a modern parenting touchstone. To understand the place of gender in modern society, we need to look at its role in each of these areas and the connections between them. Disney's dimorphism didn't create gender differentiation, and it doesn't force parents to approach their children's development differently by sex. But the ideals and norms matter, and segregation in an unequal society is rarely benign.

In the long run, the desperate defense of difference in the social conflicts over marriage equality and sexual civil rights may be a sideshow in the historical development of gender and its inequalities—which live on in popular media and culture. But those conflicts, in the context of continuing gender inequality, offer a revealing window into the cultural workings of gender and its reach into our social and personal lives. They also lead us into a more direct discussion of gender inequality, the subject of the next chapter.

6 Gender Inequality

Difference is a precondition of inequality between groups. The condition of inequality requires a referent—one group has more or less of something than another. With regard to gender inequality, it is not the case that men have more of everything desirable than women, or that all men have more of anything desirable than all women do, or that gender inequality results from a single, coherent set of sexist motivations or the actions they inspire. Yet it is reasonable for practical—or political—purposes to refer to gender inequality as a systemic property of contemporary US society (and all other societies). To do so responsibly, however, requires grappling with a complicated set of facts that change over time according to patterns that are linked but not synchronized. Retreating behind the gauzy haze of terms like *nuance* and *complexity* is not a solution to this problem; rather, we need to name and measure the quantities we hope to understand and to explain them in both specific and systemic terms, quantitatively and qualitatively. We need facts and theory, and intelligible descriptions of both.[1]

This chapter deals mostly with economic inequality—jobs and incomes and wealth. That's partly because economic inequality is very important and partly because it's easier to measure than a lot of other things, like sexual assault, mansplaining, childhood socialization, and other kinds of inequality that I discuss in other essays. Because I often come at gender inequality through critiques of media accounts, I start here with what the news people call a "deep dive" into one highly influential publication: the *New York Times*.

1. GENDER SEGREGATION AT THE *NEW YORK TIMES*

The Women's Media Center (WMC) reported in 2015 that women wrote 37 percent of print news stories in major newspapers. Levels ranged from a low of 31 percent female at the *New York Daily News* to a high of 54 percent at the *Chicago Sun-Times*. The *New York Times* is near the bottom of the major newspapers, with just 32 percent female bylines in the last quarter of 2014.[2]

The WMC report focused on the front section of each newspaper. Thanks to a data collection by my colleague Neal Caren, we can do better (figure 27).[3] Neal extracted everything the *Times* published online from October 23, 2013, to February 25, 2014—a total of 29,880 items, including online-only as well as print items. After eliminating the 7,669 pieces that had no author listed (mostly wire stories), we tried to determine the gender of the first author of each piece. Neal identified the gender for all first names that were more than 90 percent male or female in the Social Security name database in the years 1945–70. That covered 97 percent of the bylines. For the remainder, I investigated the gender of all writers who had published ten pieces or more during the period (attempting to find both images and gendered pronouns). That resolved all but 255 pieces, leaving me with a sample of 21,440.[4]

This analysis showed:

- 1. Women were the first or only author on 34 percent of the articles.
- 2. Women wrote the majority of stories in five out of twenty-one major sections, from Fashion (52 percent women), to Dining, Home, Travel, and Health (76 percent women). Those five sections, however, account for only 11 percent of the total.
- 3. Men wrote the majority of stories in the seven largest sections. Two sections were more than three-fourths male: Sports (89 percent) and Opinion (76 percent). US, World, and Business were between 66 and 73 percent male.

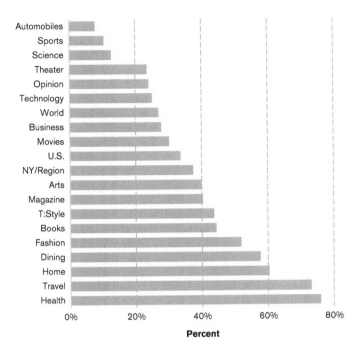

Figure 27. Percentage of stories with female first or only author, by section, for 21,440 *New York Times* articles, October 23, 2013, to February 25, 2014.

Since we have all this text, we can go a little beyond the section breakdown in the *Times*. What are men and women writing about? Using the words in the headlines, I compiled a list of those headline words with the biggest gender difference in rates of appearance. To get that, I calculated the frequency of occurrence of each headline word, as a fraction of all headline words in female-authored versus male-authored stories. For example, *children* occurred thirty-six times in women's headlines and twenty-four times in men's headlines. Since men used more than twice as many headline words as women, this produced a very big gender spread in favor of women for the word *children*. On the other hand, women's headlines had ten instances of *Iran*, versus eighty-five for men. Repeating this comparison for every headline word, I generated the ranked lists in table 2, with the most gender-tilted words at the top of each list.

Table 2. *New York Times* headline words used disproportionately in stories written by women versus
men, October 23, 2013, to February 25, 2014

Women	Men
Scene	US
Israel	Deal
London	Business
Hotel	Iran
Her	Game
Beauty	Knicks
Children	Court
Home	NFL
Women	Billion
Holiday	Nets
Food	Music
Sales	Case
Wedding	Test
Museum	His
Cover	Games
Quiz	Bitcoin
Work	Jets
Christie	Chief
German	Firm
Menu	Nuclear
Commercial	Talks
Fall	Egypt
Shoe	Bowl
Israeli	Broadway
Family	Oil
Restaurant	Shows
Variety	Super
Cancer	Football
Artists	Hits
Shopping	UN
Breakfast	Face
Loans	Russia
Google	Ukraine
Living	Yankees
Party	Milan

Vows	Mets
Clothes	Kerry
Life	Gas
Child	Investors
Credit	Plans
Health	Calls
Chinese	Fans
India	Model
France	Fed
Park	Protesters
Doctors	Team
Hunting	Texas
Christmas	Play

WHAT DOES IT MEAN?

With some exceptions, the list of words gives the impression that men cover the important geopolitical questions of the day (*Iran, nuclear*), the economy (*deal, billion, oil*), and the masculine world of sports while more women spend their days writing about *hotels, beauty, children, weddings, shoes,* and *Christmas.* However, this doesn't mean most women write about hotels and most men write about Iran. It means these are the words with the biggest gender disparities, so they show where the extreme differences lie—it's an indicator of segregation. Surely this segregation reflects the influence of diverse factors, including editor and reader expectations, gender socialization, and women's ways of adapting to work in a male-dominated industry. But the bottom line of male domination is clearly evident.

This is just one newspaper, but it matters a lot. According to the Alexa Web traffic analysts, NYTimes.com is the 32nd most popular website in the United States and the 117th most popular in the world—and the most popular website of a printed newspaper in the United States.[5] By my count, in the JSTOR database of academic scholarship, the *Times* was mentioned almost four times more frequently than the next most frequently mentioned newspaper, the *Washington Post.*

A growing body of research (some by me and Matt Huffman, among others) suggests that having women in charge produces better average outcomes for women below them in the organizational hierarchy.[6] Jill Abramson, the *Times*'s executive editor for the period I studied here, was listed as the nineteenth most powerful woman in the world by *Forbes*, behind only Sheryl Sandberg and Oprah Winfrey among media executives. Abramson was aware of the gender issue and proudly told the Women's Media Center that she had reached the "significant milestone" of having a half-female news masthead. So why are women underrepresented in such prominent sections? Under Abramson the *Times* didn't even do as well as the national average: 39 percent of the 61,500 news reporters working full time, year round in 2014 were women, according to the American Community Survey.[7]

Organizational research finds that large companies are less likely to discriminate against women, and we suspect three main reasons: greater visibility to the public, which leads to complaints about bias; greater visibility to the government, which may enforce antidiscrimination laws; and greater use of formal personnel procedures, which limits managerial discretion and weakens old-boy networks. Among writers, however, an informal, backchannel norm still apparently prevails in hiring decisions—at least according to recent personal accounts.[8] Maybe the *Times*'s big-company, formalized practices apply more to departments other than those that select and hire writers, where subjective assessment remains the dominant mode of assessing performance—perhaps even more in this most elite of journalism workplaces. Several weeks after I posted this analysis on my blog, Abramson was fired by the *Times*'s publisher, Arthur Sulzberger, who said she had lost the confidence of her staff (reports described her as abrasive and alienating); her allies said she had recently complained about being paid less than the previous (male) executive editor.[9] After her replacement by a (Black) man, she is no longer on the *Forbes* list of most powerful women.

2. THE GENDER GAP GETS IT FROM ALL SIDES

The "gender gap" is a regular feature of public debate over gender inequality. This hardworking statistic is as often abused and attacked by antifemi-

Figure 28. Female-to-male earnings ratio, 1960–2015. Median earnings of full-time, year-round workers. Source: Current Population Survey via IPUMS.org.

nists as it is misused and misunderstood by those sympathetic to feminism. But it is good for one thing: information.

The statistic is released each year with the US Census Bureau's income and poverty report. The Current Population Survey (CPS) reports annual incomes from 2015: the median earnings of full-time, year-round working women ($40,742) was 80 percent of men's ($51,212).[10] That is the source of (accurate, at the time) statements such as Barack Obama's "Women still earn only 79 cents to every dollar that men make."[11]

This statistic has the undeniable advantage of being relatively easy to calculate and comparable over time, so we can use it to assess one trend in gender inequality. The Institute for Women's Policy Research (IWPR), for example, informs us that "if change continues at the same slow pace as it has done for the past 50 years, it will take 44 years—or until 2059—for women to finally reach pay parity."[12] The trend that forms the basis for that prediction is shown in figure 28.

There is no reason to think the future will follow a linear trend established by this distinctly nonlinear history. If you did want to fit a line to the trend, the bad news is that a third-order polynomial fits very well—that is, an S-shaped line fits almost perfectly, and predicts the gap will never narrow further. Fortunately, this kind of math doesn't actually tell us what will happen in the social world. But it does caution against resting on our laurels and simply waiting for equality.

Some defenders of equal pay for women misstate the statistic, as President Bill Clinton did when he said: "How would you like to show up for work every day, but only get to take home three out of every four paychecks? . . . If you get paid 75 percent for the same kind of work, it's as if you were only picking up three paychecks, instead of four, in four pay periods. The average woman has to work, therefore, an extra 17 weeks a year to earn what a similarly-qualified man in the same kind of job makes."[13]

The mistake here is that he said "same kind of work" and "similarly-qualified man." This statistic is not designed to identify that sort of close-up discrimination. It's a broad indicator of earnings inequality, not a measure of employer discrimination. Clinton's comment led to a screaming headline on the American Enterprise Institute website, "Still Hyping the Phony Pay Gap."[14] But Clinton also went on to say: "Yes, some of this can be explained—by differences in education, experience and occupation." So he belatedly acknowledged the complexities. Oh, and that exchange occurred in 2000. How far we've come.

When Bill Clinton, ever a repository for handy statistics, essentially repeated his statement in 2013, he played right into the screaming headlines of today's antifeminists, including Hanna Rosin, who declared, "I feel the need to set the record straight" in a piece she titled "The Gender Gap Lie."[15] Kay Hymowitz also has written extensively to debunk the gender gap, arguing that it mostly results from women's choices—the educations and occupations they choose, the hours they choose, the "mommy track" they prefer.[16]

There is no single number that can tell us the true state of gender inequality. But if you had to pick one, this one is actually pretty good. That's because it reflects a combination of factors that affect gender inequality. Men and women have different employment levels, work experience, and occupational distributions, some of which reflect employer discrimination; many people aren't in the job of their "choice," maybe because someone decided not to hire or promote them to a better job. And there is pay discrimination, too, though it's almost impossible to measure in a survey. This single statistic ends up giving a sense of the place of the typical worker after all those factors come into play. As long as pay is not equal, there is a gender inequality problem to discuss, whether it results from socialization, family demands, educational sorting and tracking, hiring and promotion discrimination, or pay discrimination.

Consider the case of Angelica Valencia, whose story was told in 2014 by one of the women writing at the *New York Times*, Rachel Swarns.[17] Valencia was fired from her $8.70-an-hour job packing produce after her doctor said she couldn't work overtime because she was three months into a risky pregnancy. The state actually had a new law against pregnancy discrimination on her side, but her employer somehow didn't get around to notifying her of her right to a reasonable accommodation.[18] It's important to keep cases like this in mind when critics complain that the gender gap statistic doesn't account for occupational choice, time out of the labor force, women's reduced hours, and so on.

Such critics include Ruth Davis Konigsberg, who had a piece in *Time* with the sneering subtitle "Women don't make 77 cents to a man's dollar. They make more like 93 cents, as long as they don't major in art history."[19] I guess Angelica Valencia should have thought of that, although it's really only something that the 29 percent of adults with bachelor's degrees need to lose sleep over. Hanna Rosin offered a similarly helpful explanation: "Women congregate in different professions than men do, and the largely male professions tend to be higher-paying."[20]

So what does the story of Angelica Valencia's pregnancy tell us, besides the pitfalls of majoring in art history or congregating in the wrong profession? I don't know what happened in her case, but let's assume that she, or someone in a situation like hers, took a while to find a new job and then ended up in a lower-paying job as a result of that discrimination. If we insist on statistically controlling for occupation, hours, job tenure, and time out of the labor force in order to see the "real" wage gap, someone like her may not show up as underpaid—if they're paid the same as men in the same jobs, working the same hours, for the same length of time, and so on. So the very thing that makes Valencia earn less—being fired for getting pregnant—disappears from the wage gap analysis. Instead, the data shows that women take more time off work, work fewer hours, change jobs more often, and "choose" less lucrative occupations. Of course, a lot of women choose to get pregnant (and a lot of men choose to become fathers). But getting fired and ending up in a lower-paid job as a result is not part of that choice (and it rarely happens to fathers). That's why the overall difference in pay between men and women, which reflects a complicated mix of factors, is a good indicator of inequality.

Segregation

But let's look more closely at those college graduates that journalists often assume represent all workers. The ACS asks college graduates what their major was. In figure 29 I've taken full-time, full-year workers who have a bachelor's degree and no further education (to remove the influence of later degrees), by college major, and arranged them from most to least male dominated. The level of gender segregation itself is remarkable, as the majors range from construction services, at 6 percent female, to family and consumer sciences, which is 87 percent female. The figure shows the average earnings as well as the spread between men's and women's average earnings. The male-dominated majors do pay more than the female-dominated ones, as engineering majors earn the most, while education majors earn the least. But there is also a male advantage within every group. Women's earnings range from a low of 75 percent of men's for area studies majors at the worst, all the way up to 92 percent for engineering technologies majors at the best. Seeing the gap within each major is especially useful for those who think the gender gap results from women choosing less lucrative majors.

College majors, of course, are closely related to the jobs people have (if they've graduated from college), so the sorting of people into majors—like the sorting of workers into jobs more generally, is a key issue. One way to look at that is by breaking occupations down by education level, as I have done with the twenty-five largest occupations in figure 30. This illustrates how much segregation there is at every education level. A separate analysis (not shown) confirms that within each group of occupations, the

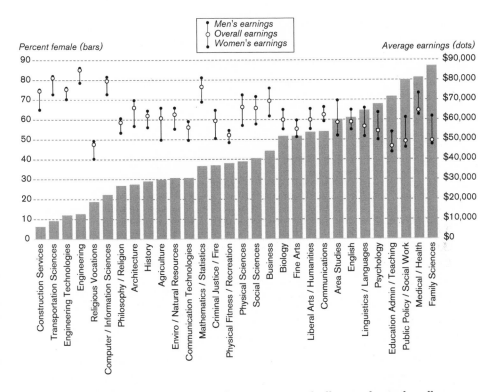

Figure 29. Average earnings and gender composition of college graduates, by college major. Source: Author calculations from the 2014 American Community Survey via IPUMS.org. Includes only full-time, year-round workers, ages twenty-five to fifty-four, with a bachelor's degree and no further degrees.

female-dominated jobs have lower average earnings than those dominated by men—a finding consistent with decades of research.[21]

Job segregation lies behind much of the gender gap in pay—representing the culmination of historical and contemporary processes of allocating people to tasks. If women earn less than men on average, than the jobs in which they are crowded will tend to have lower pay. And then discrimination pushes, or pulls, women into those lower-paying jobs. In fact, there is evidence that the presence of women in an occupation itself leads to lower average pay, as a result of what we call gender devaluation.

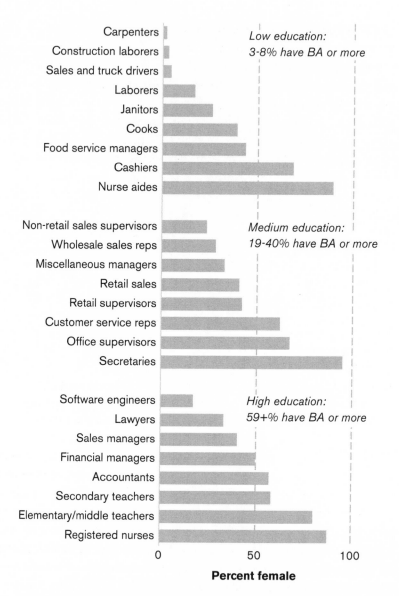

Figure 30. Percentage female in twenty-five largest occupations, by education level. Source: Author analysis of 2015 March Current Population Survey data from IPUMS.org. Full-time, full-year workers (excluding chief executives).

I developed one comparison to illustrate this devaluation process—the process of rewarding "male" work more than "female" work. Consider two of the occupations in the low-education group: sales workers and truck drivers versus nursing aides. These are narrowly defined occupations, but they include millions of workers: in 2014 there were 2 million nursing aides and 3.2 million sales workers and truck drivers (I'll call them truck drivers for short, but this category excludes big industrial trucks).[22] The nursing aides are 88 percent female, the truck drivers are 94 percent male. Drawn from Census Bureau data, and information from the US Department of Labor's O*Net job classification system, here are some other facts:

- The nursing assistants are better educated on average, with only 50 percent having no education beyond high school, compared with 67 percent of the light truck drivers.
- But in terms of job skills, they are both in the O*Net "Job Zone Two," meaning three months to one year of training is "required by a typical worker to learn the techniques, acquire the information, and develop the facility needed for average performance in a specific job-worker situation."
- The O*Net reported median wage for 2012 was $11.74 for nursing assistants, compared with $14.13 for light truck drivers, so nursing assistants earn 83 percent of light truck drivers' hourly earnings.

To make a stricter apples-to-apples comparison, I took just those workers from the two occupations who fit these narrow criteria: age twenty to twenty-nine, high school graduate with no further education, employed fifty to fifty-two weeks in the previous year, with usual hours of forty per week, never married, no children. In the 2009–11 ACS, this gave me a sample of 748 light truck drivers and 693 nursing assistants, with median annual earnings of $22,564 and $20,000, respectively—the light truck drivers earn 13 percent more. Why?

The typical argument for heavy truck drivers' higher pay is that they spend a lot of time on the road away from home. But that's not the case with these light truck drivers, and I restricted this comparison to forty-hour workers only. The O*Net database includes a long list of abilities and working conditions for people to evaluate jobs and the workers who do them. There are clues in here about why men and women with similar skill and education levels are separated across these two occupations, but not much to explain why the truck drivers earn more. In terms of abilities, the nursing aide job requires more explosive strength and trunk strength, but less dynamic strength and static strength. The nursing aides have more language skills while the truck drivers have more coordination and dexterity. In terms of working conditions, the nursing aides face disease and infection, spend more time on their feet as well as stooping, crouching, bending, and twisting—and dealing with physically aggressive people. The truck drivers, on the other hand, spend more time exposed to the weather and experience more loud sounds and lights that are too bright or not bright enough.

You can stare at these lists and try to figure out which skills should be rewarded more, or which conditions compensated more. Or you could derive some formula based on the pay of the hundreds of occupations, to see which skills or conditions "the market" values more. But the problem for understanding gender inequality is that you will not be able to divine a fair market value for these differences that doesn't already have gender composition baked into it. By *baked in*, I mean: things men do—have always done—are more valuable in our market system than things women do. It's hard to pin down, because "the market" doesn't make this comparison directly, because nursing aides and light truck drivers generally don't work for the same employers or get hired from the same labor pools. Sociologists who have studied these patterns over time conclude that gender composition itself is a strong independent driver of pay differences, with inequalities derived more from the traditional division of labor than from individual actions of today's employers.[23]

The only solution I know of to the problem of unequal pay according to gender composition is government wage scales according to a "comparable worth" scheme. That was the subject of an extensive debate several decades ago, but such radical state intervention is not high on the current political agenda, despite repeated promises by Democratic leaders (including Barack Obama and Hillary Clinton) that they would address the gender gap.[24] Under our current legal regime it is virtually impossible for one woman, or even a class of women, to successfully bring a suit to challenge this kind of disparity—because it does not entail individuals being paid unequally for the same work. That means occupational integration might be the best way to reduce the pay gap.[25]

Each of these comparisons tells us something different. We must be careful not to read into these numbers more than they can tell us. None of the numbers I've shown can fully distinguish occupational choice from employer discrimination, for example, or the cumulative effects of family time out of the labor force versus discrimination in previous jobs. But the gender gap numbers are measures of inequality. And as long as we are accurate and responsible in our use of these numbers, that's useful information about the state of gender inequality.

3. GENDER SHIFTS IN FAMILIES

Breadwinner women are all over the news, but the simple story in most versions is not good enough, and in some cases, as we will see, it's very wrong. The promotional materials for Farnoosh Torabi's book *When She Makes More* rely on a single, dramatic statistic: "The number of married couples with top-earning wives is *four* times greater than it was in the 1960s."[26] A Pew Research Center report carried the banner statistic, "Mothers are the sole or primary provider in four-in-ten households with children."[27] These numbers are quite slippery, and those without a firm grasp are likely to overreact. On cue, *Fox and Friends* host Clayton Morris expressed his concern: "Are female breadwinners a problem? Isn't there some sort of biological, innate need for men to be the caveman? Go out and bring home the dinner—is it emasculating if we don't do it?"[28]

Here are three central facts to keep in mind, illustrated in figure 31, which shows the distribution of income within married couples in 1970, 1990, and 2014. From this we can see:

1. *Yes, the balance of income within married couples has shifted toward women since the 1950s.* There is a dramatic drop in the percentage of couples in which the husband earns all the income—from 45 percent in 1970 to 20 percent in 2014. That is the plummet of the "traditional" male breadwinner.

2. *But the pace of change slowed dramatically after the 1990s.* The vast majority of that change had happened already by 1990—a generation

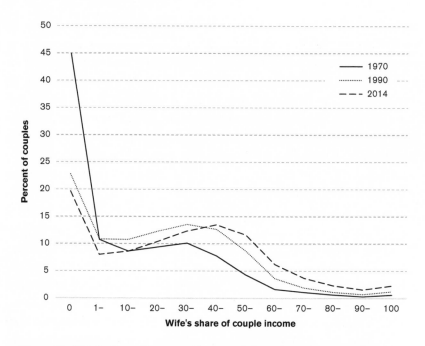

Figure 31. Distribution of income within married couples, 1970–2014. Source: Author calculations from Decennial Censuses and the American Community Survey data via IPUMS.org. Restricted to different-sex couples with positive total incomes in which the wife is age eighteen to sixty-four.

ago. The shift since 1990 has mostly been a decline in couples where the wife earns 1 to 20 percent, and a rise in those where the wife earns 50 to 70 percent, but it's modest compared with what happened before 1990.

3. *Today's female "breadwinners" are not much like the men who filled that role a half century ago.* As of 2014, only 2 percent of couples have a wife that earned all the income in the previous year. That's more than it used to be, but it's not a role reversal.

These three facts are essential to understanding the nature of changing gender inequality within families. There may be something psychologically triggering for some people who experience a wife earning anything more than her husband does, but we do nothing to help that situation by exaggerating the extent of women's dominance. Consider that, on average, in 2014 wives who earned more than their husbands brought in 68 percent of the couple's income. On the other hand, the average husband who earned more brought in 82 percent of the total. A male "breadwinner" is three times more likely to earn all the income in the couple than a female "breadwinner." In addition, those analyses, like Pew's above, that report the highest prevalence of female providers are including single mothers—who are of course primary providers for their families, but their prevalence is not a good indicator of declining gender inequality.

Actually, this triplet pattern fits a lot of trends regarding gender inequality: *yes,* lots of change, *but* most of it decades ago, *and* not quite as fundamental as it looks. Consider stay-at-home fathers—the complement to the female breadwinner.

A *New York Times* Style section piece featured a picture of a "Daddy and me" class in Central Park and reported on the rapid growth of the population of stay-at-home fathers. "Until recently, stay-at-home fathers made up a tiny sliver of the American family spectrum," wrote Alex Williams, describing the new trend as "a lifestyle choice—one that makes sense in an era in which women's surging salaries have thrown the old family hierarchy into flux."[29] The cover of the *New Yorker* on Mother's Day of that year (May 7, 2012) showed a lone mother with her toddler in a stroller, standing at the edge of a playground full of dads and children.

The data in that article were accurate. Gretchen Livingston wrote a report for Pew Social Trends on fathers staying at home with their kids. She defined stay-at-home fathers as any father age eighteen to sixty-nine living with his children who did not work for pay in the previous year. Her analysis showed a doubling of stay-at-home fathers from 1989 to 2012. There are especially pronounced spikes during recessions, which highlights the economic context of the trend, but even without the recessions the trend is upward.[30]

As with breadwinners, we also need to understand the definition. In Livingston's analysis, 21 percent of the stay-at-home fathers reported that their reason for not working was caring for their home and family; 23 percent couldn't find work, 35 percent couldn't work because of health problems, and 22 percent were in school or retired. It is reasonable to call a father "stay-at-home" regardless of his reason (after all, we never needed stay-at-home mothers to fulfill motive-based criteria before we gave them that label). And yet there is a tendency to read into this a bigger change in gender dynamics than it justifies. The Census Bureau has for years calculated a much more narrow definition that applies only to married parents of kids under fifteen: those out of the labor force all year, whose spouse was in the labor force all year, and who specified their reason as taking care of home and family.[31] You can think of people in this category as the *hardcore* stay-at-home parents, the ones who do it long term and have a carework motivation for doing it. When you define them that way, stay-at-home mothers outnumber fathers 100 to 1.

In figure 32 I show trends in two simple measures. The first, which I calculate from 1976 through 2014, includes all married parents (living with children under age fifteen) who reported no employment in the previous year. This is the broadest category of stay-at-home parents, not dependent on their reason for not working or on what anyone else in the household is doing. By this measure, the prevalence of stay-at-home mothers fell markedly from 1970s until 2000, but it has since rebounded back up over 30 percent. In the figure I also show the percentage of parents who did not work in the previous year who reported that their reason for nonemployment was "caring for home and family." This doesn't change the trend for mothers much, as the great majority of nonemployed mothers gave this as their reason. For fathers, however, only 23 percent of those who didn't work said the reason was caring for home and family. So even though the percentage of fathers in this role has more than doubled, it's never surpassed 1.5 percent of all married fathers—maybe still a "tiny sliver of the American family spectrum." As in the case of female breadwinners, then, although there has been a pronounced change in the pattern of stay-at-home parents compared with the period of extreme gender division epitomized by the 1950s, it mostly occurred decades ago. And the trend shows something more like a role shift than a revolution or role reversal.

Exaggerating Change

In the last few years, on this and other questions, I've spent a lot of time trying to combat the tendency to exaggerate the extent of change toward gender equality. My basic concern is that if we don't understand the trends

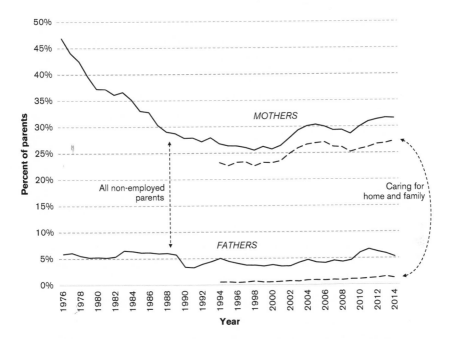

Figure 32. Stay-at-home parents as percentage of married parents living with children ages zero through fourteen. Source: Author calculations from Current Population Survey data via IPUMS.org.

we won't be able to see what remains to be done—and the obstacles to inequality that remain. Maybe it's uniquely American, but we have a strong urge to see equality approaching as an inevitable evolution of impartial social forces. Somewhere between our natural inclination toward egalitarianism and against injustice on the one hand, and techno-logical advances on the other, men and women are presumed to be head-ing toward equality in the foreseeable and not-too-distant future. Failure to see that most change toward gender equality happened decades ago also distorts our view of the importance of explicit feminist politics as a crucial factor in that change. And it prevents us from understanding how contemporary policies and practices—especially around the work-family intersection—are blocking further progress.[32]

Exaggerations of the gender equality trend also may be a natural product of the perceived need in journalism to tell a linear story with clear implications for the future. This tendency was apparent in the book by journalist Liza Mundy, *The Richer Sex*, with the wishful-thinking subtitle "How the New Majority of Female Breadwinners Is Transforming Sex, Love and Family." A more aggressive mischaracterization of reality appeared in Hanna Rosin's TED talk, *Atlantic* article, and eventually book *The End of Men*.[33] She opened the TED talk by declaring that "in many of the places where it counts the most, women are in fact taking control of everything." Unlike the feminist surges in the 1920s and 1960s, however, she added, "This time it's not about passion and it's not about any kind of movement. This is really just about the facts of this economic moment that we live in. The 200,000-year period in which men have been top dog is truly coming to an end, believe it or not, and that's why I talk about 'the end of men.'"

In the months that followed, I chronicled the amazing collection of errors and distortions that Rosin made in her articles and the book. She claimed that the majority of "managers" are now women (it's actually "managers and professionals," which includes nurses and teachers); that "young women are earning more than young men" (this is true only for single, childless women under thirty in urban areas); that "70% of fertility clinic patients" prefer to have a female child (there's just no evidence for that); that Auburn, Alabama, is "a town dominated by women" (it has the same male dominance as most US cities); that "rates [of sexual assault] are so low in parts of the country . . . that criminologists can't plot the numbers on a chart" (that's just ridiculous); that the average age of marriage for women "in Asia" is thirty-two (it's much lower); and that "the recent rise in plastic surgeries is fueled by men" (there is no rise, and men account for only 13 percent of plastic surgeries).[34]

Rosin illustrated the problem of assuming that gender trends map onto a linear progress story when, after the 2012 election, she somehow thought women made up one-third of Congress and wrote: "A record number of women were elected to Congress, bringing their number to a third of the membership, the level many sociologists cite as a tipping point when a minority becomes normalized and starts to enter the mainstream. In other words, it's no longer big news when a woman gets elected; it's expected."

This one-third tipping point theory Rosin attributes (without citation) to "many sociologists" is, not surprisingly, a myth; if there's one thing we have learned about minority representation and its effects on inequality, it's that we can't apply a simple numerical rule to the many patterns observed in the research literature. And even if her facts on the number of women in Congress were correct, the suggestion that the United States has reached the point where women's representation at the top is no longer news is obviously not true in the simplest sense. When informed that women held only 18 percent of seats in Congress, *Slate* deleted the whole passage. (The article was as clear an illustration as you could ask for of sloppy writers' tendency to advance a theory on the basis of cherry-picked facts and to distort or omit any evidence that doesn't fit.)

I eventually concluded that Rosin's story of women sweeping into dominance without the impetus of "passion" or "any kind of movement" was misleading to the point of being corrosive—it harms our ability not just to understand but to mobilize people to address gender inequality. She essentially turned several broad facts—that women are earning more degrees in higher education than men and that the service economy is growing—and manufactured around them a story of technological change (the shift from brawn to brains) tipping the power balance from male to female. This is not complete fiction, as the changing composition of the economy through the mid-twentieth century did produce rapid growth in occupations that were female dominated, such as medical, educational, and administrative occupations.[35] But the part about women becoming socially dominant remains purely hypothetical—albeit theoretically plausible.[36]

In the *New York Times* magazine excerpt from her book, Rosin wrote: "As the usual path to the middle class disappears, what's emerging in its place is a nascent middle-class matriarchy, in which women like Patsy [one of her interviewees] pay the mortgage and the cable bills while the men try to find their place."[37] This is completely inaccurate. There has of course been movement toward gender equality (with the caveats I noted above), but the evidence simply does not support anything like a "matriarchy" or female dominance in families or in the economy generally. The idea that women are inevitably rising to power in politics and the economy, replacing men in the pants-wearing driver's seat, is both disempowering to feminists and enraging to sexists. With careful attention to the actual trends, we can understand the necessity of further efforts toward equality and can illuminate the ways forward, while also disarming the militant purveyors of antifeminist backlash.

4. THAT FEMINIST VIRAL STATISTIC MEME

Exaggerating the progress and promise of equality is disempowering because it undermines the urgency of calls for concerted action to address gender inequality. But exaggerating the extent of patriarchal domination is also disempowering because it presents the problem as hopelessly unchanging. In the last few years I have been fortunate to be on the receiving end of feminist criticism (and also feminist support) for criticizing both of these disempowering tendencies.

The one-hundredth anniversary of International Women's Day, in 2011, came at an auspicious time for statistical infographic memes. The coming wave of "data journalism" was as yet only nascent, but social media were already demonstrating the potential for a statistic-based meme to have outsized influence in the political arena: not just a political statement, not just an empirical fact, but a single fact (or a few of them) propelling a perspective, making it visually as well as verbally memorable, and anchoring it in a base of credibility.

That year I was reminded of something that had been nagging at me for at least ten years, since I read it in Judith Lorber's excellent 1994 book, *Paradoxes of Gender*. She wrote: "An often-cited United Nations Report (1980) claims that women do two-thirds of the world's work, receive 10 percent of the income, and own 1 percent of the property."[38] The reference wasn't helpful (a 1980 report I couldn't access), but those facts had never seemed plausible to me.

Then, in 2011, as International Women's Day approached, we were treated to a barrage of mainstream, corporate-backed liberal feminism, including a collaboration between Google and a nonprofit called Women for Women, which encouraged women to march across bridges around the world on March 8. To promote the effort, they produced a video, which has now been viewed almost a million times, that includes this in the narration: "Did you know that women perform two-thirds of the world's work and produce half the world's food, but earn just 10 percent of the income and own just one percent of the property?"[39]

The inequality described in that video is easily understood as outrageously immoral. But why would a 2011 infographic include a statistic from a 1995 book that cited a 1980 report? As memes travel from mind to mind, like viruses, such questions are lost. A statistical meme just needs a plausible link or citation to make the leap from one host to another and—unlike a virus—can be transmitted from one person to millions more instantly, without the need for face-to-face contact.

For example, *Wall Street Journal* writer Sudeep Reddy (later an economics editor) wrote a blog post titled "New Facts on the Gender Gap from the World Bank." The first of his bullet point facts was dramatic: "Women represent 40 percent of the world's labor force but hold just one percent of the world's wealth." The labor force statistic was in the World Bank report (in the first paragraph, actually, giving some hint of the depth of his research), but the wealth statistic, which isn't true, was not. The *Journal*'s Twitter account fit that fact into a tweet, and by the next day it was being reported on ThinkProgress as a "newsflash," which got repeated by *Ms.*, and then became the "number of the day" on the feminist site Shakesville.[40] And so on.

On the Trail

Because I'm concerned about both kinds of disempowering errors—the optimistic and pessimistic overstatements—and generally want to promote the responsible use of social statistics, I wanted to find out where the meme came from and then repair or retire it. It really only took a few hours of research, and some interlibrary loan requests, to track it down.

That 2011 International Women's Day version—which gave the meme new global momentum—was more or less verbatim how it had appeared in Lorber's book and a decade earlier, on page 1 of Robin Morgan's introduction to the classic collection called *Sisterhood Is Global: The International Women's Movement Anthology*.[41] Beyond that, I quickly found three sources offered by bona fide scholars. The first was the footnote from Morgan's book, which says: "Statistics from Development Issue Paper No. 12, UNDP." Produced as part of the UN's Decade for Women (1975–85), this report was titled "Women and the New International Economic Order" and was probably published in 1980. That document is fascinating reading, but on the key point it is just a restatement of the meme, without documentation.[42] It is not the true source. The second was a report called "World Conference of the United Nations Decade for

Women: Equality, Development and Peace" (UN document buffs might call it A/Conf. 94/20), or the "Programme of Action" that emerged from that 1980 meeting, which was in Copenhagen. That document was released under the name of Kurt Waldheim, who (before his Nazi past was revealed) was secretary general to the UN at the start of the Decade for Women.[43] This was Lorber's source, but it is not the true source.

Finally, the Copenhagen report contains a footnote to a 1978 edition of a Decade for Women–inspired journal published by the International Labour Organization, called *Women at Work*. This, I eventually discovered, is the true source.[44] It occurs in the editor's introduction to the journal. Unfortunately, the sum total of what it provides is this: "A world profile on women, using selected economic and social indicators, reveals that women constitute one half of the world population and one third of the official labour force; perform nearly two-thirds of work hours; but according to some estimates receive only one-tenth of the world income and possess less than one-hundredth of world property."

There is no information on the indicators used or their sources, or what is meant by "some estimates." That is where the trail went cold, until I found the testimonial of Krishna Ahooja-Patel, who took credit for the passage. In 2007, Ahooja-Patel, the editor over whose initials that editorial appeared, published a book called *Development Has a Woman's Face: Insights from within the U.N.*, in which she offers an unsourced sketch of the methods she used to derive the famous statement. "Several assumptions had to be made," she concedes, "based on some available global data and others derived by use of fragmentary indicators at the time, in the late 1970s."[45]

The figures used were crude estimates at best. Women were 33 percent of the world's formal workforce, and they were "only on the low income level in the pyramid of employment," where (on the basis of data from "several countries") they earned 10 to 30 percent of men's income. Therefore, "One could assume that women's income is only one-third of the average income of men." Since women were one-third of the workforce and earned one-third as much as men, their total income was .33 × .33, or 11 percent (which she rounded down to 10 percent). In short, the statistic was a guess based on an extrapolation wrapped round an estimate.

What about the dramatic conclusion, that women "possess less than one-hundredth of world property"? Ahooja-Patel offers only this explanation: "If the average wage of women is so low, it can be assumed that they do not normally have any surplus to invest in reproducible or non-reproducible assets." Hence, their share of those assets is less than 1 percent. That's it. In fact, she adds, "In reality the figure may be much lower" (than 1 percent). Her source? "Various UN Statistics."

The Inequality between Women

These things are hard to measure, hard to know, and hard to explain. Setting aside the problem that the data didn't (and still don't, completely) exist to fill in the true numbers in this famous sequence of facts—the first and perhaps greatest problem is that we can't easily define the concepts, which is part of a larger feminist problem. Defining work as a quantity is fraught, as is property. Even in 1970, how could women own only 1 percent of property, when most women were married and in many countries had at least some legal claim to their families' property? Similarly, what claim did women who worked without pay in private homes and fields have to their husbands' cash incomes? And what about socialist countries (which were a big deal back then), where a lot of payment was in the form of in-kind transfers, and where various forms of collective ownership were pervasive? Did "women" own state or commune land in socialist China? Was their food ration "income"? So it's too simple to say the famous facts are wrong.

One of the complaints I have heard often from feminists (of which, to repeat, I am one) is that debunking this meme without offering the true statistics is harmful to the movement. This complaint reflects the common conflation of data and argument—the belief that citing a fact is making an argument, so that debunking the fact undermines the argument. Angry with my apparent attack on feminism, one commenter on my blog wrote, "I'm sorry but in order to claim something is false you have to be able to prove it by showing the truth." But the burden of proof is not on us (me) to show it is wrong. My responsibility is rather to point out that it was never demonstrably true, which is enough to conclude we shouldn't use it.

One of the potential negative consequences of this meme is also one of its attractions: the claim that, despite all the work women do, they own virtually nothing the world over, supports a call to global unity for women. But it is undermined by the fact that a large number of women are, of course, rich. The meme doesn't just represent a failure of education in the areas of ballpark demography and statistical critical thinking. People who fall for it also aren't realizing how rich the rich countries are—including the women in them—in the global scheme of things. If global feminist unity is to be had, it simply won't be built from a shared experience of poverty. We need to understand that so we can move on to a more fruitful approach. I eventually decided to give up on the argument that the meme needs no refuting and instead tried to show how it couldn't be true, that it must be off by orders of magnitude. Debunking this is a good exercise for statistical and demographic literacy and helps drive home the extent of global inequality *between women,* which is what's missing from the appeals that employ the meme.

So let's consider some facts. Start with the statement that women earn only 10 percent of the world's income. With a combination of arithmetic and basic knowledge of a few demographic orders of magnitude, it's straightforward to identify and conduct a simple test of the claim.

In the United States in 2015, the 112.6 million adult women reported average incomes in the previous year of $32,588 each. That is a total of $3.67 trillion. The whole world's gross domestic product—a rough measure of total income—is $77.96 trillion. So, US women *alone* earn 4.7 percent of world income today.[46] Unless the rest of the world's women combined earn less than US women (they don't), it's impossible that women earn less than 10 percent of global income. Ballpark, but you see the point. We needed only five minutes to prove the income statistic isn't true.

What about property? Recall that Ahooja-Patel described her original 1 percent estimate as referring to women's "reproducible or non-reproducible assets," which she wrote as "property." (Since then people have changed it to "land," or even "titled land," changing the words to make the claim seem more plausible without doing any real research.) My strategy for debunking this, similar to the one I used for income, is to find a small group of women who themselves own more than 1 percent of all world wealth and let that set the matter to rest.

For practical reasons, I decided to figure out the wealth owned by single women in the United States. That's because US data are pretty good, the women are pretty rich (in the scheme of things) so they're likely to satisfy the goal, and single women are simpler because you don't have to worry about defining or identifying shared wealth. (If married men and women jointly own their wealth, the "Women own 1 percent" claim is obviously implausible from the start.)

The Credit Suisse Research Institute estimated global household wealth at $243.1 trillion in 2013.[47] To estimate the share of global household wealth held by single women in the United States, I compared this with data from the 2013 Survey of Consumer Finances (SCF).[48] By my calculations, the SCF shows a total household net worth of $65.2 trillion. That works out to about $294,000 per adult (the average is so high because rich people are really rich)—a figure pretty close to the CSRI estimate of $348,000 per US adult, which is good for confidence in making this comparison.

The SCF is useful because it includes a breakdown of households by sex and marital status. Using that, I calculate that US single women (not married or living with a partner, in their own households), have a total net worth of $6.2 trillion. So single women in the United States are not doing well by US standards. They are 28 percent of the households but have only 9.5 percent of the wealth. But by global standards they look much better. They are just 0.7 percent of the world's adult population but have 2.6 percent of the global household wealth. That means that no matter how much property the billions of other women in the world own—including all married women in the United States, all single and married women in every other country—the women of the world own more than 2.6 percent of total, and the meme is wrong.

As an aside, what about extremely rich women? Sample surveys like the SCF are unlikely to call on the tiny sliver of people who are super-rich (and if they did, those people probably wouldn't talk). But when outsiders, such as Forbes, estimate the wealth of the wealthy, they can give us some clue of the share owned by women at the very top. I looked at the 2016 Forbes list of billionaire women, led by the ninety-four-year-old L'Oreal heir Liliane Bettencourt ($36 billion in 2016) and the Wal-Mart heir Alice Walton ($32 billion), all the way down to the barely billionaires such as tech executive Meg Whitman.[49] These lists bounce around a lot, so the estimates will vary, but they are good for a ballpark figure. By my count, the 108 women billionaires on the list have a combined net worth at $536 billion, which is about one-fifth of 1 percent of global household wealth.

There are very few women among the richest rich (if you don't count wives), but so vast is their wealth that alone they do a lot to push "all women" up toward the 1 percent threshold needed to debunk the meme.

A final empirical point about this meme concerns geography and land. Although Ahooja-Patel was guesstimating wealth, as I noted, some people have turned this into a statement about land ownership. This is the case even when their own evidence provides enough data to refute the meme. For example, in a post on the *Ms.* magazine blog, Jessica Mack describes the problem of women's land ownership in China. Land ownership has been a big problem there ever since the breakup of the collective owner-ship system in the 1980s, with massive land-grabbing and the migration of tens of millions of people to the cities. She writes: "In China, women have equal rights to inherit and own land, yet rarely do. A recent survey in 17 Chinese provinces, undertaken by the global land rights group Landesa, found that only 17.1 percent of existing land contracts and 38.2 percent of existing land certificates include women's names."[50]

I don't doubt there is a serious gender inequality problem. But what does it mean that "17.1 percent of existing land contracts and 38.2 percent of existing land certificates include women's names"? Does it mean women "own" that land? Are they part owners? That's a question she should have considered before writing, later in the post: "Yet women globally own only one to two percent of all titled land." This was really a rhetorical flourish, though, not a fact. For a source she reached into the meme's giant grab bag and came up with a blog post from World Food Program USA, which says that women "own less than 2 percent of the world's titled land."[51] That fact in turn is sourced to someone just repeating the classic meme.[52]

Anyway, the good news is that the seeds of the meme's undoing are in Jessica Mack's own post. You just to have a sense of the size of the world, and China within it. If women "own" either 17 percent or 38 percent of land in China, could they really own just 1 percent of land in the world? No. China has 7 percent of the world's total land area and 20 percent of the world's harvested land area.[53] Assuming all land parcels are the same size (not a safe assumption, but we have nothing else to go on), if women in China have their names on 17 percent of land contracts and 38 percent of land certifi-cates, that represents 1 to 3 percent of the total land, or 3 to 8 percent of the harvested land. That's in China alone, so the meme is killed again.[54]

Why?

Despite being included in antifeminist Christina Hoff Sommers's list of "five feminist myths that will not die," this meme may in fact finally be dying.[55] I didn't see it used at all around the most recent International Women's Day. The old online references by the UN and international development organizations have all been revised or taken down. The fact-checking sites PolitiFact and Washington Post Fact Checker eventually did debunking pieces, relying in part on my research (the *Post* gave Oxfam four "Pinocchios" for using it in 2015).[56]

But why did this thing, which never had many legs to stand on, ever become so pervasive even decades after it was devised? I have seen it used by legislators in South Africa, international universities, feminist organizations, journalists, humanitarians, activists, sociologists, economists—and, amazingly, UN organizations speaking in the present tense in the 2010s. There is a great, much longer story here, which is beyond my capacity to tell, having to do with statistical memes in general as well as this one in particular. The story involves access to information and deference to, and cynicism about, statistical authorities—in the context of statistical and demographic (sorry to say) illiteracy; the relationship between feminism and science; and even the role of social media in social movements. I can't explain why it happened, but I'm quite sure that debunking it hasn't hurt feminism.

Gender inequality is not simple, one-dimensional, or universal. And it's not always easy to measure. But that must not deter us from trying to understand and act upon it. As Alan Alda likes to say in his science communication workshops, we need to "surf uncertainty rather than avoiding it."[57] We can know enough to make sound generalizations, and to inform our social interventions, even while our knowledge remains partial. Of course, the risk of being wrong is real, but so are the potential consequences of inaction. This is what makes the social science of inequality important (and also sometimes fun). When we turn, in the next chapter, to the intersections of different kinds of inequality, it will be especially helpful to maintain a perspective that is empirically rigorous while also avoiding the fatalistic surrender to uncertainty.

7 Race, Gender, and Families

In the previous chapter I argued for taking into account the vast inequalities between women globally. The intersection of race and gender in the United States presents a similar problem. There are unique qualities of gender inequality, separate from race or class or other inequalities, mostly having to do with sex and sexuality, rape and sexual assault. But the people for whom those gender dynamics are most central—or most readily identified—are the women with the most advantages in other ways. For example, although any woman may be the victim of sexual harassment at work, for those lower in the class or race hierarchy that sexual harassment is intertwined with the other qualities of their subordination—with the imminent threat of being fired, for example. Only for those women at the top is sexual harassment likely to be purely sexual, you might say. And their political activism is most likely to appear more purely feminist—in the sense of being unconnected with other forms of subordination. If this is true, it may help explain why it so often seems that feminism focuses on women in the upper levels of the social hierarchy—and why the uncritical application of such feminism to women at the lower ends of the hierarchy so often falls flat (or just seems racist).

In the work on race, gender, and family inequality that I have pursued for the last several years, this tension is a recurring theme. I got into studying families partly because I wanted a way to unravel "intersecting" inequalities, in that place where race, class, and gender collide intimately as well as structurally—families.[1] Rather than solve these problems theoretically, on the blog I have mostly chipped away at questions from the news or in the research literature. The result has been a loosely connected set of data analyses that attempt to take down myths, illuminate ambiguities, and raise questions about how race and ethnicity work within our system of inequality, especially in interaction with gender and families. I hope that the analyses, collected here, help readers at least think about how these inequalities fit together today, if not solve the practical and political problems present in the intersections.

1. BLACK IS NOT A COLOR

When I saw Rihanna on the cover of *Black Hair* magazine in May 2012 I did a double take (figure 33). At a glance that Black woman with her Black hair didn't look very black (in the way the capitalization in that sentence implies). It also reminded me of an old schoolyard debate in which some elementary school science nerd declared, "Black is not a color."

In many quarters, such as among those publishing under the rules of the *Chicago Manual of Style*, black is a color, which means it's not capitalized: "*Color.* Common designations of ethnic groups by color are usually lowercased unless a particular publisher or author prefers otherwise . . . (black people; blacks; people of color; white people; whites)."

That's rule 8.39 from the sixteenth edition, which is progress from the fifteenth edition's rule that "capitalization may be appropriate if the writer *strongly* prefers it" (8.43, emphasis added). Working under that older rule, in 1996, I added a footnote to my first journal publication that read, "I . . . capitalize Black to signify its reference to a people rather than a color or a 'race.'"[2] I can't remember if at the time I had read an essay by Catharine MacKinnon from *Signs* in 1982, for which she also was asked to provide a justification. She wrote:

Figure 33. Black Hair magazine cover, May 2012.

Black is conventionally (I am told) regarded as a color rather than a racial or national designation, hence is not usually capitalized. I do not regard Black as merely a color of skin pigmentation, but as a heritage, an experience, a cultural and personal identity, the meaning of which becomes specifically stigmatic and/or glorious and/or ordinary under specific social conditions. It is as much socially created as, and at least in the American context no less specifically meaningful or definitive than, any linguistic, tribal, or religious ethnicity, all of which are conventionally recognized by capitalization.[3]

Today, most news media still do not capitalize *Black* or *White*. The *Associated Press Stylebook* reads: "*black.* Acceptable for a person of the black race. *African-American* is acceptable for an American black person of African descent. (Use *Negro* only in names of organizations or in quotations.) Do not use *colored* as a synonym."[4]

Sociology journals are inconsistent. The *American Sociological Review* has gone both ways at different times.[5] On the other hand, some sociology journals follow the more progressive American Psychological Association style, in which *Black* and *White* are capitalized. In the wider American world—at least as measured by the Google Books ngrams database, *black* outnumbers *Black* by almost 4 to 1.[6]

The federal Office of Management and Budget, which directs the government in its collection and use of data related to race, has not addressed capitalization.[7] The Census Bureau does capitalize, as in this report on the 2010 Census: "'Black or African American' refers to a person having origins in any of the Black racial groups of Africa. It includes people who indicated their race(s) as 'Black, African Am., or Negro' or reported entries such as African American, Kenyan, Nigerian, or Haitian."[8]

Clearly the movement is toward capitalizing. That is consistent with the rise since the 1980s of the term *African American*, which applies an ethnic formulation to the group. However, when asked whether they preferred *black* or *African American*, two-thirds of the people in question told the Gallup poll that they didn't care—and the rest were evenly split between the two terms (it was a telephone poll that didn't discuss capitalization).[9] In any event, *African American* doesn't solve the problem, since it is not appropriate when the subject really is race rather than ethnicity—which is when people are acting on or perceiving the appearance of a person's body rather than the origins of their identity (to the extent that this is sometimes possible). I feel for the poor interview subject described in this report of a Census Bureau test on racial identity measurement: "She is an immigrant to the US from Africa. However, roughly six generations ago her ancestors were from India. She lived in an Indian community in Africa prior to immigrating to the United States. She answered 'no' to . . . 'Black or African American' because she was from an African country, but of Indian origin. She answered 'yes' to the Asian question and 'yes' to Asian Indian. She also reported 'some other race' [on the form], saying 'African, not African American, African from Africa, Asian African.'"[10]

Anyway, *Black* and *White* are racial terms. They are social constructions and not biological classifications. We use them socially. Whether or not that's okay, I think it's better to capitalize them at least to help make that clear.

2. BLACK WOMEN'S EDUCATIONAL SUCCESS

US women are outperforming men in educational attainment, although women still complete degrees in disciplines that are less lucrative than men's. At the same time, Whites have an educational advantage over Blacks. The coexistence of these facts causes some confusion, which is exacerbated by the interventions of two very different groups: one conservative group that thinks feminism has gone too far, resulting in men's systematic disempowerment, and another progressive group that wants to recognize and celebrate the accomplishments of Black women in the face of historical adversity and oppression. Here's a case of this confusion, driven by a basic misunderstanding of descriptive statistics.

The meme distributor ATTN got great viral traction in 2016 with millions of views for a video slugged "Black women are now America's most educated group." I don't know who started it, but within a few days it was all over social media, and the same headline appeared on *The Root, Upworthy, Salon,* and *Good,* among others—with everyone trying to get a slice of the viral phenomenon's clicks.

There was nothing new in this news, although it falsely described as new a report on 2010 academic-year graduation rates. What is true is that Black women in that year received a higher percentage of degrees *within* their race/ethnic group than did women in any other major group. So, for example, of all the MA degrees awarded to Black students, Black women got 71 percent of them. In comparison, White women only got 62 percent of all White MA degrees. In demography you might call this a "denominator problem." Black women are receiving degrees at a high rate only when the denominator is all Black degrees, rather than all degrees in the population. Of course this is useful information, but only if it's used usefully. As figure 34 shows, when it comes to attaining a bachelor's degree or higher

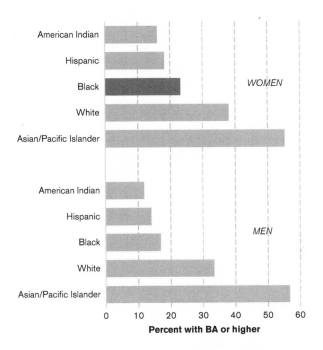

Figure 34. Percentage with a BA or higher degree, by gender and race/ethnicity, ages twenty-five to fifty-four. Source: Author analysis of 2010–14 American Community Survey data via IPUMS.org.

education, there are four groups ahead of Black women: White and Asian men and women. White women are substantially more likely than Black women to have bachelor's degrees, 38 percent versus 23 percent.

With advanced degrees such as PhDs, the numbers are smaller but the relative gaps are larger. Just over half of 1 percent of Black women have PhDs, compared with just over 1 percent of White women—and almost 3 percent of Asian women (some of whom arrived in the United States as highly educated workers or students). White women are almost twice as likely to have a PhD as Black women, and Asian women are more than five times as likely. There is no reasonable basis for calling Black women the "most educated group" in the country.

The other wrong part of meme on Black women's education also reflected a denominator problem: the claim that Black women go to college more than any other group. In her version of the story, Asha Parker in *Salon* wrote: "By both race and gender there is a higher percentage of black women (9.7 percent) enrolled in college than any other group including Asian women (8.7 percent), white women (7.1 percent) and white men (6.1 percent), according to the 2011 U.S. Census Bureau."[11]

This is a case of literally true but substantively false. And here I have to blame the Census Bureau a little, because on the table Parker referenced they do show those numbers, but what they don't say is that 9.7 percent (in the case of Black women) is the percentage of all Black "women" *age 3 or older* who are attending college. On that same table you can see that about 2 percent of Black "women" are attending nursery school or kindergarten (more relevant, probably, would be the attendance rate for those ages three to four, which is 59 percent).

So it's sort of true. Particularly odd on that table is the low overall college attendance rate of Asian women, who are far and away the most likely to go to college at the "traditional" college ages of eighteen to twenty-four. That's because they are disproportionately over age twenty-five (again, many immigrated as adults). When you break out the rates of college attendance for women, by race/ethnicity and age (figure 35), you see that Asian women clearly are the most likely of the race/ethnicity groups to be in college during the years eighteen to twenty-four but that Black women—by a much slimmer margin—are the most likely of the groups to be enrolled after age twenty-five (this figure includes graduate school enrollment).

The data in figure 35 can be used to estimate the lifetime years of higher education for each group. For example, 50 percent of Hispanic women ages eighteen to nineteen are enrolled in college, so over those two years that's an average of one year of enrollment for each Hispanic woman. If you add up those years across each age group you can estimate how many years a person from each group would be in college from ages eighteen to fifty-four. By this measure, Asian women are projected to spend the most time enrolled, 6.2 years. But Black women are projected to spend more time in college than White women, 5.5 versus 4.9 years. Unfortunately, as we have seen, this does not translate into higher rates of bachelor's degree attainment. So either Black women are more likely to be in school part time, or part of the year, or they are more likely to attend college without graduating (because of academic problems, financial constraints, or other

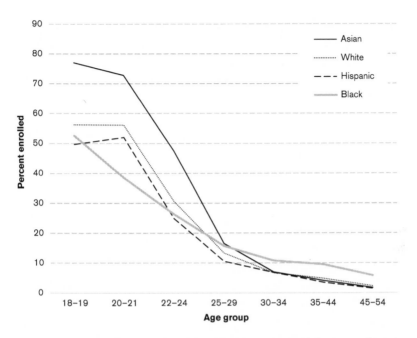

Figure 35. Percentage of women enrolled in college, by race/ethnicity and age. Source: US Census Bureau, October 2014 Current Population Survey via IPUMS.org.

life circumstances). Maybe, then, these data tell a story of hardship and subordination as well as resilience and determination for Black women.

Facts

Racism is racism, inequality is inequality, facts are facts. Debunking these superficial reports doesn't make me racist or not racist, and it doesn't change the situation of Black women, who are absolutely undervalued in America in all kinds of ways (and one of those ways is that they don't have the same educational opportunities as other groups). At the same time, why Black women (and women in general) are getting more degrees than men (in their own race/ethnic groups) is an important question. But pointing out the obvious inaccuracies here will only help us get to the bottom of what's going on. People don't need false memes to do the good work they're trying to do.

Our current information economy rewards speed and clickability. Journalists who know what they're doing work slower and cost more. Making good graphics and funny GIFs is a good skill, but it's a different skill than interpreting and presenting accurate information. We can each help a little by pausing before we share. And those of us with the skills and training to track these things down should all pitch in and do some debunking once in a while. For academics, there is usually little reward in this work, beyond the rewards we already get for our cushy jobs, but it should be part of our mission nonetheless.

3. DETROIT'S GRUELING DEMOGRAPHIC DECLINE

After Darren Wilson, a Ferguson, Missouri, police officer, shot to death Michael Brown, an eighteen-year-old Black man, the police left his body face down in the middle of Canfield Drive—not quite covered with a sheet, a pool of blood four feet long extending from his head—for four hours. Dozens of police, including dogs, held back the horrified crowd of Brown's neighbors.[12]

Whatever logistical details of police procedure led to that treatment of his body, it seemed obvious that the callousness of their response—like the killing itself—was thinkable in America only because he was Black. Whether or not that brutal image was intended as a message of domination from the town's White establishment to its Black residents, that was its profound effect.

"Dictators leave bodies in the street," wrote columnist Charles Pierce.[13] This reminds me of Detroit.

For the last six decades or so we have witnessed—or, mostly, not witnessed—the collapse and decay of one of the country's great cities. Nowhere in the world has a city with a population of more than one million people collapsed as much as Detroit's has since 1950 (at least not in peacetime, and since ancient Rome).[14] Detroit's demise has been plain for all to see, and the lack of response from those with the power to intervene, whether intentional or not, has sent a strong signal about the relative worth of its people. Maybe it would have happened that way if it weren't also a Black city, but I doubt it.

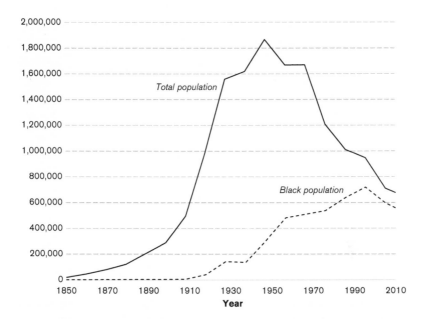

Figure 36. Detroit's population, 1850–2015. Source: Author's tabulation from Decennial Census and American Community Survey data via IPUMS.org and FactFinder.census.gov.

Figure 36 shows the rise and fall of Detroit from 1850 to 2015. From its peak at almost 1.9 million residents in 1950, the city has lost 64 percent of its population. Put another way, after growing at an average rate of thirty-two thousand people per year from 1900 to 1950, since that time it has fallen at an annual rate of eighteen thousand. The overall population decline has coincided with the rise of the Black population, however. That is, Blacks were moving into a shrinking city—and the city was shrinking because Blacks were moving in. Detroit is now 83 percent Black. You don't have to be a conspiracy theorist, which I'm not, to suspect that this is not a coincidence.

This population trend is for the city of Detroit proper. Of course, one of the major demographic trends in the country during this period was the migration of people—mostly White people—to the suburbs of major metropolitan areas. What happened in Detroit is the most extreme case of this pattern, a hallmark of our particular brand of deindustrialization.[15] The

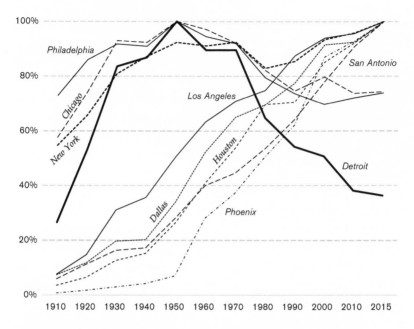

Figure 37. City population, as percentage of peak year. Source: Author's tabulation from Decennial Census and American Community Survey data via IPUMS.org and FactFinder.census.gov. Includes cities that ever had more than one million residents.

surrounding counties actually witnessed population growth as the urban core was hollowing out—Whites moved to the suburbs and Blacks could not or did not.[16]

In addition to suburbanization, the US population also migrated south and west during this period. These two trends produced two distinct patterns of population change in the biggest cities, as shown in figure 37, which includes population trends for all nine cities that ever had more than one million residents. One northern group—Philadelphia, Chicago, Detroit—peaked in 1950 and declined thereafter; these cities now range from 33 percent to 83 percent Black. The other group, in the South and West—Dallas, Houston, Los Angeles, San Antonio, Phoenix—are still growing. These range from 7 to 24 percent Black. (The exception is New York City, which has more than recovered from its much smaller population decline, but that is partly because it includes the equivalent of large White suburbs within its city limits.)

Detroit's condition has bobbed into the national news now and then. For example, there was a flurry of reporting on the infant mortality rate, which spiked up to 15 per 1,000 live births in 2012, higher than any other US city (it has since fallen back down to 10.5, now a little lower than Cleveland).[17] Reporters observed that the odds of surviving to the age of one year are better in Thailand, Mexico, or China. But it's better to compare cities to other urban areas rather than to whole countries. Detroit's infant mortality is now 2.4 times the rate in urban Cuba, twice the rate of urban El Salvador, and just a little lower than the rate of urban Mexico.[18] Compared with the largest cities in twenty-four other rich countries, Detroit's infant mortality rate is more than 3 times higher than sixteen of them and at least twice the rate of the rest.[19] But except for the occasional sensational news story, for the most part the country and its media are silent on the condition of Detroit or, as important, what we should do about it.

Detroit is the most extreme case of city dismemberment that we have been able to monitor with the tools and data of modern demography. Figure 38 shows Detroit compared with a group of nineteen large cities for which there were data from the American Community Survey. These indicators are all interrelated, and the causal order between them cannot be definitively established. But together they spell hard times for the people of Detroit and hard times for the city.

These patterns show the effects of chronic, severe social and economic hardship and isolation. From left to right in figure 38, we see:

- The marriage rate is lowest in Detroit by a lot; women in most of the cities are more than twice as likely to marry in a given year as those in Detroit. For people to marry, they need to be in relationships in the first place, and both partners need to believe the relationship is stable and rewarding. With a shortage of employed single men, poverty, and housing troubles (to name a few issues), the conditions are not conducive to marriage.[20]

- The conditions are not conducive to stable marriages, either—which may be one reason people are reluctant to marry. Among those married, the women of Detroit are most likely to experience divorce, with almost

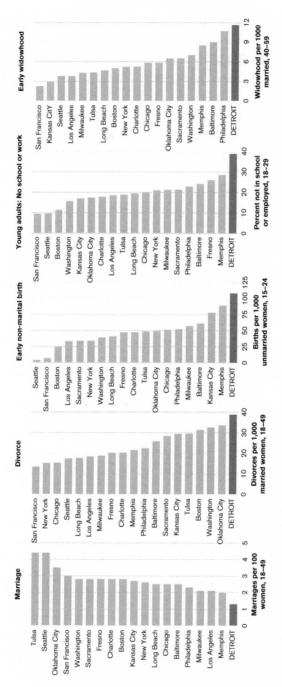

Figure 38. Demographic indicators for nineteen selected cities. Source: Author tabulations from the 2009–11 American Community Survey data via IPUMS.org.

4 percent of those ages eighteen to forty-nine divorcing per year—more than twice the rate seen in cities like Chicago, Seattle, and New York, and almost three times the rate in San Francisco.

- Partly because their marriage prospects are so poor, young, unmarried women in Detroit are extremely likely to bear children. That is, the child-bearing women who may be married in other places are single in Detroit. They are more than twice as likely to have a baby as women in fourteen of the nineteen cities listed, and many times more likely than those in San Francisco and Seattle, where many more single women that age are still in school.

- To assess the level of social and economic isolation, consider the young adults who are neither in school nor employed, a situation that for young adults in Detroit is extremely common. Compared with Detroit's 39 percent, the closest city, Memphis, has only 29 percent out of school and work, and the figure is less than 10 percent in Seattle and San Francisco. Exclusion from these major institutions is both cause and effect of the low marriage rate and the high unmarried birth rate.

- Finally, for those who manage to find and marry someone, and avoid divorce, what is the chance they will be widowed young—say, between the ages of forty and fifty-nine? Depressingly high: a brutal 1.2 percent of married Detroiters in that age range experience widowhood in a given year, compared with .23 percent in San Francisco and less than 1.0 percent in all but one other city. If widowhood at a young age is common, besides the heartache of the loss itself, I expect that would undermine the perception of security associated with marriage.

The demographic data set the context for social life in Detroit. Rates of population decline, social isolation, divorce, and widowhood are observable and become part of the consciousness of the population. These harsh demographic facts are sort of like living next to an abandoned, burned-out house—which thousands of people in Detroit are doing, of course. They're warnings about the uncertainty of the future as well as the hardships of the present. How those warnings affect social life and interaction, how they are internalized, is something we should study more.[21]

In light of these potent markers of social crisis—so obvious to so many people who live in Detroit—the willful lack of attention or compassion from the US government and the obliviousness of the mainstream culture must feel as cold as they look. With what consequence? Not to overdramatize (well, to overdramatize), it's like leaving a Black body in the street for four hours and then feigning surprise when someone accuses you of not caring about his human life and death.

4. WHAT THEY SAY ABOUT RACE WHEN THEY DON'T SAY ANYTHING ABOUT RACE

Referring to the infamous book *The Bell Curve*, Paul Krugman recently wrote that Charles Murray was "famous for arguing that blacks are genetically inferior to whites." In response, Murray wants us to know that the book was not about race and IQ.[22] The data analysis in the book, purporting to show the powerful effect of genes on intelligence and success in America, was in fact based on data for Whites. Its sole concrete statement about race, Murray says, was this: "It seems highly likely to us that both genes and the environment have something to do with racial differences. What might the mix be? We are resolutely agnostic on that issue; as far as we can determine, the evidence does not justify an estimate."

That led to a Twitter exchange in which I said: "Charles Murray's defense that *The Bell Curve* wasn't about race is: 'I yelled "Smoke!" not "Fire!"'."

And he replied: "Precisely. In a crowded theater with smoke, Dick Herrnstein and I said quietly and unhysterically, 'There's smoke.'"

Why do so many people think the book was a racist tract, when it made only indirect claims about genetic racial hierarchies? Context matters. In the United States, you can practice racism without speaking about race.[23]

Racism and Race

In my teaching, I often discuss the role of male incarceration, mortality, and unemployment in contributing to the difference in marriage rates between Black and White women. And when I show that Black men have incarceration rates many times higher than White men's, I focus on racism more than race. That is, these inequalities are not the outcomes of race, but of the way racial inequality works—explicit and implicit racism, unequal opportunity, policing practices, incarceration policies, and so on. Sometimes I do use phrases like "low-income communities," or "inner-city areas," but I try to be specific about race and racism when it's called for—even though of course it can be uncomfortable, for me and my students, to do that. It's important because in the US system of inequality racial inequality is not just an outcome: the system doesn't just differentiate people by class or gender or skills or something else, with a lower-class population that "just happens" to be disproportionately from racial minority groups.

One thing that frustrates me in the growing conversation about economic inequality is the appearance of a perhaps-too-comfortable stance in which being explicit about economic inequality means not having to address racial inequality. It is true, and important, that economic inequality exacerbates racial (and gender) inequality. That's why this stance frustrates me rather than angering me. But there is a certain politeness involved in talking about class instead of race that sometimes doesn't help. Of course, this issue is not new at all, having been litigated especially extensively in the 1980s around the sociological work of William Julius Wilson.[24]

Wilson's research—on the "declining significance of race," or, the increasing significance of class—contributed to today's movement against class inequality. But it has also been co-opted by people taking the really racist position that inequality is caused by race (rather than racism). That is: poor minorities cause poverty. This position ironically doesn't have to discuss race at all, because the framing is the dog whistle.

Take the 2014 flap over Congressman Paul Ryan's remarks about poverty and "inner-city" men, in which he didn't reference race. Here is a series of quotes, in logical (not chronological) order, to put this in the context of a history of using "work" to describe racial inequality in progressively more racialized ways. You can see where Ryan fits in:

- William Julius Wilson: "Inner-city social isolation also generates behavior not conducive to good work histories. The patterns of behavior that are associated with a life of casual work (tardiness and absenteeism) are quite different from those that accompany a life of regular or steady work (e.g., the habit of waking up early in the morning to a ringing alarm clock)."[25]

- Newt Gingrich: "Really poor children, in really poor neighborhoods, have no habits of working, and have nobody around them who works. So they literally have no habit of showing up on Monday, they have no habit of staying all day."[26]

- Paul Ryan: "We have got this tailspin of culture, in our inner cities in particular, of men not working and just generations of men not even thinking about working or learning the value and the culture of work."[27]

- Charles Murray: "Try to imagine a GOP presidential candidate saying in front of the cameras, 'One reason that we still have poverty in the United States is that a lot of poor people are born lazy.' You cannot imagine it because that kind of thing cannot be said. And yet this unimaginable statement merely implies that when we know the complete genetic story, it will turn out that the population below the poverty line in the United States has a configuration of the relevant genetic makeup that is significantly different from the configuration of the population above the poverty line. This is not unimaginable. It is almost certainly true."[28]

Each analyst describes the problem of Black people not working, referring to "patterns of behavior," then "habits," then "culture," and finally "genetic makeup"—all without mentioning race. We go from children not being sufficiently exposed to steady work, to children seeing no one working in their daily lives, to multiple generations not even thinking about working, to people who are genetically lazy.

Writing in response to the Paul Ryan comment, Shawn Fremstad compared Ryan to Murray and concluded that Murray is more apocalyptic because he's warning against a White cultural collapse, not just complaining about a Black one.[29] Murray has perfected the strategy of writing about Whites, which he did again in the more recent *Coming Apart*.[30] But I usually think of this as a dog whistle device to protect his mainstream image while whipping up his racist base. That is, if you show that genetic intelligence determines economic inequality among Whites (*Bell Curve*) or that declining moral standards undermine families and the work ethic among Whites (*Coming Apart*), then the implications for Blacks—poorer and therefore supposedly more morally degenerate and less intelligent on a population level—are obvious and need not be repeated in polite company. Just say, calmly, "Smoke," and let (racist) nature takes its course.

What Does Brad Wilcox Have to Not Say about This?

Another recent entry in this tradition is none other than W. Bradford Wilcox (from whom we heard so much in chapters 3 and 4), a sometime

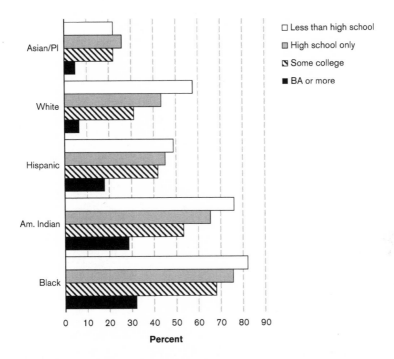

Figure 39. Percentage of new mothers not married, by race/ethnicity and education. Source: Author tabulation from the 2010–14 American Community Survey via IPUMS.org.

colleague of Murray's at the American Enterprise Institute (AEI). While promoting early marriage in his Knot Yet report, Wilcox wrote about the "education and class divide" in nonmarital births—and avoided race almost entirely.[31] But seriously, if you claim to be serious about the issue of unmarried women having babies, you can't politely ignore race and racism. It's ridiculous. This issue simply does not reduce to social class or education level. Black (and American Indian) mothers are much more likely than White (and Asian) mothers to be unmarried at every education level, as shown in figure 39.

Among college graduates, Black mothers are almost five times more likely than White mothers to be unmarried; for high school graduates the ratio is 1.4 to 1. Asian mothers who are high school dropouts are less likely to be unmarried than Black college graduates. However you want to address this issue, if you ignore this pattern and talk about it only in terms of education or social class, you're either uninformed or dishonest.

Or you don't care about Black families. This is exactly what Wilcox exhibited in a shocking interview with James Pethokoukis for AEI.[32] Wilcox said the government should lead a public education campaign to convince people to get married before they have children. Then the question was, "What would be the nature of that sort of PR campaign, and to whom would it be directed?" Wilcox answered, in part:

> Basically, since the 1970s, you've seen pretty high levels of single parenthood and non-marital child bearing among poor Americans and Americans who are high school dropouts. And we've also seen in the last really 20 or 30 years that in some important respects, marriage is stronger among college-educated Americans. So, for instance, divorce has come down from the '70s to the present for college-educated Americans. So there's been progress there.
>
> But I think in terms of where all the sort of movement is recently, and it's primarily in a negative direction, it's among moderately-educated Americans who have got a high school degree or some college or kind of classic working-class or lower middle-class Americans. And it's this particular portion of the population where about half of their births are outside of marriage today. And they're at a tipping point. They can go down the road of not having marriage as the keystone to their family formation, family life, or we can hold the line, if you will, and try to figure out creative strategies for strengthening marriage in this particular middle demographic.

What is the "classic working-class or lower middle-class American"? Hm. Here I'll switch from the edited transcript to my own transcription of the audio file, because the details they edited out are interesting. Pethokoukis asks Wilcox to elaborate, "Is this the bottom 20 percent we're talking about?" "No, no. I'm talking about, essentially, from the 25th percentile, if you will, to the 65th percentile. So, one way to talk about it would be, sort of, you know, in some ways the NASCAR demographic would be one way to talk about it. Actually a large share of the Hispanic population in the United States would fit into this demographic group. You know, it's sort of this middle American group, both white and Hispanic, where, once again, they're at kind of a tipping point."

Really. The twenty-fifth to the sixty-fifth percentile of family income? In income terms, that ranges from $32,500 to $85,000 per year, and includes 33 percent of the African American population, 37 percent of Whites, and 38 percent of Latinos.[33] So, it's more or less the middle third of each group. Or, you know—Whites and Hispanics (and NASCAR people).

Wilcox is raising the alarm about Whites, "classic" Americans, who are "at kind of a tipping point"—in danger of heading the way Blacks have gone. The clear implication is that Blacks have passed that "tipping point" already. In this view, we have to pull up the ladder behind us, even if that means some less-than-"classic" Americans get left behind.

Sometimes not talking about race is pretty racist.

5. RACE, RACISM, AND MISSING MARRIAGES

Why are Whites more likely than Blacks to be married? A common conservative explanation these days is that although economic circumstances play a role there is also just something wrong with people—the people who have children without being married. Conservative curmudgeon Ron Haskins put it this way in a panel discussion at the AEI in July 2016: "I have no brief or criticism of single parents. Many of them are victims of circumstances and societal trends and so forth. But still, the fact remains that if you're really dedicated to your kids you're gonna figure out how to have two parents in the household—that could be more important than almost any other factor."[34]

That's Haskins giving a nod to the liberal argument but then doubling down on the conservative side. In polite (liberal) society, this kind of talk seems racist—blaming the victim with "culture" talk. On the other hand, attributing low marriage rates to economics in a race-neutral way paints the cause as beyond the motivation and choices of Blacks. This seems like a good choice if you think marriage is good and racism is bad, which most people do. The problem is this kind of explanation ends up throwing out the baby of racism with the bathwater of race.

The explanation is complicated and contested, but racial differences in marriage patterns are certainly not just a special case of economic inequality—as we saw with the education levels in the previous essay. You can't understand this without tackling racism. That is one of the reasons

I wrote the essay on Detroit's demography, to show the depth and breadth of the racial divide in family demography. To look at the marriage rates in Detroit as the outcome of the choices and preferences of young Black adults—or as the result of poverty alone—is to deny the very structural nature of racism and racial inequality.

Who's Afraid of Black Men?

Structural explanations don't preclude psychological or interpersonal mechanisms; rather, the two reinforce each other. For example, Whites fear Black men partly because residential segregation, poverty, and institutional neglect create a reality of scary, crime-ridden ghettos—which is amplified back as an exaggerated, racist image.

The fear is pervasive in our society. It helps explain why police who kill unarmed Black men so often don't get indicted or convicted when they face juries of their peers, peers who readily believe their tales of terror in the face of menacing Black monsters. More egregiously, Black boys have by far the highest rates of out-of-school suspensions, starting in preschool. In addition, Black boys are more likely to be viewed as older than they are.[35] Although the underlying motivations for these patterns are difficult to prove, they are consistent with the presumption that Blacks are more violent. The image of future violent perpetration is projected across even the faces of four-year-olds, denying their very childhood.

The 2013 murder trial of George Zimmerman—the neighborhood vigilante who stalked and killed seventeen-year-old Trayvon Martin and then claimed self-defense—put the fear of Black men on graphic display. In fact, as the trial was going on, I kept accidentally referring to Zimmerman's lawyers as "the prosecution," so complete was the transformation of victim into perpetrator.[36] The defense was a defense only in the technical sense of the law; substantively, it was a prosecution of Trayvon Martin, whose death made it impossible for him to defend himself. In making the case that Martin was guilty in his own murder, Zimmerman's lawyers had the burden of proof on their side, as the state had to prove beyond a reasonable doubt that Martin wasn't a violent criminal.

This raises the more general question, who's afraid of young Black men? Zimmerman's lawyers, sizing up the jury, took the not-too-risky approach of assuming that a group of five white women and one Hispanic woman might be. "This is the person who ... attacked George Zimmerman," defense attorney Mark O'Mara said in his closing argument, holding up two pictures of Trayvon Martin, one of which showed him shirtless and looking down at the camera with a deadpan expression. He held that shirtless one up right in front of the jury for almost three minutes. "Nice kid, actually," he said, with feigned sincerity.[37] Experts had warned that female jurors might be sympathetic to the young Trayvon, but O'Mara thought the intersection of gender and race would work in his favor: White women could be convinced that a young Black man was dangerous. (His defense also included a life-sized cutout of Trayvon to show how big he was.)

The classical way of framing the question is to ask whether White women's racial identity is strong enough to overcome their gender-socialized overall prosocial attitudes or political liberalness when it comes to attitudes toward minority groups. But Zimmerman's lawyers appeared to be invoking a very specific American story: White women's fear of Black male aggression. Of course the "victim" in their story was Zimmerman, but as he lingered over the shirtless photo, O'Mara was tempting the women on the jury to put themselves in Zimmerman's fearful shoes.

White women's sense of threat from Black men raises an old, blood-stained history. In the twentieth century 455 American men were (legally) executed for rape, and 89 percent of them were Black—mostly accused of raping White women.[38] And that was just the legal executions; far more prevalent was the Jim Crow era's phenomenon of (illegal) lynching, partly driven by White men asserting ownership over White women in the name of protection. The image lives on, although the observable violence has diminished. Today, the Internet is rife with White supremacist memes about Black men raping White women (some of which are tweeted at me, along with anti-Semitic slurs, whenever I mention this subject). My own analysis of 2016 polling data shows that 53 percent of White women say the word *violent* describes Blacks moderately well, very well, or extremely well.[39] I don't know what was in the hearts and minds of the jurors in the Zimmerman trial, of course. But whether they were right or not, Zimmerman's lawyers clearly thought there was a vein of fear of Black men inside the jurors' psyches, waiting to be mined.

Who Is Attracted to Black Women?

Meanwhile, Black women are excluded from the dominant American ideal of femininity, which was built around the social gulf and division of labor between White and Black women, privileging a domesticity unavailable to Blacks and excluding women who performed hard physical labor or wielded authority within their households. Let's look at contemporary extensions of these racialized processes.

In addition to low rates of marriage altogether, Black women have the lowest intermarriage rates of any minority group; 91 percent of Black women marry men from their same race/ethnic group, compared with 74 percent for Hispanic women, 64 percent for Asian or Pacific Islander women, and 32 percent for American Indian women.[40] If marriage were color-blind, of course, smaller groups would have higher intermarriage rates. So the intermarriage rate relative to population size is a measure of social distance—and it shows that Black women are the most socially isolated, at least in terms of marriage.

The structural side of that isolation is residential segregation and its attendant institutional subordination, including the division of labor and disproportionate incarceration. The cultural and psychological side is the construction and internalization of a beauty standard by which Black women are considered less attractive. On the innovative dating site OK Cupid, Christian Rudder examined millions of accounts and determined that White, Latino, and Asian men all rate Black women the least attractive. And this pattern holds even though, on the basis of their personality and preference questionnaire responses, their compatibility with men of different race/ethnic groups is virtually identical. So it's not surprising that, even though they should (on the basis of their stated preferences) respond at equal rates to women of each group, men of every group are far less likely to reply to dating overtures from Black women. (The lack of interest is one-sided; Black women sent more messages per person than every other group.)[41]

The failure to see the beauty in Black women may be rooted in their exclusion from the American definition of femininity itself—going back to White feminists' tendency, in the nineteenth century, to refer to the rights of women and the rights of former slaves as if these were distinct, nonoverlapping categories.[42] This bias is apparent in the social sciences as well. In the very influential National Longitudinal Study of Adolescent Health (Add Health), the interviewers recorded their assessment of each interviewee's attractiveness. Black female teens and young adults in the survey were coded as having lower average attractiveness, leading the evolutionary psychologist Satoshi Kanazawa to declare on his *Psychology Today* blog that Black women "are objectively less physically attractive than other women" and to offer some baseless evolutionary speculation about the cause of this disparity.[43] The founder of the Add Health survey, Richard Udry, also created a composite measure of "femininity" in which "facial attractiveness" was one factor (along with having a positive attitude toward marriage). This completed the loop, creating a definition of femininity based on female attractiveness, after that attractiveness was constructed from the beauty standard for the dominant group of women.[44]

Black men Are Missing

By discouraging intermarriage, the relative paucity of romantic interest in Black women contributes to their relatively low marriage rates. This compounds what is probably a more important demographic factor—the shortage of Black men for Black women to marry.

For the great majority of women, employability is an important quality in a spouse. In a 2014 Pew survey, 78 percent of never-married women, compared with 46 percent of never-married men, said "a steady job" is "very important" in choosing a spouse or partner.[45] So, as the job prospects of working-class men have slipped—becoming less secure, predictable, and lucrative because of "globalization, the decline of labor unions, technological change and other tidal economic forces"—it is not surprising that fewer women are rushing to marry them.[46] That situation is worse for Black women, however, and not just because of poverty. For them, the supply of economically viable spouses is further reduced by disproportionate unemployment, mortality, incarceration, and unbalanced intermarriage rates (only 79 percent of Black men marry Black women).[47]

Here's a simple illustration. I counted up the number of unmarried men per unmarried woman in the age range eighteen to thirty-four, separately for non-Hispanic Blacks and Whites, for all metropolitan areas with

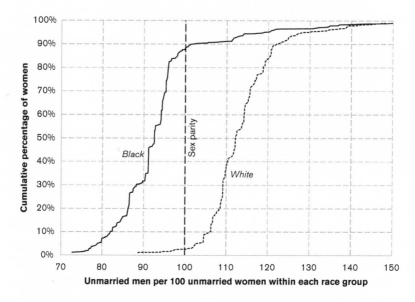

Figure 40. Distribution of unmarried women by within-race unmarried sex ratio. Source: Author analysis of 2010–214 American Community Survey via IPUMS.org.

sufficient data (240 metro areas for Whites, 183 for Blacks), which approximate marriage markets. The result is presented in figure 40, which shows the distribution of these single-young-adult sex ratios for non-Hispanic Black and White women. Here we see that 88 percent of single Black women live in metro areas where they outnumber Black single men, those with sex ratios below 100. In contrast, only 3 percent of White women live in markets that skew female. The consequences of this extreme demographic disparity include a lower marriage rate for Black women.

The salience of incarceration increased with the release of a powerful piece by Ta-Nehisi Coates in the *Atlantic,* which exposed the long reach of mass incarceration into Black families in ways that go way beyond the simple statistics about available men.[48] The large ripple effects implied by his analysis—drawing from his own reporting as well as research by Deva Pager, Bruce Western, and Robert Sampson—suggest that any statistical model attempting to identify the impact of incarceration on family structure is likely to miss a lot of the action. That's because people who've been out of prison for years are still affected by it, as are their relationships, their communities, and their children in the next generation.

However, the difference in marriage rates is not as simple as it looks. By my calculations, 85 percent of White women and 78 percent of Black women are projected to marry before they die—a surprisingly small gap. The difference in the *timing* of those marriages is bigger, with Black women marrying at much later ages. For example, just 16 percent of White women, compared with 37 percent of Black women, are projected to marry after age thirty-three. A White woman who lives to age forty-five without marrying has a 26 percent chance of someday marrying, compared with a whopping 49 percent for Black women.[49]

This delay for Black women fits the data pattern of an uphill climb in their marriage markets, which includes the White beauty standard, economic and social exclusion, and Black men's higher intermarriage rates. That might also explain why Black women are more likely to marry men further from them in age: 74 percent of White women marry a man within five years of their own age, compared with 65 percent of Black women.[50] And the paucity of choices they face might affect the marriages in which Black women end up. Blacks have the highest divorce rates of any group except American Indians, and Black women are much less likely than White women to say their marriages are "very happy" (50 percent versus 63 percent).[51]

Finally, one of the most important consequences of marriage delayed and denied for Black women is the uncoupling of marriage and childbearing—which brings us back to Haskins's comment at the start of this essay. Given the difficulty of finding partners and maintaining relationships under the demographic and cultural pressures described here, Black women face a conundrum when it comes to marriage and childbearing. Most people want to be stably married when they have children. But waiting for marriage—into their thirties—puts Black women and their children at risk of health problems (much more so than among Whites, among whom delayed parenting is associated with lower risks).[52]

These forces conspire to make it so that 71 percent of new Black mothers are not married.[53] And that means Black women who do get married are much more likely to have children already (or to have partners who do). In fact, among those married for the first time in the previous year, Census data show that 50 percent of Black women have children (biological or step) in their households already, compared with just 28 percent of White women. With the possible cost of delaying marriage on the one hand, and the challenges associated with blended families on the other, the marriage choices of Black women are forced through an awfully narrow pincer.

It is important to pay attention to the impersonal, structural forces that undermine people's aspirations for relationships and family life—things like an unpredictable and unreliable employment outlook, for women as well as men. But that should not displace our concern with race and racism. These institutional influences do not operate in a race-neutral way, and they feed back into the cultural and interpersonal drivers of racial inequality. As with the problem of measuring gender inequality, sorting out these issues is difficult and must be imperfect. In the next chapter I turn more directly toward gender, but this time with a focus on feminism and sexuality—and that's not going to make the empirical questions we face any easier to resolve.

8 Feminism and Sexuality

There are different kinds of feminist theory, which use different social and institutional points of entry into the problem of gender inequality. Naturally, there are lots of ways to categorize feminisms, but for my purposes it is useful to divide them according to the place of labor and economics versus sexuality in their conceptual schemes. For some feminists, drawing from the Marxist tradition, gender inequality flows from the division of labor. As a result, their emphasis is on the nature and organization of work and on the place of gender in that system. Others, drawing from the writing of radical feminists, see gender inequality as based primarily in the realm of sex and sexuality.[1]

Families are centers of both work and sexuality. There is a gender division of labor within families—one that has weakened substantially but remains strong. And there is a further division of labor between families and the market economy, which has implications for gender because of the different gender dynamics in those two arenas. To oversimplify: one arena, the family, is more regulated by tradition and informal interactions, while the other, the market, falls under the rule of law and more impersonal economic forces.[2]

I addressed work-related aspects of gender inequality most closely in chapter 6. Here I turn toward sexuality, which also appears both inside and outside of families—and at the border between families and the wider world (as when sex leads to marriage or children). The concepts are not so clearly separated, of course. For example, are the gender questions around motherhood and reproduction really about work or sexuality? And what about politics—which arena requires most attention? Consider this collection of essays an introductory shove toward these issues—which I hope will stimulate your own discussions about gender, sexuality, and families.

1. NOT YOUR FEMINIST GRANDMOTHER'S PATRIARCHY

It would be wrong to look at Donald Trump's election and say, "See, nothing changes!" Leading up to November 2016, it appeared from election polling that Hillary Clinton would win because of a strong lead among women, while Donald Trump would lose despite drawing the majority of male votes.[3] And that would not have been new. In the 2012 election, women were the majority of voters, and the majority of them voted for Obama; the weaker sex clearly was men. The same thing happened 1996, when men couldn't stop the reelection of Bill Clinton.[4] In the end, Hillary Clinton did win the majority of female votes (although enough White women came out for Trump to push him over the top in the swing states needed to win the Electoral College). Nevertheless, if women contribute substantially to the election of the most powerful man in the world, this fact tests our ability to think systematically about power and inequality. How is it possible to see the unprecedented transformation in women's relative status and still claim men's continued dominance? A common approach is to list data points and have more of them on the side you prefer. For example, you could say, "Women are closing the earnings gap and increasing their presence in leadership positions, and men are doing more housework; but on the other hand, a lot of women are raped and Donald Trump won the election." That's three facts to two in favor of progress, so your overall interpretation is communicated implicitly. But describing a complex situation does not require vague or opaque prose. We can be specific and accurate while also making concrete general statements at a higher level of abstraction.

For giving critical responses to generalizations about women's relative progress, I have been described as part of a "feminist academic establishment" that is "uneasy when women make progress" and "prefers to use statistics that are least favorable to signs of women's progress."[5] Hana Rosin, whose record of misstating facts in the service of inaccurate conclusions I documented extensively (see chapter 6), described me as someone who likes to engage in "data wars" over the details of gender inequality.[6] But an attention to data is necessary for gaining perspective on the big picture—it would be wrong to simply point to Trump and drop the mic.

In our academic research on gender inequality, my colleagues and I study variation and change. That means figuring out why women's employment increased so rapidly, why some labor markets have smaller gender gaps than others, why some workplaces are less segregated than others, why couples in some countries share housework more than those in other countries, why women in some ethnic groups have relatively high employment rates, and so on.[7] These patterns of variation and change help us understand gender in our system of inequality. Systemic patterns don't just happen. People (in the aggregate) have to get up in the morning and do inequality every day. To understand how it works and why it doesn't, we need to see how and why it varies—for example, why and to what extent some people resist equality while others dedicate their lives to perpetuating it. Someone who studies inequality but doesn't care about change and variation is not a social scientist.

Patriarchy

"It's easy to find references to patriarchs, patriarchy or patriarchal attitudes in reporting on other countries," writes economist Nancy Folbre. "Yet these terms seem largely absent from discussions of current economic and political debates in the United States. Perhaps they are no longer applicable. Or perhaps we mistakenly assume their irrelevance."[8]

The United States, like every society in the world, remains a patriarchy: all societies today are ruled by men. That is not just because every country (except Rwanda and Bolivia) has a majority-male national parliament, and it is the case despite the handful of countries with women heads of state (including, now, the United Kingdom).[9] It is a systemic characteristic that combines dynamics at the level of the family, the economy, the culture, and the political arena. Top political and economic leaders are the low-hanging fruit of patriarchy statistics. But they probably are in the end the most important—the telling pattern is that the higher you look, the more male it gets. If a society really had a stable, female-dominated power structure for an extended period of time, even I would eventually question whether it was really still a patriarchy. Female heads of state are important, but they are not a female power structure.

In my own area of research things are messier because families and workplaces differ so much and power is usually jointly held. But I'm confident in describing American families as mostly patriarchal. Maybe the most basic indicator is the apparently quaint custom of wives assuming their husbands' names, which is one literal definition of *patriarchal*. This hasn't generated much feminist controversy lately. But to an anthropologist from another planet, this *patrilineality* would be a major signal that American families are male dominated. Among US-born married women, only 6 percent had a surname that differed from their husband's in 2004 (it was not until the 1970s that married women could even function legally using their "maiden" names).[10] Only half of respondents think it should be required for a woman to take her husband's name, but 68 percent of women and 78 percent of men think it's "generally better." Among younger women it is more common for women to keep their names, which is one indicator of the direction of change.[11] But there is no end to the tradition in sight. In fact, progress may have slowed. A (small) study that compared attitudes among college students between 1990 and 2006 found no change in the percentage of women who planned to keep their birth names upon marriage, around 8 percent.[12]

Of course, the proportion of people getting married has fallen, and the number of children born to unmarried parents has risen. Single parenthood—and the fact that this usually means single motherhood—reflects both women's growing independence and the burdens of care that fall on them.[13] At the elite end of the social scale, the growing single-mother-by-choice movement looks like evidence of women's growing dominance in the family—well-off women choosing to go it alone and run their families from a position of strength. But at the lower end single parenthood is more complicated. There is an element of women's improving position relative to men, as in "I'm already poor, I don't need a poor man to help with that." But single motherhood also reflects, and creates, the heavy burden of child rearing that mothers bear. What researchers called the "feminization of poverty" a few decades ago—as single-mother families increased their representation among the poor population—doesn't go in the win column for feminism. That's why I don't share Liza Mundy and Hana Rosin's view that single mothers should be called "breadwinners," using the term formerly applied to men who held dominant positions in families that included subordinate wives.

Differences That Matter

The social critic Barbara Ehrenreich—in a 1976 essay she might or might not like to be reminded of—urged feminists to acknowledge distinctions that matter rather than to tar everything with the simplistic brush of "patriarchy." In China, one of the world's most entrenched patriarchal systems, women undeniably made tremendous progress over the twentieth century, but the revolution was far from complete. Ehrenreich wrote: "There is a difference between a society in which sexism is expressed in the form of female infanticide and a society in which sexism takes the form of unequal representation on the Central Committee. And the difference is worth dying for."[14]

China presents an extreme case. Its extremely harsh patriarchy was fundamentally transformed—into a different sort of patriarchy. By the late 1970s female infanticide (as well as the brutal practice of footbinding) had indeed been all but eradicated—tremendous improvements for women, saving millions of lives.[15] With the advent of the one-child policy in the 1980s, however, female infanticide gave way to sex-selective abortion (and female representation on the ruling committees dropped), representing an important transformation.[16] It's important to acknowledge the continued male dominance of Chinese society but also to pay attention to, and learn from, the pattern of and prospects for change.

Like Ehrenreich, I think we need to look at the variations to understand the systemic features of our society. Men losing out to women in national elections is an important one. Given the choice between two male-dominated parties with wide differences on social policy in 2008 and 2012 (and almost in 2016), women voters (along with Blacks, Latinos, and the poor) bested men and got their way. I wouldn't minimize that, or ignore the scale and direction of change. The American patriarchy has weakened.

I expect some readers will go right to their favorite statistics or personal experiences in order to challenge my description of our society as patriarchal. In that tit-for-tat, men (like Trump) leading the vast majority of the most powerful institutions, and American family names usually following the male line, become just another couple of data points. But they shouldn't be, because some facts are more important than others.

2. DOES SLEEPING WITH A GUY ON THE FIRST DATE MAKE HIM LESS LIKELY TO CALL BACK?

Let's imagine that a woman—we'll call her "you," the way they do in the relationship advice columns—is trying to calculate the odds that a man will call back after sex. Everyone tells you that if you sleep with a guy on the first date he is less likely to call back.[17] The theory is that giving sex away at a such a low "price" lowers the man's opinion of you because everyone thinks sluts are disgusting. Also, shame on you. (Note, this is *not* my theory; I will return to it more systematically in the next essay.)

So, you ask, does the chance that he will call back improve if you wait till more dates before having sex with him? Say you do an informal survey of your friends and find that this is actually true: the times you or your friends waited till the seventh date, two-thirds of the guys called back, but when you slept with guys on the first date, only one in five called back. From the data, it sure looks as if sleeping with a guy on the first date reduces the odds he'll call back. So does this mean that women make men disrespect them by having sex right away? If that's true, then the historical trend toward sex earlier in relationships could be really bad for women, and maybe feminism really is ruining society.

Like all theories, this one assumes a lot. It assumes that you (women) decide when couples will have sex, because it assumes that men always want to, and it assumes that men's opinion of you is based on your sexual behavior. With these assumptions in place, the data appear to confirm the theory. But what if the assumptions aren't true? What if couples just have more dates when they enjoy each other's company, and men actually just call back

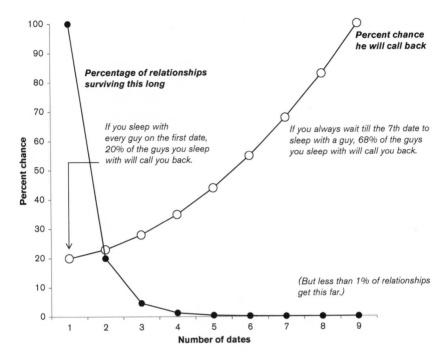

Figure 41. Chance a man will call again and couple survival rate, by number of dates (simulated).

when they like you? If this is the case, then what really determines whether the guy calls back is how well matched the couple is, and how the relationship is going, which also determines how many dates you have. What was missing in the study design was relationship survival odds. Figure 41 is a closer look at the same data underlying your informal survey, with couple survival added (to repeat: this is just an illustration, not real data).

By this interpretation, the decision about when to have sex is arbitrary and doesn't affect anything. All that matters is how much the couple like and are attracted to each other, which determines how many dates they have and whether the guy calls back. Every couple has a first date, but only a few make it to the seventh date. It appears that the first-date-sex couples usually don't last because people don't know each other very well on first dates and they have a high rate of failure regardless of sex. The seventh-date-sex couples, on the other hand, usually like each other more and they're very likely to have more dates. And there are many more first-date couples than seventh-date couples.

This is a lot like those sports statistics you hear, such as "Nine times out of ten, the team that goes up three games to one wins the series." Sure, it helps to be up by two games, but chances are they're also the better team!

So the original study design was wrong. It should have compared callback rates after first *dates*, not after first *sex*. But when you assume sex runs everything, you don't design the study that way. And by "design the study" I mean "decide how to judge people."

I have no idea why men call women back after dates. It is possible, of course, that the timing of having sex affects the curves in the figure. (And I know even talking about relationships in this anachronistic way isn't helping.) But even if sex doesn't affect the curves, I would expect higher callback rates after more dates. Anyway, if you want to go on blaming everything bad on women's sexual behavior, you have a lot of company. I just thought I'd mention the possibility of a more benign explanation for the observed pattern that men are less likely to call back after sex if the sex takes place on the first date.

3. IS THE PRICE OF SEX TOO DAMN LOW?

The accusation that women are ruining relationships—and their own lives and everything else, actually—by giving up sex too easily is a special case of a much broader antifeminist argument, which was on display in an animated video rant by Mark Regnerus (the marriage equality opponent we met in chapter 4). The video is the ten-minute version of an essay he published in the journal *Society* in 2012 (with a *Slate* companion piece)— using professional drawing hands and narrators. It has been viewed, according to YouTube, more than 1.6 million times.[18]

The premise, described by the narrator of the video, is that in the market for sex women sell and men buy.

> On average, men initiate sex more than women, they're more sexually permissive than women, and they connect sex to romance less often than women. No one's saying this is the way it ought to be. It's just the way it is! Women, on the other hand, are likely to have sex for reasons beyond just

simple pleasure. Her motivations for sex often include expressing and receiving love, strengthening commitment, affirming desirability, and relationship security. So in an exchange relationship where men want sex more often than women do, who decides when it will happen? She does, of course. Sex is her resource.

Let me stop it here for a minute. If I grant you that, on average, contemporary American men want sex with women more than the reverse, does the size of this difference matter at all? In a response to Regnerus, Elaine Hatfield and colleagues remind us that differences within the genders are greater than the differences between them (which, in turn, are shrinking over time).[19] If the difference between men's and women's attitudes toward sex were observable but tiny, would it still be true that the whole system is one in which women sell and men buy? Of course not. The difference has to be big enough to drive everything. No one can say how big it is, or needs to be, because the crackpots running this theory don't care. They are just spinning out the why-pay-for-milk-when-the-cow-is-free analogy without regard to the specifics of the model—and preying on the abundant credulity of their audience.

Anyway, what is the "price" women charge for sex? It's "a few drinks and compliments," or "a month of dates and respectful attention," or "a lifetime promise to share all of his affections, wealth, and earnings with her exclusively." Marriage is the high price men used to have to pay.

"When supplies are high, prices drop," the narrator says, "since people won't pay more for something that's easy to find. But if it's hard to find, people will pay a premium." Cow, milk, et cetera. To Regnerus, the falling marriage rate (the only fact offered as evidence for all this) means the supply of sex has increased and its price has fallen. The narrator asks, "So how did we get here? How did the market value of sex decline so drastically?" Answer: the Pill, which "profoundly lower[ed] the cost of sex." From there the video goes on to blame women for abandoning their centuries-old "cartel," which restricted the supply of sex and propped up its price. The video says:

In the past, it really wasn't the patriarchy that policed women's relational interests [because isn't that what you thought patriarchy was all about?], it was women. But . . . this unspoken pact to set a high market value of sex has all but vanished. But in a brave new world where sex no longer means babies, and marriage has become optional, the solidarity women once felt toward each other in the mating market has dissolved. Women no longer have each other's backs. On the contrary, they're now each other's competition. And when women compete for men, they tend to do so by appealing to what men want.

So, in the descent from Eden (which is about as serious as this history gets) women have sold each other out. As a result, they've lost their leverage, and now men have an advantage they don't deserve, given their randy minds. In the article version, Regnerus writes: "I assert that if women were more in charge of how their romantic relationships transpired—more in charge of the 'pricing' negotiations around sex—we'd be seeing, on average, more impressive wooing efforts by men, fewer hook-ups, fewer premarital sexual partners, shorter cohabitations, and more marrying going on (and perhaps even at a slightly earlier age, too). In other words, the 'price' of sex would be higher: it would cost men more to access it."

Yes, that does contradict the point earlier about how women always decide when they will have sex, because it's inherently their resource. But who cares, feminism is bad. (It's interesting that in popular culture men want women to "give it" to them—as in Tom Petty's song "Breakdown"—but also speak of "giving it" to women in the more violent or aggressive sense.)

Economics

A few thoughts on this big ball of wrong. First, what about actual economics? If women sell sex and men buy it, and women set the price by how slutty they act, there is still the issue of the value of what men have to offer to women. Regnerus assumes unchanging men. When it comes to sex, that's presumably because it comes from God, evolution, or (in Regnerus's Catholic view) God acting through evolution. But even if all they care about is sex, the value of what they have to offer for it—relative to what women have and need—has surely changed a lot. So, as the relative value of the men's lifetime promise of wealth and earnings (marriage) falls toward the value of a couple drinks and compliments (hookup), it's only natural that women will be less and less able to distinguish the two.

As Paula England notes in her (disappointingly mild) critique of Regnerus, his theory has a problem explaining why marriage has declined so much more for the less-than-college-educated population. Among those men and women, the relative number of men has grown markedly as women move up to get higher education. So, with the relative shortage of women, women should be in command—and they could demand marriage.[20] If women insist on marrying a man with a job, however, they actually face a shortage of men. But that's only because women insist on a man with a job. In other words, the value of what men have to offer (relative to what women need) matters. So why doesn't Regnerus talk about actual economics—the money that men and women have?

In the *Society* version, Regnerus says he gets this sexual economics theory from Roy Baumeister and colleagues, including the basic story that sex is something women sell and men buy, and the thing about how feminism dissolved female solidarity. Interestingly, however, Baumeister and his coauthors are much more keyed in to the economic questions that Regnerus all but ignores. While Regnerus focuses on the Pill, they wrote in the 2004 paper he relies on that one of the "preconditions of market exchange" in sex is that, "in general, men have resources women want." It's not just the Pill that has changed things, in other words, it's also the decline of men: "Once women had been granted wide opportunities for education and wealth, they no longer had to hold sex hostage."[21]

Regnerus really does the theory a disservice by leaving all this out. In another recent article, Baumeister and Mendoza reiterate: "According to sexual economics theory, when women lack direct or easy access to resources such as political influence, health care, money, education, and jobs, then sex becomes a crucial means by which women can gain access to a good life, and so it is vital to female self-interest to keep the price of sex high."[22]

The real problem now, according to the intellectual godfather of Regnerus's version of this theory, is gender *equality*, but Regnerus doesn't want to say that—in fact, Regnerus wants to tell a story about the Pill that doesn't include implications for women's careers and independence (which presumably are important to the young people he's trying to influence). Baumeister and Mendoza write: "When women have direct economic clout, they do not need to use sex to bargain for other resources, and so they can make sex more freely available."[23] Thus they show that casual sex is more common in countries with more gender equality.

But the logic here is approaching random. When women were poor, they needed to *withhold* sex to get money. Now that they have more money—and are *less* dependent on men—they don't need to withhold it, so they give it away. Wait, what? If they don't need to sell it anymore, and we already know they don't want to "have" it (that is, *do* it), then why don't those Scandinavian women just keep it, for fuck's sake?[24]

It seems likely that the differences between Regnerus and Baumeister are of emphasis rather than principle. Regnerus's explanation would be stronger if he latched onto this crazy economics argument. But perhaps he stays away from that because taking a stand against women's equality is a political and cultural nonstarter, and Regnerus's ambition is social influence.

You Asked for It

Baumeister has no such qualms about offending women, and it's telling to see where this leads (even though it gets extremely offensive). In their response to Regnerus in *Society*, Baumeister and Kathleen Vohs blame women's sexual permissiveness for just about everything wrong with civilization these days. That's because "giving young men easy access to abundant sexual satisfaction deprives society of one of its ways to motivate them to contribute valuable achievements to the culture."[25] Women giving away sex is literally ruining society.

In the feminist era that Baumeister and Vohs describe (the one we live in now), rather than just seeking marriage in exchange for sex, women have upped their demands: "Women, meanwhile, want not only marriage but also access to careers and preferential treatment in the workplace." (I'm not sure how this fits with the idea that women have lowered the "price of sex," but logic isn't the point here, hating feminism is.) And then the piece descends into an unhinged screed. Women are now given "preferential treatment in the huge institutions that make up society, which men created," where "it is standard practice to hire or promote a woman ahead of an equally qualified man." This is "ironic," they repeat, because these "large institutions have almost all been created by men." The scientific importance of this unsubstantiated fact is never explained, obviously, but it sure seems to rankle them, because they return to it yet again, complaining that "all over the world and throughout history (and prehistory), the contribution of large groups of women to cultural progress has been vanishingly small."[26]

You're starting to see why the politically ambitious Regnerus doesn't more fully embrace this line of thinking. It's one of those *Saturday Night Live* sketches that just won't end. After *repeating* the thing about large organizations again, they wonder why, given women's "lesser motivation and ambition," men would give them such "preferential treatment." The answer is sex, which is "a high priority" for men:

> The male who beds multiple women is enjoying life quite a bit, and so he may not notice or mind the fact that his educational and occupational advancement is vaguely hampered by all the laws and policies that push women ahead of him. After all, one key reason he wanted that advancement was to get sex, and he already has that. Climbing the corporate ladder for its own sake may still hold some appeal, but undoubtedly it was more compelling when it was vital for obtaining sex. Success isn't as important as it once was, when it was a prerequisite for sex.[27]

And then there's marriage. In Baumeister and Vohs's view, casual sex is ruining marriage because it's increasing the crushing depression that marriage in this feminist dystopia already creates (for men). Women age and lose their sex appeal and desire, forcing men to pay more and more for less and less, even for a wife "whose contribution of sex dwindles sharply in both quantity and quality."

And now it's just a straight-up men's rights rant. Far from the Regnerus ideal in which men give their "affections, wealth and earnings" in exchange for a lifetime of sex, today's femitopia is considerably less rewarding for men than promised: "The traditional view that a wife should sexually satisfy her husband regardless of her own lack of desire has been eroded if not demolished by feminist ideology that has encouraged wives to expect husbands to wait patiently until the wife actually desires sex, with the result that marriage is a prolonged episode of sexual starvation for the husband. . . . Today's young men spend their young adulthood having abundant sex with multiple partners, and that seems to us to be an exceptionally poor preparation for a lifetime of sexual starvation."[28]

There were actually three references to "sexual starvation" in that paragraph, but I cut one for brevity. Regnerus cites Baumeister up and down, so I think it would be reasonable to ask him to comment on this (which I did), but he has so far declined.

What About Lesbians?

Oh, that. When Regnerus wrote his post in *Slate*, Belle Waring wrote a nice piece about it, which included this:

> Please note also that under the economic model, lesbians can't exist, since they have nothing of value to exchange for sex, except for . . . um . . . sex? And since women only use sex as a means to an end, and exchange it with men; and since further, sex has been explicitly devalued to something cheap, well, hm. I submit that if you propose a model of human sexual behavior, and it *positively forbids* the existence of a whole class of people who nonetheless actually exist, then maybe there's a problem with the theory?[29]

Regnerus actually has addressed the issue of lesbians—though not to explain how they sell sex without a buyer. Speaking at Franciscan University of Steubenville, he produced a weird hybrid of modernity theory and evolutionary psychology. First he suggested that homosexuality emerged partly because of the Pill, on the basis of his reading of Anthony Giddens's *Transformation of Intimacy*. He said: "Giddens draws an arrow from contraception to sexual malleability to the expansion of homosexuality."[30] Then, since he thinks lesbians are an unnatural creation of modern sexual plasticity, he took the pseudoevolutionary (Lamarckian?) leap to the implication that lesbians biologically produce asexual children. For the record—and I can't believe I'm saying this—I don't believe this is true.[31] But it does show Regnerus indeed has a theory of lesbianism, and—surprise—it is that women are ruining society (again), this time by destroying sexuality itself.

Anyway, it would be tempting (and more enjoyable) to simply ignore Mark Regnerus forever. His record of scientific manipulation and dishonesty in the service of the movement to deny equal rights to gays and lesbians is well documented, and social scientists of good will won't trust him again unless he comes clean. I wish that he and the people of good will could just agree never to interact again. But he's young and ambitious, and it's likely that he'll be back, so we should keep an eye on him.

4. GETTING BEYOND HOW *THE FACTUAL FEMINIST* IS WRONG ABOUT THE PREVALENCE OF RAPE

Christina Sommers, who produces the *Factual Feminist* videos from the American Enterprise Institute, thinks the federal government and the feminist establishment are exaggerating how much rape there is. I'm not an expert on measuring rape—and neither is she—but I've looked into it enough to say her debunking is basically bunk. But we need to go further than that.

Sommers quotes former president Obama as saying, "One in five women will be a victim of rape in their lifetime."[32] Obama got that statistic from the 2010 National Intimate Partner and Sexual Violence Survey (NISVS), conducted by the Centers for Disease Control (CDC).[33] Sommers complains that the NISVS finds a higher rate of rape than the National Crime Victimization Survey, which she asserts is the gold standard in this area. "By using a non-representative sample, and vaguely-worded questions," she charges, "the CDC yielded the one-in-five lifetime rate, and the 1.3 million female rape victims per year."

The NISVS did report that 18.3 percent of women had ever been the victim of rape, comprising three (nonexclusive) components: completed forced penetration, attempted forced penetration, or completed alcohol- or drug-facilitated penetration. That equals 21.8 million women overall, and 1.3 million who experienced one or more of these assaults in the year prior to the survey. Sommers claims the CDC has too broad a definition of rape, including lots of namby-pamby complaints from women brainwashed by a victimhood-obsessed feminist establishment.

The most important point is that the lifetime reported rape rate in the NISVS is comparable to findings in other major surveys. The CDC's long-running National Survey of Family Growth (NSFG) most recently reported that 19.5 percent of women ages eighteen to forty-four said they had "ever been forced by a male to have vaginal intercourse against your will"—similar to levels reported since 2002.[34] This is surprising because the NISVS measure is broader: it includes attempted rape as well as oral or anal penetration, and penetration by objects other than a man's penis, including acts performed by women. The NSFG asked only about vaginal intercourse by a man. So the NISVS has a broader definition and finds a lower rate of lifetime rape prevalence. Given the difficulties in defining and measuring these experiences, this seems within the realm of reasonable.

Sommers's only specific complaint about the NISVS rape prevalence statistic is that it includes alcohol- or drug-facilitated penetration. To make this point she engages in a misleading rant about sex under the influence of alcohol and drugs, not exactly misstating the NISVS method but carefully not describing it accurately. "What about sex while inebriated?" she asks. "Few people would say that sex while intoxicated alone constitutes rape." Right, and neither does the NISVS. The survey asked, "When you were drunk, high, drugged, or passed out and unable to consent. . . ." The key phrase there is *and unable to consent*. The NISVS is not saying all drunk or drugged sex is rape.

Sommers also claims that the NISVS is unrepresentative because it had a low response rate of about 30 percent. That's life in the big city of surveys these days, unfortunately, and the researchers attempted to compensate for it by using a weighting scheme to make the results representative of the national population. It's not ideal but it's not terrible, and that just means it should be interpreted cautiously and corroborated—neither Sommers nor I have any reason to believe this contributes to an inflated estimate of rape prevalence (though of course that's possible). In summary: if you have to pick a number to put to the lifetime prevalence of rape, "one in five" is a reasonable choice.

What Is Rape?

The NSFG survey combined two sets of responses to reach its figure for eighteen- to forty-four-year-old respondents. These questions were in the self-administered portion of the survey because of the sensitivity of the topic. In one section of the survey was the simple question, "At any time in your life, have you ever been forced by a male to have vaginal intercourse against your will?" In another section was a two-part question. First:

Think back to the very first time you had vaginal intercourse with a male. Which would you say comes closest to describing how much you wanted that first vaginal intercourse to happen?

- I really didn't want it to happen at the time.
- I had mixed feelings—part of me wanted it to happen at the time and part of me didn't.
- I really wanted it to happen at the time.

And then, this follow-up:

Would you say then that this first vaginal intercourse was voluntary or not voluntary, that is, did you choose to have sex of your own free will or not?

If the respondents said it was not voluntary, that counted as ever having forced sex. This is not a criminal definition of rape. Rather, it identifies people who had sex involuntarily—from their perspective. It is understandable that this measure produces higher estimates than the criminal legal system does.

I think we need a definition of rape that is not the same as the criminal law's definition, because the law is not intended to make criminal all of the ways that people experience sexual violation or coercion. The routine coercion of sex within unequal marriages, for example, must lie outside the reach of criminal law—or the next thing you know we'd have workers claiming that their employers' profits constituted theft. In that sense, the definition used by NSFG seems reasonable. Extending this further, however, we might find that drawing the line between sex and violence, or between sex and rape, not only is difficult but may be the wrong question.

Look back at the NISVS. It includes "sexual coercion" under the category of "other sexual violence"—"other" meaning not rising to the level of rape. (To be clear, this is not part of the rape prevalence estimates I discussed above). They offer this definition:

Sexual coercion is defined as unwanted sexual penetration that occurs after a person is pressured in a nonphysical way. In NISVS, sexual coercion refers to unwanted vaginal, oral, or anal sex after being pressured in ways that included being worn down by someone who repeatedly asked for sex or showed they were unhappy; feeling pressured by being lied to, being told promises that were untrue, having someone threaten to end a relationship or spread rumors; and sexual pressure due to someone using their influence or authority.

Sommers is incensed that this counts as "violence." Her voice drips with contempt as she recites the description, at how feminism's pretty little flowers are upset that somebody lied to them. I don't share this contempt. But neither would I insist that these forms of coercion be counted as "violence." Sexual coercion does not have to be defined as violence in order to be important, or bad, or an essential element of many people's sexual experience.

You Can't Handle the Truth?

The feminist argument for the distinction between sex and violence is partly a defense of "normal" sexual relationships, against the accusation that it is normal sexual relationships that feminists oppose. This is exactly the tone Sommers takes: feminists treat women as passive victims who can't handle normal relationships—you can't even get drunk and have sex with your spouse anymore! Arguing with her over the definition of violence is a losing battle. I'll give up "violence" if you agree that sexual coercion is systematically related to patriarchal power and gender inequality.

Here's an excerpt from Catharine MacKinnon's old discussion of rape *versus* sex from the 1981 essay "Sex and Violence," which influenced my attitude on this question. She said it is

> potentially cooptive [to formulate the question by saying] these are issues of violence, *not* sex: rape is a crime of violence, not sexuality. . . . I hear in the formulation that these issues are violence against women, not sex, that we are in the shadow of Freud, intimidated at being called repressive Victorians. We're saying we're *oppressed* and they say we're *re*pressed. That is, when we say we're against rape the immediate response is, "Does that mean you're against sex?" "Are you attempting to impose neo-Victorian prudery on sexual expression?" . . . To distinguish ourselves from this, and in reaction to it, we call these abuses violence.[35]

To argue with Sommers about where to draw the line for sexual violence is to inhabit the shadow of Freud, in MacKinnon's view. Rather than adopt that defensive posture, MacKinnon argued, feminists should own women's fundamental, nonobjective (in the sense of "not disinterested") position: "We have a deeper critique of what has been done to women's sexuality and who controls access to it. What we are saying is that sexuality in exactly these normal forms often *does* violate us. So long as we say that those things are abuses of violence, not sex, we fail to criticize what has been made of *sex*, what has been done to us *through* sex, because we leave the line between rape and intercourse . . . right where it is."[36]

In other words, if feminists argue over whether women's perception of involuntary sex matches the legal definition, then we lose the ability to explain that unequal sex is systematic rather than deviant. It may not be that one in five women has experienced rape according to the definition within criminal law (though that is certainly within the realm of the possible). But if that many women have had sex involuntarily, and many more have experienced sexual coercion of various kinds, isn't that bad enough?

5. WHY I DON'T DEFEND THE SEX-VERSUS-GENDER DISTINCTION

In a discussion about how the American Sociological Association should collect data on the gender of its members, I suggested putting just three options on the form—"female," "male," and "write-in"—with the association staff then coding and interpreting the write-in answers. This seemed preferable to specifying several (or many) alternative options that relatively few people would choose and maybe more people would misunderstand.[37] Because we were talking about gender, I was corrected by another sociologist, who wrote: "'Female' and 'male' refer to one's sex, not gender."

Feminists—including feminist sociologists—have made important progress by drawing the conceptual distinction between sex and gender, with sex the biological and gender the social category. From this, maybe, we could recognize that gendered behavior was not simply an expression of sex categories—related to the term "sex roles"—but a socially constructed set of practices layered on top of a crude biological base. We may date this to Simone de Beauvoir in *The Second Sex* (1949), who wrote: "It would appear, then, that every female human being is not necessarily a woman; to be so considered she must share in that mysterious and threat-ened reality known as femininity."[38]

Later she added, "One is not born, but rather becomes, a woman." And this is what Judith Butler put down as the root of the gender/sex distinc-tion: "The distinction between sex and gender has been crucial to the long-standing feminist effort to debunk the claim that anatomy is destiny. . . . At its limit, then, the sex/gender distinction implies a radical heteronomy of natural bodies and constructed genders with the consequence that 'being' female and 'being' a woman are two very different sort of being."[39]

In their famous article "Doing Gender," Candace West and Don Zimmerman reported making the sex/gender distinction in their sociol-ogy classes starting in the late 1960s.[40] I'm guessing this really started to catch on among sociologists in the 1970s, as the phrase "social construc-tion of gender" starts taking off at that point, according to the Google ngrams database. The spread of this distinction in the popular under-standing—and I don't know how far it has spread—seems to be credited to sociologists, maybe because people learn it in introductory sociology courses.

Lots of people devote energy to defending the sex-versus-gender dis-tinction, but I'm not one of them. It's that dichotomy of nature versus culture. I got turned on to turning off this distinction by Catharine MacKinnon, who wrote: "I see sexuality as fundamental to gender and as fundamentally social. Biology becomes the social meaning of biology within the system of sex inequality much as race becomes ethnicity within a system of racial inequality. Both are social and political in a system that does not rest independently on biological differences in any respect. In this light, the sex/gender distinction looks like a nature/culture distinc-tion in the sense criticized by Sherry Ortner in 'Is Female to Male as Nature Is to Culture?' I use sex and gender relatively interchangeably."[41]

From another perspective, Joan Fujimura has argued for mixing more social construction into that biological scheme, in what she calls a "socio-material view of sex": "We need to think of the categories male and female not as representing stable, fundamental differences but as already and always social categories. They form a set of concepts, a set of social catego-ries of difference to be deployed for particular purposes. Ergo, what counts as male and female must be evaluated in their context of use. The categories male and female, like the categories men and women, may be useful for organizing particular kinds of social investigation or action, but they may also inhibit actions."[42]

A less commonly cited passage in that West and Zimmerman article describes how the authors "learned that the relationship between biological and cultural processes was far more complex—and reflexive—than we previously had supposed." To help smooth the relationship between sex and gender, they use "sex category," which "stands as a proxy" for sex but actually is created by identificatory displays, which in turn lead to gender. As I see it, the sex category concept makes the story about the social construction of sex as well as gender. Consider, for example, Erving Goffman's discussion of bathroom equipment: "Toilet segregation is presented as a natural consequence of the difference between the sex-classes, when in fact it is rather a means of honoring, if not producing, this difference."[43]

The US Census Bureau, in its data definitions, says, "For the purpose of Census Bureau surveys and the decennial census, sex refers to a person's biological sex," and their forms ask, "What is Person X's Sex: Male/Female." But that explanation is never on the form, and there's no (longer) policing of people filling it out—like race, it's based on self-identification. So for any reason anyone can choose either "male" or "female." What they can't do is write in an alternative or leave it blank (it will be made up for you if you do).

So the Census Bureau's words are asking for something "biological," but people are social animals, and they check the box they want. I think it's eliciting sex category identification, which is socially produced, which is gender.

This all means that, to me, it would be okay if the form said, "Gender: Male/Female." I'm just not sure the benefits of defending the theoretical sex/gender distinction outweigh the costs of treating biological sex as outside the realm of the social.

6. DOES DOING DIFFERENCE DENY DOMINANCE?

Does women's behavior make them less equal?

"Guess what," critic-of-feminism Camille Paglia said in a *Salon* interview. "Women are different than men!"[44] Usually when people point out gender differences, they don't just mean men and women are different, they mean "women are different than men." As an archetypal example, in the essay "Do Women Really Want Equality?" Kay Hymowitz argued that women don't want to model their professional lives on male standards and therefore don't really want equality: "This hints at the problem with the equality-by-the-numbers approach: it presumes women *want* absolute parity in all things measurable, and that the average woman wants to work as many hours as the average man, that they want to be CEOs, heads of state, surgeons and Cabinet heads just as much as men do."[45]

So the male professional standard is just *there*, and the question is what women will do if they want equality with it. Of course, what women (and men) want is a product of social interaction, so it's not an abstract quality separate from social context. Also, I'm no statistician but I know that when there is a gap between two variable quantities (such as men's and women's average hours in paid work), moving one of them isn't the only way to bring them closer together. In other words—men could change, too.

What about Vocal Fry and Uptalk?

Naomi Wolf would add vocal fry and uptalk to the list of women's self-inflicted impediments: "'Vocal fry' has joined more traditional young-women voice mannerisms such as run-ons, breathiness and the dreaded question marks in sentences (known by linguists as uptalk) to undermine these women's authority in newly distinctive ways."[46] So the male speech pattern is just there, and the question is what women will do if they want equality. Debbie Cameron objected that coaching women on how to talk like men is "doing the patriarchy's work for it."[47] So some feminists want more respect for vocal fry, saying: "When your dads bitch about the way you talk it's because they're just trying to not listen to you talk, period, so fuck your dads."[48]

Elevating vocal fry to a virtue would be more persuasive if the common examples weren't mostly privileged women talking about basically nothing. As an old dad, I personally bitched about the way the two women interviewed on NPR uptalk-and-vocal-fried their way through an excruciating seven-minute conversation about the awesomeness of selfie culture: "I actually do edit my selfiieees, occasionally, just because, after

I discoverrrred there were so many apps that can, you know, make you look so much better, I felt like I was kind of, not doing myself a favor by posting unedited selfiieees to Instagram."[49]

Of course, this being a patriarchal society, double standards abound. When men fry their vocals hardly anyone complains. And then there's resting bitch face (RBF), "a face that, when at ease, is perceived as angry, irritated or simply ... expressionless," according to Jessica Bennett. But only for women: "When a man looks stern, or serious, or grumpy, it's simply the default," said Rachel Simmons, an author and leadership consultant at Smith College. "We don't inherently judge the moodiness of a male face. But as women, we are almost expected to put on a smile. So if we don't, it's deemed 'bitchy.'"[50] Many men feel that RBF is a blight on their scenery—one they have the right to demand improvement upon—which is why they yell "Smile!" at random women on the street.

Sometimes women should act more like men, because some of the behavior that men would otherwise own is about power and access and self-determination and other things that women want and deserve. And some gender differences are just little pieces of the symbolic architecture that helps establish that men and women are different, which means women are different, which means men are dominant. Difference for its own sake is bad for gender equality.

It's tricky because we don't have different audiences for different messages anymore, but we need two true messages at once: it's wrong to discriminate against and shame women for their speech patterns, and it's a good idea not to undermine yourself with speech patterns that annoy or distract men and old people.

What about Sports?

One process people use to essentialize sex categories—to enhance rather than downplay gender differences—is sex-segregated sports. This has emerged in the defining case of Caster Semenya, who finally won her first Olympic gold medal in 2016. Semenya is said to have an intersex condition known as androgen-insensitivity syndrome, in which a person with XY chromosomes (considered genetically male) does not respond to testosterone and so does not develop male reproductive organs, and as a result has a vagina but undescended testes instead of ovaries. A likely result is higher than average (for a woman) testosterone, or hyperandrogenism, which may provide an athletic advantage relative to other women.[51]

As is the case with many gender differences, our sports establishment and culture is built around male standards, which is why women are granted a protected sphere of difference. Vanessa Heggie writes in a fascinating historical review of sex testing in international sports:

> Sex testing, after all, is a tautological (or at least circular) process: the activities which we recognise as sports are overwhelmingly those which favour a physiology which we consider "masculine." . . . What the sex test effectively does, therefore, is provide an upper limit for women's sporting performance; there is a point at which your masculine-style body is declared "too masculine," and you are disqualified, regardless of your personal gender identity. For men there is no equivalent upper *physiological* limit—no kind of genetic, or hormonal, or physiological advantage is tested for, even if these would give a "super masculine" athlete a distinct advantage over the merely very athletic "normal" male.[52]

Thus there is no height limit in men's basketball, even though extreme tallness provides a clear biological advantage.

Heggie adds that, for every claim of gender fraud that turns out to be "true"—that is, a male or intersex person with an unfair advantage competing as a woman, which is very rare—there are countless cases of "suspicions, rumour, and innuendo" regarding women who are simply unusually big and muscular. As in wide swaths of the professional world, men are the standard, and successful women often look or act more like men—and then they are shamed or penalized for not performing their gender correctly.

There is a sex-versus-gender issue here, however. When men's behavior or activity is the standard by which all are judged, there may be gendered (social) reasons women have trouble competing—such as exclusion from training, hiring, promotion, and social networks, or socially defined burdens (such as child care) impeding their progress toward the top ranks. And then sometimes there are sex (biological) reasons women can't win, such as in the extreme elite ranks of many organized sports.

Figure 42 shows the world record times in the eight-hundred-meter footrace for men and women, from 1922 to 2016 (before the Olympics). All the fuss over Caster Semenya's natural hormone levels—her high level

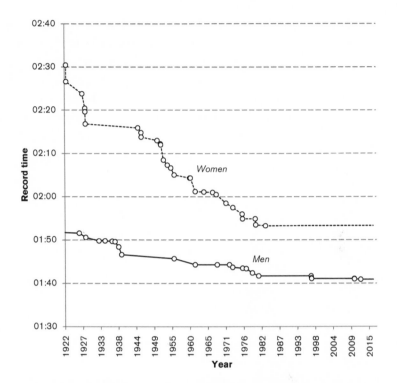

Figure 42. World record times in eight-hundred-meter footrace: women and men, 1922–2016. Source: Author chart from International Association of Athletics Federations data, available at www.iaaf.org.

of testosterone—broke out before she ever got within two seconds of Jarmila Kratochvílová's 1983 record of 1:53.3. (It's presumed that Kratochvílová was taking steroids, but not proven.) And she will never approach even the qualifying times of Olympic men.

It's very telling that no woman has beaten Kratochvílová's record. In fact, after women made steady progress toward equality for four decades, men's lead has increased by almost a second in the last four decades. In this contest of physiology, the fastest women apparently cannot compete with the fastest men. This makes a strong case for sex, not gender, as the difference maker. That does not mean we're outside the realm of social construction, because the line has to be drawn somewhere to create the protective arena in which women can compete with each other, and that line is defined socially. (It also means that those—like Malcolm Gladwell—who think Semenya should be disqualified are effectively arguing that she should be required to run against men she can never challenge.)[53]

We solve the problem if we "stop pawning this fundamentally social question off onto scientists," say Rebecca Jordan-Young and Katrina Karkazis. They want to "let all legally recognized women compete. Period."[54] But if it is fundamentally social, instead of biological, why are men's times so much faster?

How Deep a Difference

In that Camille Paglia interview I mentioned above, she goes beyond the idea that men and women have different preferences and habits. Here is "why women are having so much trouble dealing with men in the feminist era": "Equality in the workplace is not going to solve the problems between men and women which are occurring in the private, emotional realm, where every man is subordinate to women, because he emerged as a tiny helpless thing from a woman's body. Professional women today don't want to think about this or deal with it."

Not recognizing such inherent conditions is a problem for modern feminism, she believes. "Guess what—women are different than men! When will feminism wake up to this basic reality?" In this view, which you could (she does) loosely call Freudian, the sex difference and the gender difference are nearly unified, because the psychological basis for difference is universally present at birth. The short-sighted feminist attempt to erase gender difference thus makes both women and men miserable:

> Now we're working side-by-side in offices at the same job. Women want to leave at the end of the day and have a happy marriage at home, but then they put all this pressure on men because they expect them to be exactly like their female friends. If they feel restlessness or misery or malaise, they automatically blame it on men. Men are not doing enough; men aren't sharing enough. But it's not the fault of men that we have this crazy and rather neurotic system where women are now functioning like men in the workplace, with all its material rewards.

What is out of whack is women entering men's sphere, apparently.

Difference and Dominance

Times like these, like it or not, are good times to revisit Catharine MacKinnon's essay, "Difference and Dominance: On Sex Discrimination": "Concealed is the substantive way in which man has become the measure of all things. Under the sameness standard, women are measured according to our correspondence with man, our equality judged by our proximity to his measure. Under the difference standard, we are measured according to our lack of correspondence with him, our womanhood judged by our distance from his measure. Gender neutrality is thus simply the male standard, and the special protection rule is simply the female standard, but do not be deceived: masculinity, or maleness, is the referent for both."[55]

Thus women are stuck between the rock of neutrality and the hard place of special protection—difference and dominance: "Men's physiology defines most sports . . . their socially designed biographies define workplace expectations and successful career patterns, their perspectives and concerns define quality in scholarship, their experiences and obsessions define merit, their objectification of life defines art, their military service defines citizenship, their presence defines family, their inability to get along with each other—their wars and rulerships—defines history, their image defines god, and their genitals define sex."[56]

So, as with any system of inequality: check that reference category.

Of course, those women who work more hours, adopt male speech patterns and facial expressions, and run faster may do better than those who do not (under the risk of overstepping). But why can't women embrace gender difference in things like speech patterns and wield them in the service of equality? Because under these conditions, enhancing gender differences generally works against equality.

Notes

1. MODERNITY, PARENTING, AND FAMILIES

1. The result of that work was a paper with my Census Bureau mentor (Casper and Cohen 2000).

2. Constitution Facts (n.d.).

3. D. Smith (1985).

4. The figure uses census data till 1880, then switches to the Social Security Administration numbers, which are obtainable from the Social Security website at https://www.ssa.gov/oact/babynames/. For census names, I counted people as named Mary if the first four characters of their name were "Mary," regardless of what came after, which means "Mary Anne" counts as Mary, but "Anne Mary" does not. For the years through 1880, I pooled people according to year of birth in ten-year bins, starting with 1775–84 (labeled "1780"), and so on up to 1875–84 ("1880").

5. When I was a kid, before I knew about the normal distribution, I used to roll a pair of dice and tally the sums on a piece of graph paper, always hoping 6 or 8 would somehow pull ahead of 7 in the long run. (Yes, my childhood was that great.)

6. Lieberson (2000, 24).

7. Verry (1952, 258).

8. Bain (1954, 30).

9. Zelizer (1985).

10. Trumbull (1890, 71).

11. T. Morgan (1886, 7).

12. Irwin (2009).

13. Lareau (2011).

14. Anderson and Whitaker (2010).

15. Cohen (2014b).

16. Warner (2006).

17. Stone (2007).

18. Reich (2014).

19. Perkins (2015).

20. Healy (2015).

21. I used California Department of Education (2014) for the free-lunch eligibility rates (2013–14) and California Department of Public Health (2015) for the vaccine exemption rates for kindergartners (2014–15). I weighted the analyses by the number of kindergartners enrolled in each school, so the rates shown are for students, not schools (this also helps with the outliers, which are mostly very small schools). Because there are so many schools with no PBEs, I used a tobit regression to predict exemption rates (I also excluded the top 1 percent outliers). In case the zeros were data errors, I reran the regression excluding the zero cases and got weaker but still very strong results.

22. Cohen (2014b, 324).

23. Schulte (2014); Kohn (2014).

24. Meinch (2016).

25. Shermer (2014).

26. Peter (2014).

27. I will frequently refer to data from the General Social Survey, a long-running study that is the best we have for tracking attitudes in the United States over time. For general information, visit the data site at http://gss.norc.org / (accessed July 10, 2017); I also rely on a Web access tool for the data available at http://sda.berkeley.edu/cgi-bin/hsda?harcsda+gss16 (accessed July 10, 2017).

28. Blow (2014).

29. Dyson (2014).

30. C. Ferguson (2013); C. Taylor et al. (2010).

31. Cohen (1998a). For a more recent analysis, see Fenelon (2013).

32. Kaplan (2014).

33. Pew Research Center (2014).

34. The GSS asked if "people in the group [African Americans] tend to be hard-working or if they tend to be lazy," on a scale from 1 (hardworking) to 7 (lazy). I coded them as favoring lazy if they gave scores of 5 or above. The motivation question was a yes-or-no question: "On the average African Americans have worse jobs, income, and housing than white people. Do you think these differences are because most African Americans just don't have the motivation or willpower to pull themselves up out of poverty?"

35. Mead (1932, 174).

36. Mead (1932, 186).

37. Mead (1932, 186).

38. Mead (1932, 188).

39. Vaden and Woolley (2011).

40. Woolley, Boerger, and Markman (2004).

41. Woolley and Ghossainy (2013).

42. Woolley and Ghossainy (2013).

43. Pinto (2016).

2. MARRIAGE, SINGLE MOTHERS, AND POVERTY

1. For a video of the event, see American Enterprise Institute, "Opportunity, Responsibility, and Security: A Consensus Plan for Reducing Poverty and Restoring the American Dream," December 3, 2015, www.aei.org/events/opportunity-responsibility-and-security-a-consensus-plan-for-reducing-poverty-and-restoring-the-american-dream/.

2. Sawhill (2014).

3. Meyer (2015).

4. Bruenig (2015a).

5. Sawhill (2015, 4).

6. To do the calculations, instead of the official poverty rate I used the Supplemental Poverty Measure. This measures resources versus needs for "resource units," which are either families (including cohabitors, foster children, and other people that are normally considered "nonrelatives") or people living without families. For every resource unit, the poverty threshold is based on the cost of food, clothing, shelter, and utilities, adjusted for geographic location, housing type, and family composition. In addition to money income, the resources for the calculation include noncash assistance like food stamps, school lunch, housing, and energy subsidies; then taxes, work expenses, child care expenses, medical expenses, and child support are deducted from resources. Note that I refer to resource units as "families," although some of them are single people. The Stata code I used to analyze the data, which includes the variables used from the IPUMS.org database, is at https://www.terpconnect.umd.edu/~pnc/working/eliminate%20child%20poverty/. For definitions and other statistics, see Short (2014).

7. Reeves (2013).

8. Murray (2000). At the risk of stating the obvious for readers of this book, his last sentence is not true, reflecting instead Murray's impatience with the slow pace of science in confirming what he already believes. In fact, we do not even know what the "relevant genetic makeup" is, if there is any, that differentiates

poor people from nonpoor people. On race and genetics, I have written a review piece. See Cohen (2015b).

9. Covert (2016).

10. The quote is in a speech available in full on C-SPAN. See Rubio (2014).

11. Rector (2012b).

12. For the "godfather" attribution, see Lowry (2006). It's worth noting that these statistics, like almost all statistics about poverty, are not about "being raised in . . ." and merely provide a snapshot of current family structure and poverty rates, but that's another problem.

13. Author calculations from the 2015 March Current Population Survey.

14. Jacobsen (2014).

15. Kim (2013).

16. Haskins (2013).

17. Rector (2012a).

18. Author calculations using US Census Bureau data and data from the Metropolitan Police Department through 2015.

19. Associated Press (2012).

20. Schmidt (1985).

21. P. Taylor (1991, A1).

22. Loose and Thomas (1994).

23. Cohen (2012).

24. Gallagher wrote this in a comment on a post called "Single Motherhood and Crime in One Graph," dated November 27, 2012, on a now-defunct blog called *Family Scholars Blog* (sponsored by the Institute for American Values) that is no longer accessible.

25. Douthat's tweet is from November 27, 2012, https://twitter.com /douthatnyt/status/273478522662699008; Murray's is from November 27, 2012, https://twitter.com/charlesmurray/status/273617887095291904.

26. Elizabeth Marquardt wrote this in a comment on a post called "Single Motherhood and Crime in One Graph," dated November 27, 2012, on a now-defunct blog called *Family Scholars Blog* (sponsored by the Institute for American Values) that is no longer accessible.

27. Willcox's post was on the defunct *Family Scholars Blog* but has been captured by the Wayback Machine; see Wilcox (2012).

28. Demuth and Brown (2004).

29. Hymowitz (2012).

30. Mumola and Karberg (2006).

31. Guerino, Harrison, and Sabol (2011).

32. For examples of this research, see Ingram et al. (2007); McNulty and Bellair (2003); Sokol-Katz, Dunham, and Zimmerman (1997).

3. MARRIAGE PROMOTION

1. Hoover Institution (1996).

2. From author analysis, based on Census Bureau data, of the prevalence of marriage among women ages twenty-five to fifty-four.

3. National Marriage Project (2012).

4. AEI/Brookings Working Group on Poverty and Opportunity (2015).

5. Cohen (2013g).

6. Ortega (2014).

7. Ages at marriage are from Guilmoto (2011). Gender inequality measures are from UN Human Development Reports, available at http://hdr.undp.org/en /composite/GII.

8. Edin and Nelson (2013).

9. Fremstad and Boteach (2015).

10. Personal Responsibility and Work Opportunity Reconciliation Act, Public Law 104–193, 42 USC 1305 (1996).

11. Rector and Pardue (2004).

12. Heath (2012).

13. US General Accountability Office (2008).

14. Wood et al. (2010).

15. Devaney and Dion (2010).

16. Wood et al. (2012).

17. Lundquist et al. (2014, 2).

18. Hawkins (2015); Simpson and Hawkins (2015).

19. Hawkins, Amato, and Kinghorn (2013).

20. In the first adjustment, rescaling D.C., all the standard errors at least doubled. And all of the standard errors are at least three times larger with D.C. gone. I'm not a medical doctor, but I think it's fair to say that when removing one case triples your standard errors, your regression model is not well.

21. Western, Bloome, and Percheski (2008).

22. Lerman and Wilcox (2014).

23. Kristof (2016).

24. Graham (2015).

25. AEI/Brookings Working Group on Poverty and Opportunity (2015).

26. Kearney and Levine (2015).

27. UN Statistics Division (n.d.).

28. Institute for American Values (2000).

29. Perry v. Schwarzenegger, 2010, 704 F. Supp. 2d 921. Dist. Court.

30. Templeton funded the thrift project at $1.2 million in 2004. See John Templeton Foundation (n.d.). The financial details in this essay are from my reading of the foundations' tax-exempt IRS 990 forms.

31. Marquardt had also been strongly opposed to gay marriage on moral grounds. See Marquardt (2009).

32. Blankenhorn and Marquardt (2012).

33. Institute for American Values (2013).

34. Gallagher (2013).

35. The original document is Marriage Opportunity Council (2015); the magazine version is Blankenhorn et al. (2015).

36. Bruenig (2015b).

37. Tweet from @SandyDarity, 8:11 p.m., March 23, 2015, https://twitter.com/SandyDarity/status/580175168015884288.

38. Sanneh (2015).

39. Marriage Opportunity Council (2015).

40. Reiman (2006).

4. MARRIAGE EQUALITY IN SOCIAL SCIENCE AND THE COURTS

1. Carey (2012). The paper itself is Regnerus (2012a).

2. Luscombe (2012).

3. In 2010 I had referred to the implications of same-sex parenting for social science as a "demographic revolution" (Cohen 2010b). Research at the time found no evidence of systematic disadvantage for children whose parents were lesbian or gay. See Biblarz and Stacey (2010).

4. Kaiser (2014).

5. For a CDC study, see Ward et al. (2014); for a Census Bureau study, see US Census Bureau (2011). Although studies on same-sex couples are obviously not a top research priority, the National Science Foundation has funded them going back at least to the early 1980s. See Brody (1983).

6. Regnerus (2012c).

7. A fact indicative of both the liberal bent of mainstream sociology and the extreme nature of Bradley support: my search of two hundred academic journals in the field of sociology (in the JSTOR database) reveals only eight papers that have acknowledged receipt of funding from the Bradley Foundation; none of these were in a major sociology journal, and none were written by sociology faculty.

8. American College of Pediatricians (2012).

9. Golinski v. United States Office of Personnel Management, 2012, 824 F. Supp. 2d 968. Dist. Court.

10. Regnerus (2012d).

11. Gates (2012).

12. See Pascoe (2012); Rojas (2012); Perrin (2012); Umberson (2012).

13. Johnson et al. (2012); C. Smith (2012).

14. American Psychological Association et al. (2012).

15. American Sociological Association (2012).

16. Bartlett (2012).

17. A. Ferguson (2012).

18. See UT News (2012). As much as most concerned sociologists disliked the work Regnerus had done—and how he had done it—many still breathed a sigh of relief as public university administrators dismissed a complaint from a nonacademic activist directed at a professor that demanded sanctions for politically unpopular research.

19. See Resnick (2013). The e-mails that I draw from in this account are available on reporter Sofia Resnick's Scribd site, here: https://www.scribd.com /user/65082544/Sofia-Resnick. Resnick described the e-mails in Resnick (2012). My write-up appeared the next day in Cohen (2013h).

20. Eckholm (2014b).

21. Regnerus (2012c).

22. From foundation to publication to media campaign, this narrative is a wonderful illustration of the process by which elites influence public opinion, as told in Domhoff (2009).

23. Cohen (2013i). In the Michigan case *DeBoer v. Snyder*, Regnerus, testifying as an expert witness, was confronted with Amato's criticism of the way he had politicized the results. See Cohen (2014a).

24. For the e-mails between Wright and Wilcox, which were published by the anonymous activist who goes by the name Straight Grandmother, see "Wright Agrees to Let Wilcox Peer Review Regnerus," Scribd, n.d., www.scribd.com /doc/233338987/Wright-Agrees-To-Let-Wilcox-Peer-Review-Regnerus.

25. Flaherty (2013).

26. Perrin, Cohen, and Caren (2013).

27. Cheng and Powell (2015).

28. Rosenfeld (2015).

29. The direction of the burden of proof here has been a recurring problem, which we attempted to address in Perrin, Cohen, and Caren (2013).

30. Social Science Professors (2013).

31. I was delighted to see that, in the face of such vacuous and ahistorical pronouncements, the court records from marriage equality cases also included references to the actual history, especially in the form of Coontz (2006) and Cott (2002).

32. Friess (2014).

33. Oral arguments in No. 12-144, Hollingsworth v. Perry, March 26, 2013, pp. 19–20.

34. B. Friedman (2014). Friedman's decision was reported in Eckholm (2014a).

35. Toobin (2015).

36. Tweet from @GovMikeHuckabee, June 26, 2015, https://twitter.com/GovMikeHuckabee/status/3499l1972378181632.

37. Deneen (2015).

38. I described his testimony in the case in Cohen (2014c).

39. Social Science Professors (2013).

40. Author transcription from the *Drew Marini Show*, September 17, 2014.

41. Transcript of the General Audience of Pope Francis, Saint Peter's Square, Wednesday, Holy See, April 22, 2015, https://w2.vatican.va/content/francesco/en/audiences/2015/documents/papa-francesco_20150415_udienza-generale.html.

42. Text of a joint declaration of Pope Francis and the Russian Orthodox Patriarch Kirill, para. 20, February 2, 2016, http://en.radiovaticana.va/news/2016/02/12/joint_declaration_of_pope_francis_and_patriarch_kirill/1208117.

43. The videos are no longer available free but are for sale at https://vimeo.com/ondemand/humanum.

44. Regnerus (2015) has predicted that gay marriage will cause a decline in the birth rate.

5. DOING DIMORPHISM

1. Risman (1999).

2. M. Gordon, Price, and Peralta (2016).

3. Schilt and Westbrook (2015, 27).

4. Goffman (1977).

5. Paoletti (2015).

6. Sociological Images (2016).

7. I have made the Google ngrams search available here: http://tinyurl.com/zqnu4zm.

8. Cohen (2010a).

9. One reader of my blog pointed out this was like putting a collar and tie on the cartoon character Yogi Bear, who otherwise had a sexually ambiguous body, as most bears do.

10. Wade and Ferree (2014).

11. Connellan et al. (2000).

12. The research in this area consistently finds small effect sizes. See McClure (2000).

13. See, for example, Orenstein (2012); D. England, Descartes, and Collier-Meek (2011).

14. On sex dimorphism generally, especially with regard to brains and behavior, see Fine (2011).

15. Fryar, Gu, and Ogden (2012).

16. C. Gordon et al. (1988).

17. Katha Pollitt (1991) called this the "Smurfette principle."

18. The comment is on this post: Cohen (2013e).

19. Cohen (2014b).

20. The authoritative work in this area is Paoletti (2012).

21. Frassanito and Pettorini (2008, 882).

22. Wong and Hines (2015).

23. Ellis and Ficek (2001).

24. Paoletti (2012).

25. Cohen (2013a).

26. Paoletti (2015).

27. American Society for Aesthetic Plastic Surgery (2016).

28. Sax (2016).

29. Christopherson, Briskie, and Inglehart (2009).

30. I only found this in a study from Italy, but it seems likely to hold in other countries as well. See Deli et al. (2012).

6. GENDER INEQUALITY

1. On the pitfalls of the "unconstrained" search for ever more explanatory factors, see Healy (2017).

2. Women's Media Center (2015).

3. Neal Caren has posted training materials and code for his data extraction and analysis work, including details on working with Python, at "Resources for Learning Python," http://nealcaren.github.io/.

4. This is a count of stories by the gender of their authors, not a count of authors. If men or women write more stories per person, then the figures will differ from those for the gender composition of authors. So it's not a workplace study but a content study. It asks: When you see something in the *Times,* what is the chance it was written by a woman versus a man? I combined Sunday Review (which was small) with Opinion, since they have the same editor and are the same on Sundays. I combined Style (which was small) into Fashion, since they're "Fashion and Style" in the paper. I combined *T Magazine* (which was small) into *T:Style,* since they seem to be the same thing. Also, I coded Reed Abelson's articles as female because I know she's a woman even though "Reed" is male more than 90 percent of the time.

5. The rankings are updated regularly. See Alexa's rankings at "nytimes.com Traffic Statistics," accessed July 23, 2017, www.alexa.com/siteinfo/nytimes.com.

6. See, e.g., Huffman, Cohen, and Pearlman (2010); Stainback, Kleiner, and Skaggs (2016). However, some evidence supports the contrary view, e.g., Srivastava and Sherman (2015).

7. These figures are from my use of American Community Survey data at IPUMS.org.

8. A. Friedman (2014).

9. Auletta (2014).

10. Proctor, Semega, and Kollar (2016).

11. Barack Obama Facebook status update, April 12, 2016, https://www.facebook.com/barackobama/posts/10153800980901749.

12. Institute for Women's Policy Research (2015).

13. Clinton (2000).

14. Furchtgott-Roth (2000).

15. The Clinton quote is from ABC News (2013). See Rosin (2013).

16. Hymowitz (2011).

17. Swarns (2014).

18. New York City Commission on Human Rights (n.d.).

19. Konigsberg (2013).

20. Rosin (2013).

21. For a review, see Cohen (2013j).

22. The full comparison is at Cohen (2013d). The full titles of the occupations are "Nursing, Psychiatric, and Home Health Aides," and "Driver/Sales Workers and Truck Drivers." The 2014 estimate is from the Current Population Survey. For the rest of this comparison I drew on the 2009–11 American Community Survey data at IPUMS.org. For a more in-depth analysis of the nursing aides and their occupational mobility, see Ribas, Dill, and Cohen (2012).

23. Levanon, England, and Allison (2009).

24. For the comparable-worth debates, see Acker (1991); P. England (1992). Neither the Lilly Ledbetter Fair Pay Act, signed by Obama in 2009, nor the Paycheck Fairness Act, backed by Clinton, would have imposed a comparable worth scheme, although the latter law would have narrowed the scope of justifications allowed for disparities in pay between different jobs.

25. One exception is the public sector in Minnesota, which has something like comparable worth, in which local jurisdictions have their pay structures reviewed at regular intervals for evidence of gender bias, based on the required conditions and abilities of their jobs. See Legislative Office on the Economic Status of Women (2016).

26. Torabi (2015).

27. Wang, Parker, and Taylor (2013).

28. Luscombe (2014).

29. Williams (2012).

30. Livingston (2014).

31. US Census Bureau (2015b).

32. I made this case in an op-ed (Cohen 2013f). For the general stalling of progress on gender equality, see Cotter, Hermsen, and Vanneman (2011). On stalled progress toward equality in the division of labor, see Sayer (2015).

33. See Mundy (2012a); Rosin (2012a). I reviewed Mundy and Rosin's books together in Cohen (2013k). My full-length critique of Rosin was published in a law review article (Cohen 2013c).

34. I detailed these specific errors in Cohen (2013b).

35. Cotter, Hermsen, and Vanneman (2001).

36. For an extended version of this theory, see Jackson (1998).

37. The cover of the magazine showed a man with no pants, and the subtitle for the article was "Welcome to the New Middle-Class Matriarchy" (Rosin 2012c).

38. Lorber (1994, 288).

39. Women for Women (2011).

40. The chain of links is detailed in Cohen (2011).

41. R. Morgan (1984).

42. I have placed a copy of this document online at philipncohen.com /working/WNIEO.pdf.

43. Zinsser (2002).

44. International Labour Office (1978).

45. Ahooja-Patel (2007, 367). In 2015, in response to a *Washington Post* reporter who got her name from my post, she wrote, reasonably: "Please understand that the knowledge of statistics we have now in 2015 is not the same as what we knew earlier, especially in the 1970s and 80s. Some of the statistics we were looking at in that period were estimates and the national statistical offices of the period did not cover women's issues or data" (Kessler 2015).

46. US women's income is from US Census Bureau (2015a); global gross domestic product figures are from World Bank (2016).

47. Credit Suisse AG (2014).

48. Data are from Board of Governors of the Federal Reserve System (2014).

49. Forbes (2016).

50. Mack (2012).

51. World Food Program USA (2010).

52. Hanstad (2009).

53. Food and Agriculture Organization of the United Nations (2016).

54. Others have investigated the land question also, finding that while of course women own less land than men, there's no way it's as low as 1 percent. For example, an analysis of sub-Saharan African countries found that women owned anywhere from a few percent to almost half of the privately held land. See Doss et al. (2013).

55. Sommers (2014).

56. Greenberg (2014); Kessler (2015).

57. See the promotion video at Alan Alda Center for Communicating Science, Facebook page, December 24, 2014, https://www.facebook.com/aldacenter /posts/764774310245069.

7. RACE, GENDER, AND FAMILIES

1. I first attempted to contribute to theorizing about "intersectionality" in my master's thesis, published as Cohen (1996); my first approach at an empirical analysis was Cohen (1998b).

2. Cohen (1996).

3. MacKinnon (1982, 516).

4. Associated Press (2015).

5. The American Sociological Association presidential address by Evelyn Nakano Glenn used uncapitalized *black*; see Glenn (2011). On the other hand, our article's capitalization sailed through without objection: Cohen and Huffman (2007).

6. To check that, I compared frequency of "black people" and "Black people," to exclude references to the color in other contexts. See GoogleBooks, Ngram Viewer, https://books.google.com/ngrams/graph?content=black+people+%2F+B lack+people&year_start=1988&year_end=2008&corpus=17.

7. Office of Management and Budget (1997).

8. Rastogi et al. (2011). The census practice of capitalizing started sometime between the publication of the 1990 and 1991 editions of the Statistical Abstract of the United States, although I can't find a policy statement to this effect. See the *Statistical Abstracts* website at www.census.gov/library/publications/time-series /statistical_abstracts.html.

9. Jones (2013).

10. Childs et al. (2010).

11. Parker (2016). You know the rewrite journalists are playing telephone when they all cite the same out-of-date statistics, in this case a census report that had been updated three times since 2011.

12. Hunn and Bell (2014).

13. Pierce (2014).

14. Seoul, Korea, probably suffered greater losses temporarily during the Korean War. Mosul in Iraq and Aleppo in Syria—which each had more than one million people before their countries fell apart in the 2000s—might end up worse, but we don't know yet (and wartime exoduses might be in a different category). The population of the ancient city of Angkor Wat, in Cambodia, is not known but appears to have been somewhat less than one million. See Fletcher et al. (2015). In the United States, the city of St. Louis lost population at a rate

similar to Detroit's, but it never had one million residents, and it had less than half the population of Detroit in 1950.

15. Wilson (1987).

16. Mouw (2000).

17. Kids Count Data Center (2016).

18. United Nations Statistics Division (2014).

19. Save the Children (2015).

20. Edin and Nelson (2013).

21. Just from the demographer's sanitized, data-driven vantage point Detroit's collapse is excruciating enough. To get deeper you could read many books, including Sugrue (2014); Binelli (2014); and LeDuff (2014).

22. Krugman (2014). For Murray's response, see Murray (2016). The book in question is Herrnstein and Murray (1994).

23. Bonilla-Silva (2013).

24. See, for example, the essays in Katz (1992).

25. Wilson (1987, 60).

26. Huisenga (2011).

27. Volsky (2014).

28. Murray (2000).

29. Fremstad (2014).

30. Murray (2012).

31. Wilcox (2013).

32. Pethokoukis (2014).

33. US Census Bureau. (n.d.).

34. Author's transcript of the American Enterprise Institute panel, "Does Welfare Policy Discourage Marriage?" July 26, 2016.

35. US Department of Education (2014); Goff et al. (2014).

36. Cobb (2013).

37. Muskal and Hennessy-Fiske (2013); Buckley (2013). This segment of the closing argument is available at *George Zimmerman Trial* (2013).

38. US Census Bureau (1996, 222).

39. Data are from American National Election Study (2016). White women generally report feeling warmer toward Blacks than White men do, and White women are more progressive on antiracist policy issues, a finding attributable to their more liberal attitudes generally. See M. Taylor and Mateyka (2011); Maxwell (2015). A majority of White men (62 percent) and White women (56 percent) voted for Mitt Romney over Barack Obama in 2012; see NBC News (2012).

40. Cohen (2014b, 269).

41. Rudder (2014, 2009).

42. Cohen (1996).

43. The blog post was removed after public outcry. See Psychology Today (2011). The original post, Satoshi Kanazawa, "Why Are Black Women Less

Physically Attractive Than Other Women?," *The Scientific Fundamentalist*, May 15, 2011, is archived at https://web.archive.org/web/20110608130823/http://forums.somethingawful.com/showthread.php?threadid=3412493. The Add Health interviewers were 80 percent women and 65 percent White and had an average age of fifty years. See Richmond et al. (2012).

44. See Udry (2000).

45. Although they don't provide the breakdown by gender and race, Blacks are more likely than Whites to say that a steady job is very important in a partner (77 percent versus 59 percent). Wang and Parker (2014).

46. Lowrey (2014).

47. Cohen (2014b, 279).

48. Coates (2015).

49. More details and results from these projections are in Cohen (2015c).

50. Cohen (2015d).

51. I report the divorce rates in Cohen (2014b, 352). Marital happiness is from my tabulation of data from the 2010–14 General Social Survey.

52. Cohen (2016).

53. Hamilton et al. (2015).

8. FEMINISM AND SEXUALITY

1. For a different way of categorizing feminisms, and a more thorough introduction, I recommend Lorber's (2011) edited collection.

2. I describe the institutional arenas concept to structure my textbook (Cohen 2014b).

3. Presidential Gender Watch (n.d.).

4. In the same vein, the majority of Whites voted against Obama in 2008. These results are based on exit polls. See CNN.com (1996, 2008); NBC News (2012).

5. Mundy (2012b).

6. Rosin (2012b).

7. Cohen and Bianchi (1999); Cohen and Huffman (2003); Huffman, Cohen, and Pearlman (2010); Geist and Cohen (2011); Read and Cohen (2007).

8. Folbre (2012).

9. Inter-Parliamentary Union (2016).

10. Gooding and Kreider (2010).

11. Powell et al. (2012).

12. Scheuble, Johnson, and Johnson (2011).

13. Folbre (2010).

14. Ehrenreich (1976).

15. Coale and Banister (1996); Mackie (1996).

16. Hvistendahl (2011).

17. Lachmann (2014).

18. For the video, see *The Economics of Sex* (2012). For the article version, see Regnerus (2012b). The journal *Society* is a hub for conservative intellectuals.

19. Hatfield, Forbes, and Rapson (2012).

20. P. England (2012).

21. Baumeister and Vohs (2004, 253).

22. Baumeister and Mendoza (2011, 351).

23. Baumeister and Mendoza (2011, 352).

24. For a similar argument about Baumeister, see Marcotte (2011).

25. Baumeister and Vohs (2012) .

26. Baumeister and Vohs (2012, all quotes from 522).

27. Baumeister and Vohs (2012, 523).

28. Baumeister and Vohs (2012, 523).

29. Waring (2012).

30. Regnerus (2014).

31. I expanded on this in Cohen (2015a).

32. American Enterprise Institute (2014).

33. The statistic Obama gave is from the 2010 National Intimate Partner and Sexual Violence Survey; the executive summary is available at www.cdc.gov /violenceprevention/pdf/NISVS_Executive_Summary-a.pdf.

34. Special tabulation by National Center for Health Statistics, reported at www.cdc.gov/nchs/nsfg/key_statistics/f.htm.

35. MacKinnon (1988, 85).

36. MacKinnon (1988, 87).

37. I was fortunate to have the research assistance of Lucia Lykke for this essay. The discussion referenced here was in response to a post on the *Scatterplot* blog by Tina Fetner (2013). For a much more complete discussion of gender data collection schemes, including the one I describe here, see GenIUSS Group (2014).

38. Beauvoir (1953, xix).

39. Butler (1986, 35).

40. West and Zimmerman (1987).

41. MacKinnon (1989, xiii).

42. Fujimura (2006, 76).

43. Goffman (1977, 316).

44. Paglia (2015).

45. Hymowitz (2013).

46. Wolf (2015).

47. Cameron (2015).

48. Shepherd (2015).

49. NPR Staff (2015).

50. Bennett (2015).

51. Levy (2009). I first wrote about Semenya in Cohen (2010c).
52. Heggie (2010).
53. Gladwell and Thompson (2016).
54. Jordan-Young and Karkazis (2012).
55. MacKinnon (1988, 34).
56. MacKinnon (1988, 36).

References

ABC News. 2013. "This Week: Bill Clinton on CGI." September 29.

Acker, Joan. 1991. *Doing Comparable Worth: Gender, Class, and Pay Equity.* Philadelphia: Temple University Press.

AEI/Brookings Working Group on Poverty and Opportunity. 2015. *Opportunity, Responsibility, and Security: A Consensus Plan for Reducing Poverty and Restoring the American Dream.* Washington, DC: American Enterprise Institute for Public Policy Research and the Brookings Institution.

Ahooja-Patel, Krishna. 2007. *Development Has a Woman's Face: Insights from within the U.N.* New Delhi: APH Publishing.

American College of Pediatricians. 2012. Brief of *Amicus Curiae*, Nos. 12–15388 and 12–15409. US Court of Appeals for the Ninth Circuit.

American Enterprise Institute. 2014. "Sexual Assault in America: Do We Know the True Numbers?" *Factual Feminist,* April 28. https://www.youtube.com/watch?v=lNsJ1DhqQ-s.

American National Election Study. 2016. "Pilot Study." www.electionstudies.org/studypages/anes_pilot_2016/anes_pilot_2016.htm.

American Psychological Association et al. 2012. Brief of *Amici Curiae.* Nos. 12–15388 and 12–15409 US Court of Appeals for the Ninth Circuit.

American Society for Aesthetic Plastic Surgery. 2016. "Cosmetic Surgery National Data Bank Statistics: 2015." https://www.surgery.org/sites/default/files/ASAPS-Stats2015.pdf.

American Sociological Association. 2012. Brief of Amicus Curiae. Nos. 12–144, 12–307. Supreme Court of the United States.

Anderson, Sarah E., and Robert C. Whitaker. 2010. "Household Routines and Obesity in US Preschool-Aged Children." *Pediatrics* 125 (3): 420–28.

Associated Press. 2012. "DC on Pace for Fewer than 100 Homicides in 2012." *Washington Examiner,* December 18.

———. 2015. *The Associated Press Stylebook 2015.* New York: Basic Books.

Auletta, Ken. 2014. "Why Jill Abramson Was Fired." *New Yorker,* May 14.

Bain, Read. 1954. "Making Normal People." *Marriage and Family Living* 16 (1): 27–31.

Bartlett, Tom. 2012. "Controversial Gay-Parenting Study Is Severely Flawed, Journal's Audit Finds." *Chronicle of Higher Education,* July 26.

Baumeister, Roy F., and Juan Pablo Mendoza. 2011. "Cultural Variations in the Sexual Marketplace: Gender Equality Correlates with More Sexual Activity." *Journal of Social Psychology* 151 (3): 350–60.

Baumeister, Roy F., and Kathleen D. Vohs. 2004. "Sexual Economics: Sex as Female Resource for Social Exchange in Heterosexual Interactions." *Personality and Social Psychology Review* 8 (4): 339–63.

———. 2012. "Sexual Economics, Culture, Men, and Modern Sexual Trends." *Society* 49 (6): 520–24.

Beauvoir, Simone de. 1953. *The Second Sex.* New York: Alfred A. Knopf.

Bennett, Jessica. 2015. "I'm Not Mad. That's Just My RBF." *New York Times,* August 1.

Biblarz, Timothy J., and Judith Stacey. 2010. "How Does the Gender of Parents Matter?" *Journal of Marriage and Family* 72 (1): 3–22.

Binelli, Mark. 2014. *The Last Days of Detroit: Motor Cars, Motown and the Collapse of an Industrial Giant.* New York: Vintage.

Blankenhorn, David, William Galston, Jonathan Rauch, and Barbara DaFoe Whitehead. 2015. "Can Gay Wedlock Break Political Gridlock?" *Washington Monthly,* May. http://washingtonmonthly.com/magazine/maraprmay-2015/can-gay-wedlock-break-political-gridlock/.

Blankenhorn, David, and Elizabeth Marquardt. 2012. "Amendment Goes Too Far." *Raleigh News Observer,* April 11.

Blow, Charles M. 2014. "On Spanking and Abuse." *New York Times,* September 17.

Board of Governors of the Federal Reserve System. 2014. "Survey of Consumer Finances." www.federalreserve.gov/econresdata/scf/scfindex.htm.

Bonilla-Silva, Eduardo. 2013. *Racism without Racists: Color-Blind Racism and the Persistence of Racial Inequality in America.* Lanham, MD: Rowman and Littlefield.

Brody, Jane E. 1983. "Sex in America: Conservative Attitudes Prevail." *New York Times,* October 4.

Bruenig, Matt. 2015a. "The Vulnerable Poor." *Demos*, August 25.

———. 2015b. "Why Ending Relationships Is Good." *Demos*, March 19.

Buckley, Cara. 2013. "6 Female Jurors Are Selected for Zimmerman Trial." *New York Times*, June 20.

Butler, Judith. 1986. "Sex and Gender in Simone de Beauvoir's *Second Sex*." *Yale French Studies* 72:35–49.

California Department of Education. 2014. "Student Poverty FRPM Data." www.cde.ca.gov/ds/sd/sd/filessp.asp.

California Department of Public Health. 2015. "Immunization Rates in Child Care and Schools." www.cdph.ca.gov/programs/immunize/pages /immunizationlevels.aspx.

Cameron, Debbie. 2015. "A Response to Naomi Wolf." Language: A Feminist Guide, July 26. https://debuk.wordpress. com/2015/07/26/a-response-to-naomi-wolf/.

Carey, Benedict. 2012. "Study Examines Effect of Having a Gay Parent." *New York Times*, June 11.

Casper, Lynne M., and Philip N. Cohen. 2000. "How Does POSSLQ Measure Up? Historical Estimates of Cohabitation." *Demography* 37 (2): 237–45.

Cheng, Simon, and Brian Powell. 2015. "Measurement, Methods, and Divergent Patterns: Reassessing the Effects of Same-Sex Parents." *Social Science Research* 52 (July): 615–26.

Childs, Jennifer Hunter, Rodney Terry, Nathan Jurgenson, Matthew Clifton, and George Higbie. 2010. *Iterative Cognitive Testing of the 2010 Race and Hispanic Origin Alternative Questionnaire Experiment Reinterview*. Study Series, Survey Methodology #2010–13. Washington, DC: US Census Bureau. https://www.census.gov/srd/papers/pdf/ssm2010-13.pdf.

Christopherson, Elizabeth A., Dan Briskie, and Marita Rohr Inglehart. 2009. "Objective, Subjective, and Self-Assessment of Preadolescent Orthodontic Treatment Need: A Function of Age, Gender, and Ethnic/Racial Background?" *Journal of Public Health Dentistry* 69 (1): 9–17.

Clinton, Bill. 2000. "Remarks by the President in Statement on Equal Pay Day." National Archives and Records Administration, January 24. http://clinton6 .nara.gov/2000/01/2000–01-24-remarks-by-the-president-in-statement-on-equal-pay.html.

CNN. 1996. "All Politics: Presidential Election Exit Poll Results." November 6. www.cnn.com/ALLPOLITICS/1996/elections/natl.exit.poll/index1.html.

———. 2008. "2008 Presidential Election Center—Results, Polls, Calendar." www.cnn.com/ELECTION/2008/results/polls/#USP00p1.

Coale, Ansley J., and Judith Banister. 1996. "Five Decades of Missing Females in China." *Proceedings of the American Philosophical Society* 140 (4): 421–50.

Coates, Ta-Nehisi. 2015. "The Black Family in the Age of Mass Incarceration." *Atlantic*, October.

Cobb, Jelani. 2013. "George Zimmerman, Not Guilty: Blood on the Leaves." *New Yorker*, July 13.

Cohen, Philip N. 1996. "Nationalism and Suffrage: Gender Struggle in Nation-Building America." *Signs* 21 (3): 707–27.

———. 1998a. "Black-White Differences in Predictors of Mortality among Older Americans: Evidence from the Longitudinal Study of Aging." Paper presented at the annual meeting of the Population Association of America, Chicago, April 2–4.

———. 1998b. "Replacing Housework in the Service Economy: Gender, Class, and Race-Ethnicity in Service Spending." *Gender and Society* 12 (2): 219–31.

———. 2010a. "The Bathroom Icon Has No Clothes." *Family Inequality*, March 30. https://familyinequality.wordpress.com/2010/03/30/the-bathroom-icon-has-no-clothes/.

———. 2010b. "Demographic Science and Gay Civil Rights." *Huffington Post*, March 18. www.huffingtonpost.com/philip-n-cohen/demographic-science-and-g_b_316760.html.

———. 2010c. "Returning to Caster Semenya's Return." *Family Inequality*, July 9.https://familyinequality.wordpress.com/2010/07/09/returning-to-semenyas-return/.

———. 2011. "Follow the Bouncing 1% Meme. . . ." *Family Inequality*, September 21. https://familyinequality.wordpress.com/2011/09/20/follow-the-bouncing-1-meme/.

———. 2012. "Single Moms Can't Be Scapegoated for the Murder Rate Anymore." *Atlantic*, November 26.

———. 2013a. "Children's Gender and Parents' Color Preferences." *Archives of Sexual Behavior* 42 (3): 393–97.

———. 2013b. "Correct That Error, Hanna Rosin Edition." *Family Inequality*, September 12. https://familyinequality.wordpress.com/2013/09/12/correct-that-error-hanna-rosin-edition/.

———. 2013c. "The 'End of Men' Is Not True: What Is Not and What Might Be on the Road toward Gender Equality." *Boston University Law Review* 93 (3): 1159–84.

———. 2013d. "Gender Devaluation, in One Comparison." *Family Inequality*, December 5. https://familyinequality.wordpress.com/2013/12/05/gender-devaluation/.

———. 2013e. "'Help, My Eyeball Is Bigger Than My Wrist!': Gender Dimorphism in *Frozen*." *Sociological Images*, December 17. https://thesocietypages.org/socimages/2013/12/17/help-my-eyeball-is-bigger-than-my-wrist-gender-dimorphism-in-frozen.

———. 2013f. "Jump-Starting the Struggle for Equality." *New York Times*, November 24, SR9.

———. 2013g. "Marriage Is Declining Globally: Can You Say That?" *Family Inequality*, June 12. https://familyinequality.wordpress.com/2013/06/12 /marriage-is-declining/.

———. 2013h. "'More Managerial Than Intellectual': How Right-Wing Christian Money Brought Us the Regnerus Study." *Family Inequality*, March 11. https://familyinequality.wordpress.com/2013/03/11/more-managerial-than-intellectual/.

———. 2013i. "Paul Amato on Reviewing Regnerus." *Family Inequality*, July 20. https://familyinequality.wordpress.com/2013/07/20/paul-amato-on-reviewing-regnerus/.

———. 2013j. "The Persistence of Workplace Gender Segregation in the US." *Sociology Compass* 7 (11): 889–99.

———. 2013k. "Still a Man's World: The Myth of Female Ascendance." *Boston Review* 38 (1): 54–58.

———. 2014a. "The Blogger Will Be Heard, Michigan Trial Edition." *Family Inequality*, March 14. https://familyinequality.wordpress.com/2014/03/14 /the-blogger-will-be-heard/.

———. 2014b. *The Family: Diversity, Inequality, and Social Change*. New York: W. W. Norton.

———. 2014c. "People Who Believe in Hell Are Allowed to Raise Children?" *Family Inequality*, March 7. https://familyinequality.wordpress.com/2014 /03/07/people-who-believe-in-hell/.

———. 2015a. "How Random Error and Dirty Data Made Regnerus Even Wronger Than We Thought." *Family Inequality*, April 30. https://familyinequality.wordpress.com/2015/04/30/how-random-error-and-dirty-data-made-regnerus-even-wronger-than-we-thought/.

———. 2015b. "How Troubling Is Our Inheritance? A Review of Genetics and Race in the Social Sciences." *Annals of the American Academy of Political and Social Science* 661 (1): 65–84.

———. 2015c. "Lifetime Chance of Marrying for Black and White Women." *Family Inequality*, September 15. https://familyinequality.wordpress. com/2015/09/15/lifetime-chance-of-marrying-for-black-and-white-women/.

———. 2015d. "Who's Your Marriage Market?" *Family Inequality*, April 2. https:// familyinequality.wordpress.com/2015/04/02/whos-your-marriage-market/.

———. 2016. "Maternal Age and Infant Mortality for White, Black, and Mexican Mothers in the United States." *Sociological Science* 3:32–38.

Cohen, Philip N., and Suzanne M. Bianchi. 1999. "Marriage, Children, and Women's Employment: What Do We Know?" *Monthly Labor Review* 122 (12): 22–31.

Cohen, Philip N., and Matt L. Huffman. 2003. "Individuals, Jobs, and Labor Markets: The Devaluation of Women's Work." *American Sociological Review* 68 (3): 443–63. doi:10.2307/1519732.

———. 2007. "Working for the Woman? Female Managers and the Gender Wage Gap." *American Sociological Review* 72 (5): 681–704.

Connellan, Jennifer, Simon Baron-Cohen, Sally Wheelwright, Anna Batki, and Jag Ahluwalia. 2000. "Sex Differences in Human Neonatal Social Perception." *Infant Behavior and Development* 23 (1): 113–18.

Constitution Facts. N.d. "The Women behind the Signers." www.constitutionfacts .com/us-constitution-amendments/women-behind-the-signers/.

Coontz, Stephanie. 2006. *Marriage, a History: How Love Conquered Marriage.* New York: Penguin Books.

Cott, Nancy F. 2002. *Public Vows: A History of Marriage and the Nation.* Cambridge, MA: Harvard University Press.

Cotter, David A., Joan M. Hermsen, and Reeve Vanneman. 2001. "Women's Work and Working Women: The Demand for Female Labor." *Gender and Society* 15 (3): 429–52.

———. 2011. "The End of the Gender Revolution? Gender Role Attitudes from 1977 to 2008." *American Journal of Sociology* 117 (1): 259–89.

Covert, Bryce. 2016. "How Jeb Bush Plans to Destroy Anti-poverty Programs." *ThinkProgress*, January 8. https://thinkprogress.org/ how-jeb-bush-plans-to-destroy-anti-poverty-programs-15bd8fbf1bdf.

Credit Suisse AG. 2014. "Credit Suisse: Global Household Wealth Increases by 8.3% to USD 263 Trillion, Driven by Wealth Growth in the United States and Europe." PR Newswire, October 14.

Deli, Roberto, Ludovica A. Macrì, Paola Radico, Francesca Pantanali, Domenico L. Grieco, Maria R. Gualano, and Giuseppe La Torre. 2012. "Orthodontic Treatment Attitude versus Orthodontic Treatment Need: Differences by Gender, Age, Socioeconomical Status and Geographical Context." *Community Dentistry and Oral Epidemiology* 40 Suppl. 1 (February): 71–76.

Demuth, Stephen, and Susan L. Brown. 2004. "Family Structure, Family Processes, and Adolescent Delinquency: The Significance of Parental Absence versus Parental Gender." *Journal of Research in Crime and Delinquency* 41 (1): 58–81.

Deneen, Patrick. 2015. "After Obergefell: A *First Things* Symposium." *First Things*, June 27. www.firstthings.com/web-exclusives/2015/06/after-obergefell-a-first-things-symposium.

Devaney, Barbara, and Robin Dion. 2010. *15-Month Impacts of Oklahoma's Family Expectations Program.* Princeton, NJ: Mathematica Policy Research.

Domhoff, G. William. 2009. *Who Rules America? Challenges to Corporate and Class Dominance.* Boston: McGraw-Hill.

Doss, Cheryl, Chiara Kovarik, Amber Peterman, Agnes R. Quisumbing, and Mara van den Bold. 2013. "Gender Inequalities in Ownership and Control of Land in Africa: Myths versus Reality." IFPRI Discussion Paper 1308.

International Food Policy Research Institute, Washington, DC. www.opening-economics.com/wp-content/uploads/2014/06/16–17juin-ose-gender-inequalities-africa.pdf.

Dyson, Michael Eric. 2014. "Punishment or Child Abuse?" *New York Times,* September 17.

Eckholm, Erik. 2014a. "Federal Judge Strikes Down Michigan's Ban on Same-Sex Marriage." *New York Times,* March 21.

——. 2014b. "Opponents of Same-Sex Marriage Take Bad-for-Children Argument to Court." *New York Times,* February 22.

The Economics of Sex. 2014. YouTube, uploaded February 14. www.youtube.com/watch?v=cO1ifNaNABY.

Edin, Kathryn, and Timothy J. Nelson. 2013. *Doing the Best I Can: Fatherhood in the Inner City.* Berkeley: University of California Press.

Ehrenreich, Barbara. 1976. "What Is Socialist Feminism?" *Win,* June 3.

Ellis, Lee, and Christopher Ficek. 2001. "Color Preferences according to Gender and Sexual Orientation." *Personality and Individual Differences* 31 (8): 1375–79.

England, Dawn Elizabeth, Lara Descartes, and Melissa A. Collier-Meek. 2011. "Gender Role Portrayal and the Disney Princesses." *Sex Roles* 64 (7–8): 555–67.

England, Paula. 1992. *Comparable Worth: Theories and Evidence.* New Brunswick, NJ: Transaction.

——. 2012. "Has the Surplus of Women over Men Driven the Increase in Premarital and Casual Sex among American Young Adults?" *Society* 49 (6): 512–14.

Fenelon, Andrew. 2013. "An Examination of Black/White Differences in the Rate of Age-Related Mortality Increase." *Demographic Research* 29 (September): 441–72.

Ferguson, Andrew. 2012. "Revenge of the Sociologists." *Weekly Standard,* July 30.

Ferguson, Christopher J. 2013. "Spanking, Corporal Punishment and Negative Long-Term Outcomes: A Meta-analytic Review of Longitudinal Studies." *Clinical Psychology Review* 33 (1): 196–208.

Fetner, Tina. 2013. "What Should ASA's Gender Categories Be?" *Scatterplot,* August 22.

Fine, Cordelia. 2011. *Delusions of Gender: How Our Minds, Society, and Neurosexism Create Difference.* New York: W. W. Norton.

Flaherty, Colleen. 2013. "Quick Takes: Controversy Continues over Gay Parenting Study." *Inside Higher Ed,* August 2.

Fletcher, Roland, Damian Evans, Christophe Pottier, and Chhay Rachna. 2015. "Special Section: New Discoveries at Angkor Wat, Angkor." *Antiquity* 89 (348): 1388–1401.

Folbre, Nancy. 2010. *Valuing Children: Rethinking the Economics of the Family*. Cambridge, MA: Harvard University Press.

———. 2012. "Patriarchal Norms Still Shape Family Care." *New York Times Economix Blog*, September 17.

Food and Agriculture Organization of the United Nations. 2016. *Statistical Yearbook 2016*. Rome: FAO Publications.

Forbes. 2016. "The World's Billionaires: 2016 Ranking." *Forbes*, March 21.

Frassanito, Paolo, and Benedetta Pettorini. 2008. "Pink and Blue: The Color of Gender." *Child's Nervous System* 24 (8): 881–82.

Fremstad, Shawn. 2014. "Will Paul Ryan Go for the Full Murray by Taking on White Working-Class 'Culture'?" *Center for Economic and Policy Research Blog*, March 13. http://cepr.net/blogs/cepr-blog/will-paul-ryan-go-for-the-full-murray-by-taking-on-white-working-class-qcultureq.

Fremstad, Shawn, and Melissa Boteach. 2015. "Valuing All Our Families: Progressive Policies That Strengthen Family Commitments and Reduce Family Disparities." Center for American Progress, January 12. https://www.americanprogress.org/issues/poverty/reports/2015/01/12/104149/valuing-all-our-families/.

Friedman, Ann. 2014. "Journalism's Hiring Transparency Problem." *Columbia Journalism Review*, April 24.

Friedman, Bernard A. 2014. "Findings of Fact and Conclusions of Law." DeBoer v. Snyder, March 21, 2014.

Friess, Steve. 2014. "Star Witness to Defend Ban on Gay Marriage Takes the Stand in Detroit." *Aljazeera America*, March 4.

Fryar, C. D., Q Gu, and C. L. Ogden. 2012. "Anthropometric Reference Data for Children and Adults: United States, 2007–2010." National Center for Health Statistics, *Vital Health Statistics* 11 (252).

Fujimura, Joan H. 2006. "Sex Genes: A Critical Sociomaterial Approach to the Politics and Molecular Genetics of Sex Determination." *Signs* 32 (1): 49–82.

Furchtgott-Roth, Diana. 2000. "Still Hyping the Phony Pay Gap." AEI Online, January 31. American Enterprise Institute.

Gallagher, Maggie. 2013. "Will We Bridge the Gender Divide?" Official website of Maggie Gallagher, February 25.

Gates, Gary J. 2012. "Letter to the Editors and Advisory Editors of Social Science Research." *Social Science Research* 41 (6): 1350–51.

Geist, Claudia, and Philip N. Cohen. 2011. "Headed toward Equality? Housework Change in Comparative Perspective." *Journal of Marriage and Family* 73 (4): 832–44. doi:10.1111/j.1741-3737.2011.00850.x.

GenIUSS Group. 2014. *Best Practices for Asking Questions to Identify Transgender and Other Gender Minority Respondents on Population-Based Surveys*. Edited by J. L. Herman. Los Angeles: Williams Institute.

George Zimmerman Trial—Defense Closing Arguments—Part 2—July 12, 2013. 2013. YouTube, uploaded July 12. https://www.youtube.com/watch?v= FCEs2fFB17s.

Gladwell, Malcolm, and Nicholas Thompson. 2016. "Caster Semenya and the Logic of Olympic Competition." *New Yorker,* August 12.

Glenn, Evelyn Nakano. 2011. "Constructing Citizenship: Exclusion, Subordination, and Resistance." *American Sociological Review* 76 (1): 1–24.

Goff, Phillip Atiba, Matthew Christian Jackson, Brooke Allison Lewis Di Leone, Carmen Marie Culotta, and Natalie Ann DiTomasso. 2014. "The Essence of Innocence: Consequences of Dehumanizing Black Children." *Journal of Personality and Social Psychology* 106 (4): 526–45.

Goffman, Erving. 1977. "The Arrangement between the Sexes." *Theory and Society* 4 (3): 301–31.

Gooding, Gretchen E., and Rose M. Kreider. 2010. "Women's Marital Naming Choices in a Nationally Representative Sample." *Journal of Family Issues* 31, no. 5 (September): 681–701.

Gordon, Claire C., Thomas Churchill, Charles E. Clauser, Bruce Bradtmiller, John T. McConville, Ilse Tebbetts, and Robert A. Walker. 1988. "Anthropometric Survey of U.S. Army Personnel: Summary Statistics, Interim Report for 1988." Accession No. ADA209600. www.dtic.mil/dtic/tr/fulltext/u2/a209600.pdf.

Gordon, Michael, Mark S. Price, and Katie Peralta. 2016. "Understanding HB2: North Carolina's Newest Law Solidifies State's Role in Defining Discrimination." *Charlotte Observer,* March 26.

Graham, Ruth. 2015. "They Do: The Scholarly About-Face on Marriage." *Boston Globe,* April 26.

Greenberg, Jon. 2014. "Do Women Own 1% of the World's Land? No." *Politifact,* August 5.

Guerino, Paul, Paige M. Harrison, and William J. Sabol. 2011. *Prisoners in 2010.* Bureau of Justice Statistics Bulletin, December. NCJ 236096. Washington, DC: Bureau of Justice Statistics.

Guilmoto, Christophe Z. 2011. "Skewed Sex Ratios at Birth and Future Marriage Squeeze in China and India, 2005–2100." *Demography* 49 (1): 77–100.

Hamilton, Brady E., Joyce A. Martin, Michelle J. K. Osterman, Sally C. Curtin, and T. J. Mathews. 2015. Births: Final Data for 2014." *National Vital Statistics Reports* 64 (12): 1–64.

Hanstad, Tim. 2009. "Access to Land Improves Women's Lives around the World." *Seattle Times,* March 10.

Haskins, Ron. 2013. "The War on Poverty: What Went Wrong?" Brookings Institution, November 19. www.brookings.edu/research/opinions/2013/11 /19-war-on-poverty-what-went-wrong-haskins.

Hatfield, Elaine, Megan Forbes, and Richard L. Rapson. 2012. "Marketing Love and Sex." *Society* 49 (6): 506–11.

Hawkins, Alan J. 2015. "Who's Being Served by Government-Funded Relationship Education Programs?" Institute for Family Studies, July 7. http://family-studies.org/whos-being-served-by-government-funded-relationship-education-programs/.

Hawkins, Alan J., Paul R. Amato, and Andrea Kinghorn. 2013. "Are Government-Supported Healthy Marriage Initiatives Affecting Family Demographics? A State-Level Analysis." *Family Relations* 62 (3): 501–13. doi:10.1111/fare.12009.

Healy, Kieran. 2015. "Another Look at the California Vaccination Data." February 3. https://kieranhealy.org/blog/archives/2015/02/03/another-look-at-the-california-vaccination-data/.

———. 2017. "Fuck Nuance." *Sociological Theory* 35(2): 118–127.

Heath, Melanie. 2012. *One Marriage under God: The Campaign to Promote Marriage in America*. New York: NYU Press.

Heggie, Vanessa. 2010. "Testing Sex and Gender in Sports: Reinventing, Reimagining and Reconstructing Histories." *Endeavour* 34 (4): 157–63.

Herrnstein, Richard J., and Charles Murray. 1994. *The Bell Curve: Intelligence and Class Structure in American Life*. New York: Free Press.

Hoover Institution. 1996. "Can Government Save the Family?" *Policy Review*, September/October.

Huffman, Matt L., Philip N. Cohen, and Jessica Pearlman. 2010. "Engendering Change: Organizational Dynamics and Workplace Gender Desegregation, 1975–2005." *Administrative Science Quarterly* 55 (2): 255–77.

Huisenga, Sarah. 2011. "Newt Gingrich: Poor Kids Don't Work 'Unless It's Illegal.'" CBS News, December 1.

Hunn, David, and Kim Bell. 2014. "Why Was Michael Brown's Body Left There for Hours?" *St. Louis Post Dispatch*, September 14.

Hvistendahl, Mara. 2011. *Unnatural Selection: Choosing Boys over Girls, and the Consequences of a World Full of Men*. New York: PublicAffairs.

Hymowitz, Kay. 2011. "Why the Gender Gap Won't Go Away. Ever." *City Journal*, Summer.

———. 2012. "The Real, Complex Connection between Single-Parent Families and Crime." *Atlantic*, December 3.

———. 2013. "Do Women Really Want Equality?" *Time*, September 4.

Ingram, Jason R., Justin W. Patchin, Beth M. Huebner, John D. McCluskey, and Timothy S. Bynum. 2007. "Parents, Friends, and Serious Delinquency: An Examination of Direct and Indirect Effects among At-Risk Early Adolescents." *Criminal Justice Review* 32 (4): 380–400.

Institute for American Values. 2000. "The Marriage Movement: A Statement of Principles." New York. http://americanvalues.org/catalog/pdfs/marriagemovement.pdf.

———. 2013. "A Call for a New Conversation on Marriage." New York. http://americanvalues.org/catalog/pdfs/2013-01.pdf.

Institute for Women's Policy Research. 2015. "Pay Equity and Discrimination." www.iwpr.org/initiatives/pay-equity-and-discrimination.

International Labour Office. 1978. *Women at Work.* No. 1. Geneva: ILO.

Inter-Parliamentary Union. 2016. "Women in National Parliaments." www.ipu.org/wmn-e/classif.htm.

Irwin, Sarah. 2009. "Locating Where the Action Is: Quantitative and Qualitative Lenses on Families, Schooling and Structures of Social Inequality." *Sociology* 43 (6): 1123–40.

Jackson, Robert Max. 1998. *Destined for Equality: The Inevitable Rise of Women's Status.* Cambridge, MA: Harvard University Press.

Jacobsen, Louis. 2014. "Marco Rubio Says Marriage 'Decreases the Probability of Child Poverty by 82 Percent.'" *PolitiFact,* January 9.

Johnson, Bryon, et al. 2012. "A Social Scientific Response to the Regnerus Controversy." June 20. www.baylorisr.org/2012/06/20/a-social-scientific-response-to-the-regnerus-controversy/.

John Templeton Foundation. N.d. "Thrift and American Culture: Exploring the Science and Practice of Thrift." https://web.archive.org/web/20160730210251/https://www.templeton.org/what-we-fund/grants/thrift-and-american-culture-exploring-the-science-and-practice-of-thrift.

Jones, Jeffrey M. 2013. "U.S. Blacks, Hispanics Have No Preferences on Group Labels." Gallup, July 26. www.gallup.com/poll/163706/blacks-hispanics-no-preferences-group-labels.aspx.

Jordan-Young, Rebecca, and Katrina Karkazis. 2012. "Olympic Sex Verification: You Say You're a Woman? That Should Be Enough." *New York Times,* June 17. www.nytimes.com/2012/06/18/sports/olympics/olympic-sex-verification-you-say-youre-a-woman-that-should-be-enough.html.

Kaiser, Jocelyn. 2014. "NIH Cancels Massive U.S. Children's Study." *Science Insider,* December 12. www.sciencemag.org/news/2014/12/nih-cancels-massive-us-children-s-study.

Kaplan, Eric. 2014. "Should We Believe in Santa Claus?" *New York Times Opinionator,* December 20.

Katz, Michael B., ed. 1992. *The "Underclass" Debate.* Princeton, NJ: Princeton University Press.

Kearney, Melissa S., and Phillip B. Levine. 2015. "Media Influences on Social Outcomes: The Impact of MTV's *16 and Pregnant* on Teen Childbearing." *American Economic Review* 105 (12): 3597–3632. doi:10.1257/aer.20140012.

Kessler, Glenn. 2015. "The Zombie Statistic about Women's Share of Income and Property." *Washington Post,* March 3.

Kids Count Data Center. 2016. "Infant Mortality." Annie E. Casey Foundation. http://datacenter.kidscount.org/data/tables/6051-infant-mortality#detailed /3/58,102/false/869,36,868,867,133/any/12718,12719.

Kim, Christine. 2013. "Marriage Combats Child Poverty." Spotlight on Poverty and Opportunity, December 6. https://web.archive.org/web/20131208191836 /http://www.spotlightonpoverty.org/ExclusiveCommentary.aspx?id=93e821a0– 46b1–4562-b499-e8646300e8bf.

Kohn, Alfie. 2014. *The Myth of the Spoiled Child: Challenging the Conventional Wisdom about Children and Parenting.* N.p.: Da Capo Press.

Konigsberg, Ruth Davis. 2013. "The Pay Gap Is Not as Bad as You (and Sheryl Sandberg) Think." *Time,* March 7.

Kristof, Nicholas. 2016. "Compassionate Conservatives, Hello?" *New York Times,* January 28.

Krugman, Paul. 2014. "That Old-Time Whistle." *New York Times,* March 16.

Lachmann, Suzanne. 2014. "Sex on the First Date? Don't Feel Ashamed." *Psychology Today,* January 29.

Lareau, Annette. 2011. *Unequal Childhoods: Class, Race, and Family Life, 2nd Edition with an Update a Decade Later.* Berkeley: University of California Press.

LeDuff, Charlie. 2014. *Detroit: An American Autopsy.* New York: Penguin.

Legislative Office on the Economic Status of Women. 2016. "Pay Equity: The Minnesota Experience (6th Edition)." www.oesw.leg.mn/PDFdocs/Pay_ Equity_Report2016.pdf.

Lerman, Robert I., and W. Bradford Wilcox. 2014. "For Richer, for Poorer: How Family Structures Economic Success in America." American Enterprise Institute. www.aei.org/wp-content/uploads/2014/10/IFS-ForRicherForPoorer-Final_Web.pdf.

Levanon, Asaf, Paula England, and Paul Allison. 2009. "Occupational Feminization and Pay: Assessing Causal Dynamics Using 1950–2000 U.S. Census Data." *Social Forces* 88 (2): 865–91.

Levy, Arial. 2009. "Either/Or." *New Yorker,* November 30.

Lieberson, Stanley. 2000. *A Matter of Taste: How Names, Fashions, and Culture Change.* New Haven, CT: Yale University Press.

Livingston, Gretchen. 2014. "Growing Number of Dads Home with the Kids." Pew Research Center's Social and Demographic Trends Project, June 5. www.pewsocialtrends.org/2014/06/05/growing-number-of-dads-home-with-the-kids/.

Loose, Cindy, and Pierre Thomas. 1994. "'Crisis of Violence' Becoming Menace to Childhood." *Washington Post,* January 2.

Lorber, Judith. 1994. *Paradoxes of Gender.* New Haven, CT: Yale University Press.

———. 2011. *Gender Inequality: Feminist Theories and Politics.* 5th ed. New York: Oxford University Press.

Lowrey, Annie. 2014. "Can Marriage Cure Poverty?" *New York Times,* February 4.

Lowry, Rich. 2006. "The Welfare-Reform Miracle." *National Review Online,* August 18. www.nationalreview.com/article/218505/welfare-reform-miracle-rich-lowry.

Lundquist, Erika, Hsueh, JoAnn, Amy E. Lowenstein, Kristen Faucetta, Daniel Gubits, Charles Michalopoulos, and Virgina Knox. 2014. "A Family Strengthening Program for Low-Income Families: Final Impacts from the Supporting Healthy Marriage Evaluation." Department of Health and Human Services, Office of Planning, Research and Evaluation. www.mdrc.org/sites/default/files/SHM2013_30-Month%20Impact%20ES.pdf.

Luscombe, Belinda. 2012. "Do Children of Same-Sex Parents Really Fare Worse?" *Time,* June 11.

———. 2014. "The Real Problem with Women as the Family Breadwinner." *Time,* May 5.

Mack, Jessica. 2012. "Women Losing Land Rights in China." *Ms. Magazine Blog,* March 8. http://msmagazine.com/blog/2012/03/08/women-losing-land-rights-in-china/.

Mackie, Gerry. 1996. "Ending Footbinding and Infibulation: A Convention Account." *American Sociological Review* 61 (6): 999–1017.

MacKinnon, Catharine A. 1982. "Feminism, Marxism, Method, and the State: An Agenda for Theory." *Signs* 7 (3): 515–44.

———. 1988. *Feminism Unmodified: Discourses on Life and Law.* Cambridge, MA: Harvard University Press.

———. 1989. *Toward a Feminist Theory of the State.* Cambridge, MA: Harvard University Press.

Marcotte, Amanda. 2011. "Do Women Like Sex?" *Slate,* August 10.

Marquardt, Elizabeth. 2009. "Is 'Marriage' Subject to Compromise?" *New York Times,* February 24.

Marriage Opportunity Council. 2015. "Marriage Opportunity: The Moment for National Action." Institute for American Values. New York. http://americanvalues.org/catalog/pdfs/Marriage-Opportunity.pdf.

Martin, Joyce A., et al. 2017. "Births: Final Data for 2015." *National Vital Statistics Reports* 66 (1).

Maxwell, Angie. 2015. "Untangling the Gender Gap in Symbolic Racist Attitudes among White Americans." *Politics, Groups, and Identities* 3 (1): 59–72.

McClure, E. B. 2000. "A Meta-analytic Review of Sex Differences in Facial Expression Processing and Their Development in Infants, Children, and Adolescents." *Psychological Bulletin* 126 (3): 424–53.

McNulty, Thomas L., and Paul E. Bellair. 2003. "Explaining Racial and Ethnic Differences in Serious Adolescent Violent Behavior." *Criminology* 41 (3): 709–47.

Mead, Margaret. 1932. "An Investigation of the Thought of Primitive Children, with Special Reference to Animism." *Journal of the Royal Anthropological Institute of Great Britain and Ireland* 62:173–90.

Meinch, Timothy. 2016. "Carson Asks Fifth-Graders 'Who's the Worst Student?'." *Des Moines Register*, January 7.

Meyer, Robinson. 2015. "Apple's Cash Reserves Would Fill 93 Olympic Swimming Pools." *Atlantic*, September 9.

Morgan, Robin. 1984. *Sisterhood Is Global: The International Women's Movement Anthology.* New York: Feminist Press at CUNY.

Morgan, Thomas J. 1886. "What Is the True Function of a Normal School?" *Education* 6:1–18.

Mouw, Ted. 2000. "Job Relocation and the Racial Gap in Unemployment in Detroit and Chicago, 1980 to 1990." *American Sociological Review* 65 (5): 730–53.

Mumola, Christopher J., and Jennifer C. Karberg. 2006. *Drug Use and Dependence, State and Federal Prisoners, 2004.* NCJ 213530. Bureau of Justice Statistics Special Report. Washington, DC: Bureau of Justice Statistics.

Mundy, Liza. 2012a. *The Richer Sex: How the New Majority of Female Breadwinners Is Transforming Sex, Love and Family.* New York: Simon and Schuster.

———. 2012b. "Why Do Some Feminists Get Uneasy When Women Make Progress?" *Atlantic*, November 13.

Murray, Charles. 2000. "Deeper into the Brain." *National Review,* January 24.

———. 2012. *Coming Apart: The State of White America, 1960–2010.* New York: Crown Forum.

———. 2016. "Charles Murray on Allegations of Racism." American Enterprise Institute, March 17. https://www.aei.org/publication/charles-murray-on-allegations-of-racism/.

Muskal, Michael, and Molly Hennessy-Fiske. 2013. "Defense, Prosecution Conclude Arguments in Zimmerman Murder Trial." *Los Angeles Times,* July 12.

National Marriage Project. 2012. "The President's Marriage Agenda." The State of Our Unions: Marriage in America 2012. www.stateofourunions.org/2012/SOOU2012.pdf.

NBC News. 2012. "Presidential Election Results." http://elections.nbcnews.com/ns/politics/2012/all/president.

New York City Commission on Human Rights. N.d. "Pregnancy and Employment Rights Poster." www.nyc.gov/html/cchr/html/publications/pregnancy-employment-poster.shtml.

NPR Staff. 2015. "Narcissistic, Maybe. But Is There More to the Art of the Selfie?" *All Tech Considered,* June 27, NPR.

Office of Management and Budget. 1997. "Revisions to the Standards for the Classification of Federal Data on Race and Ethnicity." *Federal Register*

Notice, October 30. https://obamawhitehouse.archives.gov/omb/fedreg_
1997standards.

Orenstein, Peggy. 2012. *Cinderella Ate My Daughter: Dispatches from the Front Lines of the New Girlie-Girl Culture.* New York: Harper Paperbacks.

Ortega, José Antonio. 2014. "A Characterization of World Union Patterns at the National and Regional Level." *Population Research and Policy Review* 33 (2): 161–88.

Paglia, Camille. 2015. "Camille Paglia: How Bill Clinton Is Like Bill Cosby." Interview by David Daley. *Salon*, July 28. www.salon.com/2015/07/28/camille_paglia_how_bill_clinton_is_like_bill_cosby/.

Paoletti, Jo B. 2012. *Pink and Blue: Telling the Boys from the Girls in America.* Bloomington: Indiana University Press.

———. 2015. *Sex and Unisex: Fashion, Feminism, and the Sexual Revolution.* Bloomington: Indiana University Press.

Parker, Asha. 2016. "Black Women Are Now the Most Educated Group in the United States." *Salon*, June 2.

Pascoe, C. J. 2012. "How Not to Study Families." *Social (In)Queery*, June 20. https://socialinqueery.com/2012/06/19/how-not-to-study-families/.

Perkins, Lucy. 2015. "California Governor Signs School Vaccination Law." NPR.org, June 30. www.npr.org/sections/thetwo-way/2015/06/30/418908804/california-governor-signs-school-vaccination-law.

Perrin, Andrew J. 2012. "Bad Science Not about Same-Sex Parenting." *Scatterplot*, June 23. https://scatter.wordpress.com/2012/06/23/bad-science-not-about-same-sex-parenting/.

Perrin, Andrew J., Philip N. Cohen, and Neal Caren. 2013. "Are Children of Parents Who Had Same-Sex Relationships Disadvantaged? A Scientific Evaluation of the No-Differences Hypothesis." *Journal of Gay and Lesbian Mental Health* 17 (3): 327–36.

Peter, Josh. 2014. "Whippings Part of Adrian Peterson's Childhood." *USA Today*, November 18.

Pethokoukis, James. 2014. "Can Anything Really Be Done about Family Breakdown and American Poverty? A Q&A with Brad Wilcox." *AEI Ideas*, March 11.

Pew Research Center. 2014. "Most Say Religious Holiday Displays on Public Property Are OK." Religion and Public Life Project, December 15.

Pierce, Charles P. 2014. "The Body in the Street." *Esquire*, August 22.

Pinto, Laura. 2016. "Elf et Michelf." *YouTube.* https://www.youtube.com/watch?v=s9Pn16dCWIg.

Pollitt, Katha. 1991. "Hers: The Smurfette Principle." *New York Times Magazine*, April 7.

Powell, Brian, Catherine Blozendahl, Claudia Geist, and Lala Carr Steelman. 2012. *Counted Out: Same-Sex Relations and Americans' Definitions of Family.* New York: Russell Sage Foundation.

Presidential Gender Watch. N.d. "Presidential Polling Data." Accessed July 28, 2016. http://presidentialgenderwatch.org/polls/womens-vote-watch/presidential-polling-data.

Proctor, Bernadette D., Jessica L. Semega, and Melissas A. Kollar. 2016. *Income and Poverty in the United States: 2015.* P60–256. Washington, DC: US Census Bureau.

Psychology Today. 2011. "An Apology from *Psychology Today.*" *Psychology Today,* May 27.

Rastogi, Sonya, Tallese D. Johnson, Elizabeth M. Hoeffel, and Malcolm P. Drewery. 2011. *The Black Population: 2010.* C2010BR-06. 2010 Census Briefs. Washington, DC: US Census Bureau.

Read, Jen'nan Ghazal, and Philip N. Cohen. 2007. "One Size Fits All? Explaining US-Born and Immigrant Women's Employment across 12 Ethnic Groups." *Social Forces* 85 (4): 1713–34.

Rector, Robert. 2012a. "Examining the Means-Tested Welfare State: 79 Programs and $927 Billion in Annual Spending." Heritage Foundation, May 3.http://origin.heritage.org/research/testimony/2012/05/examining-the-means-tested-welfare-state.

———. 2012b. "Marriage: America's Greatest Weapon against Child Poverty." Heritage Foundation, September 5. www.heritage.org/poverty-and-inequality/report/marriage-americas-greatest-weapon-against-child-poverty.

Rector, Robert, and Melissa G. Pardue. 2004. "Understanding the President's Healthy Marriage Initiative." Heritage Foundation, March 6. www.heritage.org/research/reports/2004/03/understanding-the-presidents-healthy-marriage-initiative.

Reeves, Richard V. 2013. "Shame Is Not a Four-Letter Word." *New York Times,* March 15.

Regnerus, Mark. 2012a. "How Different Are the Adult Children of Parents Who Have Same-Sex Relationships? Findings from the New Family Structures Study." *Social Science Research* 41 (4): 752–70.

———. 2012b. "Mating Market Dynamics, Sex-Ratio Imbalances, and Their Consequences." *Society* 49 (6): 500–505.

———. 2012c. "Q & A with Mark Regnerus about the Background of His New Study." *Patheos,* June 10. www.patheos.com/blogs/blackwhiteandgray/2012/06/q-a-with-mark-regnerus-about-the-background-of-his-new-study/.

———. 2012d. "Queers as Folk." *Slate,* June 11.

———. 2014. *Dr. Mark Regnerus: What Sexual Behavior Patterns Reveal about the Mating Market and Catholic Thought.* Video of speech given at Franciscan University, Steubenville. YouTube, uploaded January 8. https://www.youtube.com/watch?v=QcRGyytsukM.

———. 2015. "The Erosion of the Marriage Ecosystem." Heritage Foundation, July 16. https://medium.com/2015-index-of-culture-and-opportunity/marriage-rate-85c9988e78bb.

Reich, Jennifer A. 2014. "Neoliberal Mothering and Vaccine Refusal: Imagined Gated Communities and the Privilege of Choice." *Gender and Society* 28 (5): 679–704.

Reiman, Jeffrey. 2006. *The Rich Get Richer and the Poor Get Prison: Ideology, Class, and Criminal Justice.* 8th ed. Boston: Allyn and Bacon.

Resnick, Sofia. 2012. "Conservative-Backed Study Intended to Sway Court on Gay Marriage." *Huffington Post*, March 10. www.huffingtonpost.com/2013/03/10/supreme-court-gay-marriage_n_2850302.html.

———. 2013. "Journalists Win Release of Documents Tracing Right-Wing Funding for Texas Gay Marriage Study." *AlterNet*, February 3. www.alternet.org/investigations/journalists-win-release-documents-tracing-right-wing-funding-texas-gay-marriage-study.

Ribas, Vanesa, Janette S. Dill, and Philip N. Cohen. 2012. "Mobility for Care Workers: Job Changes and Wages for Nurse Aides." *Social Science and Medicine* 75 (12): 2183–90.

Richmond, Tracy K., S. Bryn Austin, Courtney E. Walls, and S. V. Subramanian. 2012. "The Association of BMI and Externally-Perceived Attractiveness across Race/Ethnicity, Gender, and Time." *Journal of Adolescent Health* 50 (1): 74–79.

Risman, Barbara J. 1999. *Gender Vertigo: American Families in Transition.* New Haven, CT: Yale University Press.

Rojas, Fabio. 2012. "Comments on Regnerus." *Orgtheory*, July 29. https://orgtheory.wordpress.com/2012/07/29/comments-on-regnerus/.

Rosenfeld, Michael. 2015. "Revisiting the Data from the New Family Structure Study: Taking Family Instability into Account." *Sociological Science* 2:478–501.

Rosin, Hanna. 2012a. *The End of Men: And the Rise of Women.* New York: Riverhead Books.

———. 2012b. "Male Decline Is No Myth." *Slate*, October 2.

———. 2012c. "Who Wears the Pants in This Economy?" *New York Times Magazine*, August 30.

———. 2013. "The Gender Wage Gap Lie." *Slate*, August 30.

Rubio, Marco. 2014. "Senator Marco Rubio on Poverty." C-SPAN, January 8. www.c-span.org/video/?317059-1/income-mobility-american-dream.

Rudder, Christian. 2009. "How Your Race Affects the Messages You Get." *OkTrends*, October 5.

———. 2014. "Race and Attraction, 2009–2014." *OkTrends*, September 10.

Sanneh, Kelefa. 2015. "Don't Be Like That." *New Yorker*, February 9.

Save the Children. 2015. *The Urban Disadvantage: State of the World's Mothers.* Fairfield, CT: Save the Children Federation. www.savethechildren.org/atf /cf/%7B9def2ebe-10ae-432c-9bd0-df91d2eba74a%7D/SOWM_EXECU-TIVE_SUMMARY.PDF.

Sawhill, Isabel V. 2014. *Generation Unbound: Drifting into Sex and Parenthood without Marriage.* Washington, DC: Brookings Institution Press.

————. 2015. "Purposeful Parenthood." *Education Next* 15 (2): 51–55.

Sax, Leonard. 2016. "Why Do Girls Tend to Have More Anxiety Than Boys?" *New York Times Well Blog*, April 21. http://well.blogs.nytimes.com/2016 /04/21/why-do-girls-have-more-anxiety-than-boys/.

Sayer, Liana C. 2015. "Trends in Women's and Men's Time Use, 1965–2012: Back to the Future?" In *Gender and Couple Relationships,* edited by Susan M. McHale, Valarie King, Jennifer Van Hook, and Alan Booth, 43–77. New York: Springer.

Scheuble, Laurie K., David R. Johnson, and Katherine M. Johnson. 2011. "Marital Name Changing Attitudes and Plans of College Students: Comparing Change over Time and across Regions." *Sex Roles* 66 (3–4): 282–92.

Schilt, Kristen, and Laurel Westbrook. 2015. "Bathroom Battlegrounds and Penis Panics." *Contexts* 14 (3): 26–31.

Schmidt, Susan. 1985. "Growing Number of Senseless Slayings by Teens Instills Concern." *Washington Post,* October 14.

Schulte, Brigid. 2014. *Overwhelmed: Work, Love, and Play When No One Has the Time.* New York: Macmillan.

Shepherd, Julianne Escobedo. 2015. "LOL Vocal Fry Rules U R All Dumb." *Jezebel*, July 30. http://jezebel.com/lol-vocal-fry-rules-u-r-all-dumb-1720927207.

Shermer, Michael. 2014. "How the Survivor Bias Distorts Reality." *Scientific American.* September 1.

Short, Kathleen. 2014. *The Supplemental Poverty Measure: 2013.* Current Population Reports P60–251. Washington, DC: US Census Bureau.

Simpson, David, and Alan J. Hawkins. 2015. "Who Is Being Served by Government-Funded Fatherhood Programs?" Institute for Family Studies, September 2. http://family-studies.org/who-is-being-served-by-government-funded-responsible-fatherhood-programs/.

Smith, Christian. 2012. "An Academic Auto-Da-Fé." *Chronicle of Higher Education*, July 23.

Smith, Daniel Scott. 1985. "Child-Naming Practices, Kinship Ties, and Change in Family Attitudes in Hingham, Massachusetts, 1641 to 1880." *Journal of Social History* 18 (4): 541–66.

Social Science Professors. 2013. Amici Curiae Brief, Nos. 12–144, 12–307. Hollingsworth v. Perry and U.S. v. Windsor.

Sociological Images. 2016. "Needlessly Gendered Products." Pinterest. https://www.pinterest.com/socimages/needlessly-gendered-products/.

Sokol-Katz, Jan, Roger Dunham, and Rick Zimmerman. 1997. "Family Structure versus Parental Attachment in Controlling Adolescent Deviant Behavior: A Social Control Model." *Adolescence* 32 (125): 199–215.

Sommers, Christina Hoff. 2014. *The Top Five Feminist Myths of All Time.* American Enterprise Institute. YouTube, uploaded September 8. https://www.youtube.com/watch?v=3TR_YuDFIFI.

Srivastava, Sameer B., and Eliot L. Sherman. 2015. "Agents of Change or Cogs in the Machine? Reexamining the Influence of Female Managers on the Gender Wage Gap." *American Journal of Sociology* 120 (6): 1778–1808.

Stainback, Kevin, Sibyl Kleiner, and Sheryl Skaggs. 2016. "Women in Power: Undoing or Redoing the Gendered Organization?" *Gender and Society* 30 (1): 109–35.

Stone, Pamela. 2007. *Opting Out? Why Women Really Quit Careers and Head Home.* Berkeley: University of California Press.

Sugrue, Thomas J. 2014. *The Origins of the Urban Crisis: Race and Inequality in Postwar Detroit.* Princeton, NJ: Princeton University Press.

Swarns, Rachel L. 2014. "Doctor Says No Overtime; Pregnant Worker's Boss Says No Job." *New York Times*, October 19.

Taylor, Catherine A., Jennifer A. Manganello, Shawna J. Lee, and Janet C. Rice. 2010. "Mothers' Spanking of 3-Year-Old Children and Subsequent Risk of Children's Aggressive Behavior." *Pediatrics* 125 (5): e1057–65.

Taylor, Marylee C., and Peter J. Mateyka. 2011. "Community Influences on White Racial Attitudes: What Matters and Why?" *Sociological Quarterly* 52 (2): 220–43.

Taylor, Paul. 1991. "Guns and Youth: HHS's Grim Statistics; More Male Teens Die from Bullets Than Natural Causes Combined." *Washington Post*, March 14, A1.

Toobin, Jeffrey. 2015. "God and Marriage Equality." *New Yorker*, June 26.

Torabi, Farnoosh. 2015. *When She Makes More: The Truth about Navigating Love and Life for a New Generation of Women.* New York: Plume.

Trumbull, H. Clay. 1890. "Honoring a Child's Individuality." In *Hints on Child Training*, 71–82. New York: Charles Scribner's Sons.

Udry, J. Richard. 2000. "Biological Limits of Gender Construction." *American Sociological Review* 65 (3): 443–57.

Umberson, Debra. 2012. "Texas Professors Respond to New Research on Gay Parenting." *Huffington Post*, August 26. http://www.huffingtonpost.com/debra-umberson/texas-professors-gay-research_b_1628988.html.

United Nations Statistics Division. 2014. *Demographic Yearbook.* New York: United Nations.

———. N.d. "Adolescent Fertility Rate." UNdata. http://data.un.org/Data.aspx?q
=birth+rate&d=WDI&f=Indicator_Code%3aSP.ADO.TFRT. Accessed May 1,
2017.

US Census Bureau. 1996. "Table No. 375. Prisoners Executed under Civil
Authority: 1930 to 1994." In *Statistical Abstract of the United States: 1996.*
Washington, DC.

———. 2011. "Census Bureau Releases Estimates of Same-Sex Married Couples." September 27. www.census.gov/newsroom/releases/archives/2010_
census/cb11-cn181.html.

———. 2015a. Annual Social and Economic Supplement, 2014 Person Income,
Table PINC-09. https://www.census.gov/data/tables/time-series/demo
/income-poverty/cps-pinc/pinc-09.2014.html.

———. 2015b. "Parents and Children in Stay at Home Parent Family Groups:
1994 to Present." https://www.census.gov/population/socdemo/hh-fam
/shp1.xls.

———. N.d. "Family Income: FINC-01." www.census.gov/data/tables/time-series
/demo/income-poverty/cps-finc/finc-01.html.

US Department of Education. 2014. "CRDC School Discipline Snapshot." Civil
Rights Data Collection, Issue Brief No. 1, March http://ocrdata.ed.gov
/downloads/crdc-school-discipline-snapshot.pdf.

US General Accountability Office. 2008. "Further Progress Is Needed in
Developing a Risk-Based Monitoring Approach to Help HHS Improve
Program Oversight." September. www.gao.gov/new.items/d081002.pdf.

UT News. 2012. "University of Texas at Austin Completes Inquiry into Allegations of Scientific Misconduct." University of Texas at Austin, August 29.
http://news.utexas.edu/2012/08/29/regnerus_scientific_misconduct_inquiry_
completed.

Vaden, Victoria Cox, and Jacqueline D. Woolley. 2011. "Does God Make It Real?
Children's Belief in Religious Stories from the Judeo-Christian Tradition."
Child Development 82 (4): 1120–35.

Verry, Ethel. 1952. "Review of Foster Care of Children in Michigan. Report of
Joint Legislative Committee: Seven Studies Concerning Foster Care of
Children." *Social Service Review* 26 (2): 258.

Volsky, Igor. 2014. "Paul Ryan Blames Poverty on Lazy 'Inner City' Men."
ThinkProgress, March 12.

Wade, Lisa, and Myra Marx Ferree. 2014. *Gender: Ideas, Interactions, Institutions.* New York: W. W. Norton.

Wang, Wendy, and Kim Parker, 2014. "Record Share of Americans Have Never
Married: As Values, Economics and Gender Patterns Change." Pew Research
Center, September 24, www.pewsocialtrends.org/2014/09/24/record-share-
of-americans-have-never-married/.

Wang, Wendy, Kim Parker, and Paul Taylor. 2013. "Breadwinner Moms." Pew
    Research Center's Social and Demographic Trends Project. May 29. www
    .pewsocialtrends.org/2013/05/29/breadwinner-moms/.
Ward, Brian W., James M. Dahlhamer, Adina M. Galinsky, and Sarah S. Joestl.
    2014. "Sexual Orientation and Health among U.S. Adults: National Health
    Interview Survey, 2013." *National Health Statistics Reports*, no. 77 (July).
Waring, Belle. 2012. "Hey Look, Some Sexist Bullshit at Slate. No Wai!" *Crooked
    Timber*, January 16. http://crookedtimber.org/2012/01/16/hey-look-some-
    sexist-bullshit-at-slate-no-wai/.
Warner, Judith. 2006. *Perfect Madness: Motherhood in the Age of Anxiety.*
    Reprint ed. New York: Riverhead Books.
West, Candace, and Don H. Zimmerman. 1987. "Doing Gender." *Gender and
    Society* 1 (2): 125–51.
Western, Bruce, Deirdre Bloome, and Christine Percheski. 2008. "Inequality
    among American Families with Children, 1975 to 2005." *American Socio-
    logical Review* 73 (6): 903–20.
Wilcox, W. Bradford. 2012. "Who Needs An Intact Family? Jail Will Do Just
    Fine." *Family Scholars Blog*, November 27. https://web.archive.org/web
    /20121201024450/http://familyscholars.org/2012/11/27/who-needs-an-intact-
    family-jail-will-do-just-fine/.
———. 2013. "The Great Crossover." In *The Knot Yet Report.* http://
    twentysomethingmarriage.org/the-great-crossover/.
Williams, Alex. 2012. "Dads Are Taking Over as Full-Time Parents (Just Wait
    Till Your Mother Gets Home)." *New York Times*, August 10.
Wilson, William Julius. 1987. *The Truly Disadvantaged: The Inner City, the
    Underclass, and Public Policy.* Chicago: University of Chicago Press.
Wolf, Naomi. 2015. "Young Women, Give Up the Vocal Fry and Reclaim
    Your Strong Female Voice." *Guardian*, July 24. www.theguardian.com
    /commentisfree/2015/jul/24/vocal-fry-strong-female-voice.
Women for Women. 2011. "Join Us on the Bridge on March 8th." *YouTube*,
    uploaded February 24. https://www.youtube.com/watch?v=hUF65dR08ic.
Women's Media Center. 2015. "The Status of Women in the U.S. Media 2015."
    http://wmc.3cdn.net/83bf6082a319460eb1_hsrm680x2.pdf.
Wong, Wang I., and Melissa Hines. 2015. "Preferences for Pink and Blue: The
    Development of Color Preferences as a Distinct Gender-Typed Behavior in
    Toddlers." *Archives of Sexual Behavior* 44 (5): 1243–54.
Wood, Robert G., Sheena McConnell, Quinn Moore, Andrew Clarkwest, and
    JoAnn Hsueh. 2010. "Strengthening Unmarried Parents' Relationships: The
    Early Impacts of Building Strong Families." Princeton, NJ: Mathematica
    Policy Research. www.acf.hhs.gov/sites/default/files/opre/15_impact_exec_
    summ.pdf.

Wood, Robert G., Quinn Moore, Andrew Clarkwest, Alexandra Killewald, and Shannon Monahan. 2012. "The Long–Term Effects of Building Strong Families: A Relationship Skills Education Program for Unmarried Parents." Princeton, NJ: Mathematica Policy Research. www.mdrc.org/sites/default /files/BSF_36month_impact_fnlrpt_0.pdf.

Woolley, Jacqueline D., Elizabeth A. Boerger, and Arthur B. Markman. 2004. "A Visit from the Candy Witch: Factors Influencing Young Children's Belief in a Novel Fantastical Being." *Developmental Science* 7 (4): 456–68.

Woolley, Jacqueline D., and Maliki Ghossainy. 2013. "Revisiting the Fantasy-Reality Distinction: Children as Naïve Skeptics." *Child Development* 84 (5): 1496–1510. https://www.ncbi.nlm.nih.gov/pmc/articles/PMC3689871/.

World Bank. 2016. "World Development Indicators, Table 4.2." http://wdi .worldbank.org/table/4.2.

World Food Program USA. 2010. "Women's Greater Access to Land Can Increase Food Security." March 5. http://wfpusa.org/blog/womens-greater-access-land-can-increase-food-security.

Zelizer, Viviana A. 1985. *Pricing the Priceless Child: The Changing Social Value of Children*. Princeton, NJ: Princeton University Press.

Zinsser, Judith P. 2002. "From Mexico to Copenhagen to Nairobi: The United Nations Decade for Women, 1975–1985." *Journal of World History* 13 (1): 139–68.

Index

Abramson, Jill, 132

"A Call for a New Conversation on Marriage" declaration, 80

Add Health survey, 179, 224n43

adults: behavior effects of, 36, 82; belief systems of, 29–32; color preference and, 122–23; gender socialization of, 8; power over children, 4, 27

African Americans. See Blacks

Ahooja-Patel, Krishna, 150–51, 152, 154, 221n45

Alito, Samuel, 103

Allen, Douglas, 96, 104

Amato, Paul, 69, 94, 99, 217n23

American Academy of Pediatrics, 94

American Community Survey, 59fig.15, 86fig.20, 132, 136–39, 137fig.29, 142, 142fig.31, 161fig.34, 165fig.36, 166fig.37, 167, 168fig.38, 173fig.39, 180fig.40

American Enterprise Institute (AEI), 37, 99, 134, 173, 197

American Medical Association (AMA), 94

American National Election Study (2016), 223n39

American Psychological Association (APA), 94, 159

American Sociological Association (ASA), 94, 99, 201, 222n5

Aristocats (1970 film), 119

Baumeister, Roy F., 193–96

Beauvoir, Simone de, 201–2

belief systems, 21fig.5; of adults, 29–32; Biblical, 29–30; family inequality and, 29–32; inequality and, 35–36; Judeo-Christian moral tradition, 98; modern credulity and, 33–35; personal belief exemptions, 21; Santa belief, 29, 30, 33–36

Belkin, Lisa, 15

Bennett, Jessica, 205

Blacks: Bible beliefs and, 30–31, 31fig.9; blog posts, 223n43; Detroit's demographic decline, 164–170, 165fig.36, 166fig.37, 168fig.38, 176; educational success of, 160–64; homicide trends among, 50–51; marriage and, 58, 66, 85–86, 86fig.20, 175–182; marriage rates of, 179–182, 180fig.40, 224n45; name trends and, 13; poverty and, 212n34; as racial identity, 157–160; racial inequality and, 170–75; racialized attraction, 178–79; racialized fear, 176–77; social attitudes

249